W9-CHC-963

"THE FISHERMAN AND HIS WIFE"

AMS Studies in Modern Literature: No. 12

ISSN: 0270-2983

Other Titles in This Series
1. Richard E. Amacher and Margaret F. Rule. *Edward Albee at Home and Abroad: A Bibliography, 1958 to June 1968.* 1973.
2. Richard G. Morgan, ed. *Kenneth Patchen: A Collection of Essays.* 1977.
3. Philip Grover, ed. *Ezra Pound: The London Years, 1908–1920.* 1978.
4. Daniel J. Casey and Robert E. Rhodes, eds. *Irish-American Fiction: Essays in Criticism.* 1979.
5. Iska Alter. *The Good Man's Dilemma: Social Criticism in the Fiction of Bernard Malamud.* 1981.
6. Charles Lee Green. *Edward Albee: An Annotated Bibliography, 1968–1977.* 1980.
7. Richard H. Goldstone and Gary Anderson. *Thornton Wilder: An Annotated Bibliography of Works By and About Thornton Wilder.* 1982.

"The Fisherman and His Wife"

Günter Grass's *The Flounder* in Critical Perspective

edited by

Siegfried Mews

AMS Press, Inc.
NEW YORK, N.Y.

Library of Congress Cataloging in Publication Data
Main entry under title

"The Fisherman and his wife".

  (AMS studies in modern literature; no. 12)
  Bibliography: pp. 209–217.
  Includes index
  Contents: "The ice age cometh," a motif in modern
German literature / Reinhold Grimm; translated by William
Bruce Armstrong — Günter Grass in search of a literary
theory / Peter Demetz — "I, down through the ages,"
reflections on the poetics of Günter Grass / Ruprecht
Wimmer; translated by Susan C. Anderson — [etc.]
  1. Grass, Günter, 1927-   . I. Mews,
Siegfried. II. Series.
PT2613.R338B834   1983   838′.91407   81-69878
ISBN 0-404-61582-1   AACR2

MANUFACTURED IN THE UNITED STATES
OF AMERICA

Contents

Introduction

Since 1963, the year in which *The Tin Drum* appeared on the American book market, the name of Günter Grass has been, for all practical purposes, a household word among the *literati* in this country. Although both Grass's career and his reception in the United States have had their ups and downs, he has been acknowledged as a writer of world rank for the last two decades or so; moreover, he has been regarded as the foremost representative of post-World War II German literature. In all probability, Grass's reputation stands to gain in the long run from the appearance of his latest major work, *The Flounder*.

When, in 1977, Grass's voluminous novel *Der Butt* was published in West Germany, the work was almost unanimously hailed by critics as a major artistic achievement. One reviewer, for example, praised Grass as the most imaginative prose writer of the decade; others marveled at the "encyclopedic" scope of the novel that embraced political, cultural, and literary history in addition to that of cooking, and a host of other subjects. Despite its almost forbidding length of nearly 700 pages in the German hardcover edition, the novel achieved sales records not usually attained by serious literature.

Less than one year later, when *Der Butt* had been on the bestseller lists in Germany for approximately eight months, the American translation by Ralph Manheim was published in this country in November 1978 under the title *The Flounder*. Although a paperback edition was to follow in November 1979, the American reception of the novel was less enthusiastic than that in Germany—in part owing to the fact that there was no comparable, skillfully nurtured publicity campaign such as the one that had preceded the publication of the novel in Germany. On the one hand, there were such laudatory comments as that in *Publisher's Weekly*, which should not be dismissed lightly as sheer hyperbole: "As rich, challenging and inventive as anything [Grass has] written . . . a large and tangy stew of history, legend, myth, religion and fantasy, laced with comic irony . . . one astonishing whole." On the other hand, Nigel Dennis, writing in the *New York Review of Books*, rather devastatingly criticized the work as a "bad novel" in which the "quality of the cookery does not improve the quality of the fiction." The one virtue Dennis did manage to find in the novel almost amounts to a flaw, that is, he preferred Manheim's translation to the German original.

Some of the puzzlement and scathing comment expressed by American critics is, without doubt, attributable to the fact that we are dealing with an extraordinarily rich and complex work with innovative techniques. Hence it is to explore the novel in some detail that the contributors to the present volume address themselves. Although critics in considerable numbers have felt obliged to proffer their observations on the novel—the comparatively high frequency of critical comments attests to its challenging complexity—and, hence, there is no dearth of secondary literature in either German or English (see Bibliography), first critical reactions, that is, reviews in newspapers and magazines tend to predominate, rather than analytical articles presenting an argument developed at some length.

In contrast to the widely scattered reviews and scholarly articles that have become available so far, a collection of essays such as this offers one obvious advantage: not only can a significant number of the novel's facets be explored in detail; in addition, different critical approaches can be brought to bear on one or several related aspects. The disadvantage of occasional overlapping is outweighed by the benefit of a more comprehensive coverage and scope. This intended scope enabled individual contributors to provide both supplementary and contrasting perspectives on, for example, the narrative stance (Gertrud Bauer Pickar, Helmut Koopman) or the role of myth in the novel (Edward Diller, Scott H. Abbott, Winnifred R. Adolph); it also permitted them to establish the larger context of which the novel forms a part. Thus Reinhold Grimm discusses the contemporary German literary scene in terms of a recurrent motif, Peter Demetz investigates the influence of Grass's most important literary mentor, Alfred Döblin, with regard to *The Flounder*, Ruprecht Wimmer traces the development of Grass's poetics on the basis of his entire prose fiction *oeuvre*, and Judith Ryan explores Grass's "narrative dialectic" beyond *The Flounder*.

Since the emphasis in the present collection is on critical analysis, it goes without saying that contributions that arrive at a negative assessment, notably those by Otto F. Best and Erhard Friedrichsmeyer, have not been excluded. In the absence of eternally valid truths in literary criticism editorial prerogative should not extend to censoring essays based on differing sensibilities and tastes—provided they are cogently argued and derive their conclusions from sound textual evidence.

In essence, then, the individual essays express the views of their respective authors who, in part, participated in the discussions held at sections devoted to Grass in general and *The Flounder* in particular at such conferences as those of the American Association of Teachers of German (1978), the Modern Language Association (1978, 1979), and the Mountain Interstate Foreign Language Conference (1980). As one German reviewer remarked, *The Flounder* is a book with which one can "live" for a long time. In a sense, the present volume is a result of the sustained interest by literary scholars whose response to the invitation to contribute to this volume has been quite gratifying.

What mostly distinguishes this collection of critical essays from the similar *Adventures of a Flounder* (see Bibliography) is that is addresses itself primarily—but on no account exclusively—to the American reading public. As a corollary, the volume also legitimately concerns itself with the American reception of *The Flounder* in a contribution by Sigrid Mayer. Owing to the linguistic preference of the intended reader, all essays—most of which are original contributions—are in English. Further, all titles of works, references and quotations given in the text are ordinarily in English—although, for the purpose of clarification, titles and quotations in German have also been used. As to the notes, full bibliographical references have been provided for only those titles (cited in the original language, unless there is an extant translation) that do not appear in the Bibliography. In all other cases, including cross references to contributions in this volume, normally only author, title and page reference have been given. The Bibliography, in turn, does not lay claim to any degree of comprehensiveness concerning the extant literature by and about Grass. Rather, it encompasses, apart from works by Grass in both German and English translation, important general works on Grass, works cited in the notes, and titles (mostly those in English) relevant to *The Flounder*.

For the convenience of the reader a number of abbreviations have been used throughout the volume (see Abbreviations). Further, the reader who is bewildered by the mass of facts and great number of characters appearing in the novel may wish to consult the Structural Diagram. Reference to the German originals of both *The Flounder* and *The Meeting at Telgte* has been facilitated by the inclusion of German-English Concordances.

*   *   *

A postscript: after the publication of Grass's hitherto latest work in the United States, the slim volume *Headbirths* (1982), the writer's renown among literary critics continues unabated. Although *Headbirths,* according to John Leonard in the *New York Times Book Review* is "minor Grass, [the book] would be major for almost any other writer." The novelist John Irving writes in *Saturday Review* that "we have no better, *general* introduction to the methods of [Grass's] genius than *Headbirths*." Irving's claim that "you can't be called well-read today if you haven't read him. Günter Grass is simply the most original and versatile writer alive," is borne out by the results of a poll conducted by the Goethe Institute in Boston. The 800 New England professors, teachers, and students of German who were asked to select their favorite post-World War II German-language works, listed *The Tin Drum*, which Irving calls "the greatest novel by a living author," in first place and ranked *The Flounder* second—ahead of Thomas Mann's *Doctor Faustus*, Heinrich Böll's *Group Portrait with Lady*, and Max Frisch's *Homo Faber*. In ninth place we encounter yet another title by Grass, *Cat and Mouse*. Surely, this is ample evidence of the recognition Grass has achieved—a recognition that suggests the desirability of facilitating access to Grass's work in general and the both voluminous and complex *The Flounder* in particular by means of critical studies.

Acknowledgments

Excerpts from *The Flounder* and *The Meeting at Telgte* by Günter Grass, translated by Ralph Manheim are reprinted by permission of Harcourt Brace Jovanovich, Inc.; copyright © 1977, 1979 by Hermann Luchterhand Verlag, Darmstadt and Neuwied; English translation copyright © 1978, 1981 by Harcourt Brace Jovanovich, Inc.

"Fire and Ice" from *The Poetry of Robert Frost* edited by Edward Connery Lathem. Copyright © 1923, 1969 by Holt, Rinehart and Winston. Copyright © 1951 by Robert Frost. Reprinted by permission of Holt, Rinehart and Winston, Publishers.

The article by Peter Demetz, "Günter Grass in Search of a Literary Theory," is published by permission of Mrs. Helen Wolff, Harcourt Brace Jovanovich, Inc.

Excerpts from *The Raw and the Cooked: Introduction to a Science of Mythology: I*, by Claude Lévi-Strauss, translated by John and Doreen Weightman are reprinted by permission of Harper & Row, Publishers, Inc.; copyright © 1964 by Librairie Plon; English translation copyright © 1969 by Harper & Row, Publishers, Inc.

The University Research Council of the University of North Carolina at Chapel Hill provided financial assistance for expenses related to the research for and editing of this volume. I gratefully acknowledge this assistance.

Abbreviations

1. Works by Grass

(for full bibliographical references, see Bibliography, A/I-II)

AL   *Aufsätze zur Literatur*
B   *Der Butt*
CM   *Cat and Mouse*
DS   *From the Diary of a Snail*
DZ   *Denkzettel*
F   *The Flounder*
KG   *Kopfgeburten*
MT   *The Meeting at Telgte*
TD   *The Tin Drum*
TT   *Das Treffen in Telgte*

2. Other Works

(for full bibliographical references, see Bibliography, B/II)

AoF   *Adventures of a Flounder*
TuK   *Text und Kritik*

"The Ice Age Cometh":
A Motif in Modern German Literature*

Reinhold Grimm

TRANSLATED BY WILLIAM BRUCE ARMSTRONG

> "Fire and Ice"
> Some say the world will end in fire,
> Some say in ice.
> From what I've tasted of desire
> I hold with those who favor fire.
> But if it had to perish twice,
> I think I know enough of hate
> To say that for destruction ice
> Is also great
> And would suffice. (Robert Frost)

A few years back—in 1972 to be exact—when the playwright Tankred Dorst used the postwar situation of the Norwegian writer Knut Hamsun as "the starting point for a fictional plot with fictional characters" and proceeded to bestow upon this work the laconic title *Eiszeit* ("Ice Age"), West German literary critics tore their hair in desperate bewilderment.[1] What was this perplexing title supposed to express? Nowhere in the play is it clarified; indeed the term itself is mentioned only once. In a scene in which "THE OLD MAN" (the Hamsun figure) is being examined by psychiatrists who are seeking to determine his mental competency, he is called upon to define a series of words projected on a screen which stands before him. Besides "sphere," "city," "revenge," and so on, there appears the phrase "ICE AGE." It is the last of the series and evokes a reaction that is as telling as it is ambiguous: *"The old man waves it away in exasperation and remains silent."*[2] Thus the

1

stage directions with which the scene closes or, more precisely, breaks off. The play's ending is equally terse and open-ended. "Yes, yes, yes, I'm still alive," cries the old man, waking from a faint that may have been only feigned. His declaration is made in a tone that is "mocking" and "arrogant" while his face is twisted in a cramped, grimacing smile.[3]

We, too, are forced to ask ourselves why Dorst entitled this play *Eiszeit*. Did he wish to allude to a certain personal attribute of his controversial protagonist, a coldness, a hardness, and rigidity brought about by exigencies of character and environment? Did he in addition to this—or perhaps in its stead—wish to indicate a general interpersonal, indeed societal cooling and rigidification, a "freezing trend" basic to the times in which we live? Or was his title simply a product of chance, something chosen at random and therefore devoid of symbolic content?

In any case, in retrospect it appears that Dorst's title was a signal. Had the critics' puzzlement been a bit less frantic, perhaps they would have remembered a text that, though published almost a decade earlier, bore a strikingly similar, in fact even more laconic, title. I am referring to Thomas Bernhard's first extensive work in prose, a book that appeared in 1963. Its full title consists of a single word: *Frost*. Appropriately enough, the book depicts the gradual transformation into ice of a man who "freezes from the inside out." This oppressive and irreversible development "logically reaches its fatal conclusion high up in the snow-covered mountains."[4] But can one even speak of such things in terms of development?[5] Hasn't this "frost" become a permanent condition, one in which time itself freezes into an ice-age stasis? "The frost devours everything," Bernhard's narrator sums up the situation. But even at the beginning of the book we are told: "The frost is omnipotent." "Frozen air," murmurs the main character, a painter, "now there is nothing but frozen air."[6] For him, for the narrator, and for Bernhard himself, "this ongoing frost, ongoing in all things and in each thing and everywhere, [possesses] in its unprecedented ability to magnify concepts . . . the largest, again and again far and away the largest meaning." One can hardly imagine a more explicit, indeed heavy-handed revelation of *fabula docet*. What Dorst hints at, Bernhard hurls in the reader's face. In order to extirpate any last shred of doubt, he goes on to declare that the findings being dealt with here are climatological as well as clinical in nature. He even coins a phrase that, as he himself emphasizes, links these two aspects together: "diluvial disintegration of the individual."[7]

But this is not all. With the concepts of frost and ice age he associates, admittedly in a somewhat casual manner, nothing less than the end of the world—"the *actual* end of the world," he assures us.[8] Certainly, Bernhard cannot be accused of an excess of subtlety. It was hardly necessary for him to refer to the "lifeless country" where "everything has died."[9] Nevertheless, he did, and in doing so he effectively anticipated the crucial element of the complex of motifs that Dorst later strove to evoke. The ice age, regardless of how inscrutable Dorst's use of this concept may seem at first glance; terminal decline, whether of the individual or the entire planet; devastation, destruction, annihilation as an individual and/or global catastrophe: all of this can be found, in an almost fully developed form, in Bernhard's book. In the intervening years, a standardized repertoire of frost and snow and ice and glaciers has developed, one which has become as common as the twittering of sparrows. It is a repertoire that our own busy sparrows, the critics of literature, have taken to whistling from their perches in the various literary supplements. But there is more. For what is played out in these apocalyptic final days is, quite obviously, the by now familiar endgame; and when the end of the world is concretized in the image of a doomed ship, then the fatal iceberg cannot be far away; hence we find ourselves at the worst ship disaster of all time, the sinking of the "Titanic" into the icy depths of the ocean. On all sides, in all genres we find ourselves confronted by a surfeit of evidence. If one were cynical—and many are—one would have to report: ice and annihilation have the upper hand. No doubt about it, the ice age cometh. Indeed, I fear that it is already here—at least in the realm of literature.

Of course, these images and visions have a history of their own, a fact that is attested to by the literary life of the story of the "Titanic." Moreover, contrary to certain ill-advised pronouncements that have been made,[10] they are by no means found only in West German literature or coined only to describe life in the Federal Republic. Any attempt to define the phenomenon in such a limited fashion is vitiated not only by Bernhard and his Austrian *Frost* but also by the novel *In Trubschachen,* written by the Swiss E. Y. Meyer, a work in which the motifs of winter, snow and coldness take on a central and obviously symbolic importance. Meyer's novel, incidentally, also appeared at a remarkably early point, that is, in 1973.[11] And are there not also East German authors, both former and current, who, together with their own society, must be mentioned in this connection? One need only think of Thomas Brasch and Heiner Müller. Even the feminist point of view comes into play, in an affirmative as well as an ambivalent manner, as an additional perspective in the general obsession with ice age, terminal decline, and the depths of the ocean. Shortly we shall examine this complex in the writings of Müller, Brasch, and Meyer. However, as regards the feminist perspective, it manifests itself most vividly, indeed—as is only to be expected—most dazzlingly, in Günter Grass's novel *The Flounder.*

Here one finds an alternative version of the Grimms' fairy tale, "The Fisherman and His Wife." This centrally located section is of key importance for the entire work. In a sense, it is out of the retold tale that the rest of the novel grows; and if the tale begins in the Stone Age rather than the Ice Age, it is then all the more striking that it eventually moves into an ice age—the new ice age which is either impending or already here. To be sure, this occurs only in the version (*Variation*) that Grass sets up, endowed with an equal degree of validity, next to the version that has "come down to us." Grass has the painter Philipp Otto Runge describe how "years ago" he carefully transcribed the "two versions" of an old woman's "tale"—Runge puts down the two versions because she "was strangely obstinate" and "kept shifting from one to the other and back" (F, 348). According to Runge, she clearly "had said both tales were true" (F, 351):

> The one made Ilsebill the quarrelsome wife credible, how she wants to have more and more and more, to be king emperor pope, but finally, when she wants the all-powerful Flounder to make her "like God," is sent back to the old thatched hut, called "pisspot" in the story. The other truth dictated to painter Runge by the old woman showed a modest Ilsebill and a fisherman with immoderate wishes: He wants to be unconquerable in war. He wants to build, traverse, inhabit bridges across the widest river, houses and towers reaching to the clouds, fast carriages drawn neither by oxen nor horses, ships that swim under water. He wants to attain goals, to rule the world, to subjugate nature, to rise above the earth. . . . And when at the end the fisherman . . . wants to rise up to the stars . . ., all the splendor, the towers, the bridges, the flying machines collapse, the dikes burst, drought parches, sandstorms devastate, the mountains spew fire, the old earth quakes, and in quaking shakes off the man's rule. And cold blasts usher in the next all-covering ice age. (F, 349)

The relevance of Grass's fairy tale of the ice age is only too obvious. Grass goes so far as to openly state the feminist "moral of the story," namely that "all masculine striving leads to chaos" (F, 350). To be sure, he puts these words, in the form of a negative hypothesis, in the mouth of one of his characters, Clemens Brentano. Brentano himself vigorously rejects such conclusions—Grass, however, insists via his character Runge that the old woman declared "both tales were true."

Such ambivalence cannot be found in the work of Heiner Müller. In his play, *Die Hamletmaschine* ("The Hamlet Machine"), which was published in the same year as *The Flounder,* he openly and unequivocally[12] commits himself to the feminist interpretation of and solution to the modern world riddle. Müller's "Tale of the Man," for that is what his *Hamletmaschine* reveals itself to be, is neither ambiguous nor irresolute; abandoning all subtlety, his unconditional affirmation culminates in a furious prophecy that is as radical in its devices as it is in its content. The ice age alone is not sufficient for Müller: he mixes in a vision of the ocean's depths and then adds to this strange brew a surrealistically observed scene of catastrophe and torture. *Die Hamletmaschine* lands quite literally at the bottom of the ocean—after a cataclysm the details of which are beyond imagination since it is obviously meant to be regarded as being both universal and virtually permanent.

At this point it is necessary to backtrack for a moment. In the beginning, during the so-called "construction phase" in the development of the German Democratic Republic (GDR), Müller in fact used the ice age as an image of the past and contrasted it with the control of nature and shaping of history made possible by socialism. His work was suffused by a limitless faith in the efficacy of technology and continually expanding production. Here Müller's play with the telling title *Der Bau* ("Construction"), which was first published in 1965, is particularly revealing. In this work the new socialist man, despite all his as yet uncorrected flaws and deficiencies, is able to declare with pride and confidence:

> My span of life is the building of bridges. I am
> The pontoon between the ice age and the commune.[13]

Clearly, Müller's "old" ice age refers to the Marxist concept of our barbaric prehistory that, even though we are only just beginning to free ourselves from it, is allegedly on the verge of being supplanted by the true history of the human race. And need I add that these lines, filled with total confidence in the future, are uttered by a man? Yet the same man—I realize I am simplifying, but so does Müller—when confronted in Müller's *Hamletmaschine* by Marx, Lenin, and Mao, each of whom appears as a naked woman, takes a hatchet and splits their skulls. It is a slaughter, half concrete, half ideological, that even the author of *Frost* could not have implemented in a more thoroughgoing manner. Afterwards we hear the word: "Snow." And then simply: "Ice Age."[14]

As for Müller's simultaneous vision of the ocean's depths, it develops as follows:

> *Depths of the ocean. Ophelia in a wheelchair. Fish rubble corpses and fragments of corpses drift by.*
> OPHELIA
> *While two men in doctor's gowns wrap her and the wheelchair from the bottom up with gauze bandages.*
> Electra speaking. . . . In the name of the victims. . . . I smother the world, to which I have given birth, between my thighs. . . . Long live hate, contempt, rebellion, death. Truth will reveal itself striding through your bedrooms with butcher knives.
> *Exit the men. Ophelia remains onstage, motionless in her white cocoon.*[15]

So ends Müller's *Hamletmaschine*. Supposedly after this play Müller was never again going to write for the theater; and thus in 1978 there promptly appeared a volume of essays entitled *Die Hamletmaschine, Heiner Müllers Endspiel* ("The Hamlet Machine: Heiner Müller's Endgame"). However, rumors of this sort should always be regarded with a certain degree of suspicion—as should all theories and conclusions that are based upon such rumors. Samuel Beckett continued to write plays after having written *Endgame,* and it seems more than likely that Heiner Müller will do the same. In fact, Müller has not only begun but has actually completed and published his next play. But in terms of the matter at hand, such news is of only peripheral interest. Much more important is the fact that the sinister prophecy of the "truth" that is to be promulgated with the help of "butcher knives" was taken, according to Müller's own statement, from Susan Atkins, a member of the murderous "family" headed by Charles Manson! How, then, are we to view emancipation that is based on the crazed ideas and cult-inspired butcheries of a clan of psychopaths who prophetically smear utopia's walls with their "satanic blood-rituals"?[16] Is this the future that is supposed to replace our ongoing, not to say growing, barbarism?

For all his terseness, Müller's use of the motifs of the ice age and the depths of the ocean can be safely described as excessive. In comparison, the use of these motifs by a woman, that is Christa Wolf, seems in all respects remarkably restrained and measured, indeed almost classic. However, the fundamental seriousness of Wolf's intent is clear from the outset; it is even manifest in the title of her book *Kein Ort. Nirgends* ("No Place. Nowhere"). This story, published in 1979, presents a fictional encounter between Heinrich von Kleist and Karoline von Günderode in a villa on the Rhine. Primarily concerned with self-analysis, it strives to reflect the present in the past.[17] Once again we encounter the familiar complex of motifs. "A crush like an icejam," muses Kleist in typical fashion: "It's as if I were standing on a chunk of ice, in a stream of ice chunks, in absolute darkness." Kleist's thought ends with the phrase, "A life sentence." Admittedly, this is the only such passage in the entire book. In it one finds no excesses and certainly no prophecies. Nevertheless, Wolf's story does contain something along the lines of a testament, one that at first seems courageous, even optimistic: "If we cease to hope, then surely our fears will come true." Yet is not the action of the story suffused from the very beginning with a sense of futility? Wolf's final sentence has a different ring to it: "We know what is coming."[18] Kleist as well as Günderode possess this knowledge. In the end, both historical figures, as we know, could no longer see any way out of the darkness and confusion and thus they both sought refuge in suicide. In spite of the faint glimmer of hope, the message with which the book leaves us is one of coldness and gloom. Nothing can save these two people, not even art. The author alone continues to feel sustained by it, although she herself does not mention this.

The validity and universality of Wolf's insight[19] is confirmed by Thomas

Brasch and Hans Magnus Enzensberger. Each is writing from his own perspective, but each openly states the paradox of art and the artist. Brasch, in particular, does so with provocative vehemence. In his collage of texts and images entitled *Kargo* ("Cargo"), with the explanatory addition, "Thirty-second Attempt on a Sinking Ship to Escape Out of My Own Skin," Brasch decrees in a tone that brooks no dissent: "Art has never been a means to change the world, but always an attempt to survive it."[20] Let us add that now, as in the past, art takes on this function most completely when it has as its object despair, death, and destruction. Enzensberger provides a striking example. His verse epic, *The Sinking of the Titanic*, labeled a "comedy" and thereby inviting a highly ambitious parallel to Dante, both embodies the phenomenon and provides a presentation of it. The poem in question, "Apokalypse," is one of many Enzensberger has woven into his report on the "Titanic" in order to provide scenes from the past and glimpses of the future, as well as variation and commentary. Unfortunately, it is too long to be quoted here. But in any case, the field of reference of the work as a whole is astoundingly complex. Even the island of Cuba, where in 1969 Enzensberger began work on his epic during the "strangely buoyant days of euphoria"[21] (a fact that in itself is an astounding phenomenon) serves as an element of the complex whole. The same iceberg that, after colliding with the "Titanic," disappears "black" and "silent" into the "darkness," reappears half a century later and floats "many times larger and whiter than all that is white, off in the distance in the dark bay" by Havana![22] This gigantic, truly global parable of the "sinking ship that is a ship and is not a ship"[23] extends from the Renaissance to the present and from the Third World to wintry, isolated Berlin. Indeed, coldness and snow[24] as well as the icy currents and inky blackness of the ocean's depths[25] all force their way into the room where the writer is sitting. And yet the poem ends ("hard to say, why") with an absurd "however," with a sense perhaps of purposeful engagement, certainly of dogged persistence. "Everything as it always is, everything is wavering, everything is under control, everything is running," Enzensberger ends his work with this ambiguous declaration—along with the statement: "I swim and weep . . ., weep and swim on."[26]

Enzensberger's *commedia non-divina* appeared in the fall of 1978. The book *Kargo,* which also deals with a sinking ship that "is a ship and is not a ship," was published in 1977. Thus it came out the same year as a closely related work, the *Hamletmaschine* of Brasch's mentor, Heiner Müller. Enzensberger's epic poem is in its rigorousness of form very different from Brasch's montage, a chaotic tangle of verses, sketches, playlets, aphorisms, theses, and stories. Nevertheless, in the realm of content these two works are remarkably similar. They both are based upon the same central concept that is alluded to in the titles chosen by the two writers. Unlike Enzensberger, Brasch com-

presses his presentation of this concept into the space of slightly more than
two pages, a section entitled *Ritas Vorstellung* ("Rita's View"). Moreover, he
coquettishly insists upon defining this section as a "Melodramatic Essay." It
is significant that the parabolic sinking of a ship in *Kargo* does not just partially occur in Berlin, as is the case in Enzensberger's epic; rather, it has the city
as its initial and primary (although by no means only) setting. Of course, in
Brasch's book we are no longer dealing with Berlin, the enclave of the West
but rather with Berlin, the capital of the GDR. Just as Enzensberger integrates Castro's Cuba into his critical vision of decline and destruction, so
Brasch employs the socialist half of Germany for this purpose—albeit to an
even greater extent.

Brasch's main character Rita takes a distinctly apocalyptic view of her
East German environment:

> When I see us walking down the Pieckstrasse, I see us on board the ship 'Euro-
> pean Culture.' Sinking: Everything shouted over the ocean from this ship is
> shouted from a sinking ship. Everything shouted from this ship is shouted by
> people who are only not yet completely dead. . . . The ship is very well equipped,
> among its passengers the opinion is widespread that this ship is unsinkable.[27]

Only in this section Brasch concentrates on the "ship 'European Culture'";
clearly, two pages out of almost 200 represent a mere fraction of what he has
assembled in his huge montage and collage. In all fairness, it must be pointed
out that *Kargo,* while not as multifaceted as Enzensberger's "comedy," does
exhibit a comparable degree of complexity; thus, like Müller's *Hamletmaschine,* it is a work that cannot be done full justice through the examination
of a single motif.

E. Y. Meyer's previously mentioned novel of coldness and snow, *In
Trubschachen,* a work set in the Emmenthal region during the winter, also
concerns itself with the critical analysis of culture. It does so in a manner that
emphasizes indirectness and a kind of sly humor and thereby represents a different, but no less effective approach to the problem. This book, too, contains the much-favored motif of decline and destruction, although it manifests the theme, along with death by freezing, only in an oblique and impres-
sionistic manner: either as a repulsive peasant "catastrophe" or, more frequently, as a dream. When dreaming, Meyer's seemingly proper hero is
haunted by a vision of a "*dead* and *lifeless* landscape, a primordial landscape, perhaps prehuman or deserted by humans and animals, a landscape
devastated by water." This diluvial vision is also connected to an accidental
encounter with carrion and nauseating putrification.[28] However, all this, as is
the case with the novel as a whole, is narrated with a distance and reticence
that are skillfully achieved; thus it is only gradually and indirectly that one
gains a sense of its traumatic function. For a considerable time Meyer man-

ages to maintain the unsuspecting reader's false sense of security. He lures us out on thin ice, as it were.

The illusion of safety is heightened by the author's detailed, positively voluptuous treatment of food. The form that this treatment takes is characteristic of Meyer's style. An exact description of the delicious, although uniformly heavy and cholesterol-ridden meals that the narrator consumes daily in Anna Soltermann-Hirschi's inn is achieved through the simple device of presenting a verbatim copy of each day's menu, a copy written out in imposing capital letters. Meyer integrates more than a dozen such culinary transcripts into his novel and does so in a way that is not without a certain caustic humor. However, in the larger context of the novel these gluttonous sections have a strangely unsatisfying, indeed sobering effect. In conjunction with the protagonist's reading, which alternates between Kant and lowbrow magazines, and set against the background of coldness, terminal decline, devastation, and the stink of carrion, they serve to ruthlessly expose the hollowness and illogic of contemporary consumer society, a society that derives its immense prosperity from a brutally exploitative and destructive economic system. The close attention to gluttony in Meyer's novel is by no means gratuitous; the detailed, misleadingly appreciative description of pleasure, indolence, and languorous efforts to be cultured, all of which is coupled to an obliviousness to all human suffering and deprivation, serves as the key element in a systematic process of alienation. In luring us out on the ice, Meyer also leads us into the ice age—a journey that, to continue the image used by Brasch and Enzensberger, takes us through the Swiss luxury cabin on board the good ship "Europe," where apparently everything is still "running."

Although we should not forget that this vessel has a wave–tossed sister ship, the "America," let us instead turn our attention to German film. Here of course everything is running—or rerunning—quite smoothly. And it is here that we arrive at the farce that follows the tragedy. Admittedly, "farce" is too noble a name for the work at hand. With its author, an "artist" by the name of Herbert Achternbusch, the pale and icy topic we have been dealing with goes not only to the dogs but, as shall be seen, to the polar bears as well. The result is an inadvertent travesty that manages to be at the same time moronic and pretentious. The work in question, Achternbusch's dubious contribution to our theme, is his text and film, *Servus Bayern* ("Bavaria Hello and Goodbye") of 1978. What does he offer us here? Primarily ice, a massive and crushing load of ice. One could say that Achternbusch is obsessed with ice, and also snow,[29] but especially with ice from Greenland, for it is there that *Servus Bayern* is set. Both the text and the film begin and end with a long "flight over the edge of Greenland's continental glacier."[30]

Yet even Achternbusch cannot entirely avoid a certain connection with what has been discussed so far. For example, according to a statement made by a reporter in the screenplay, the "people in Bavaria" have "ice within themselves."[31] What is more, Achternbusch's figures yell at one another: "You're only ice!" And in one instance Achternbusch actually stumbles upon an accurate, although by no means remarkably deep insight: "But the ice is both solace and death." Achternbusch's puerile little creation reaches its climax in a double scene in which Annamirl, his wife with whom it just doesn't work as it used to, stands "at the Straits of Messina . . . under a wind-whipped palm tree," while up in Greenland he clings to a polar bear and attempts "to fuck him from behind."[32] God—or the devil—only knows whether this is a conscious parody of Heine's famous poem from *Lyrisches Intermezzo* ("Lyrical Intermezzo"). Intentional or not, there is an unmistakable echo of the solitary "fir tree" in the north covered with "ice and snow" and the "palm tree" in the south mourning "alone and silent . . . on a wall of burning rock."[33] Of course it must be added that Heine's fir tree is overcome by drowsiness and not by some bizarre concupiscence for polar bears.

But enough of Achternbusch. His primary contribution is to provide a glaring example of an oft-repeated literary phenomenon: is it not always in the hands of the incompetents and the gasping, grimacing slaves of fashion that widely-used motifs become totally devalued and, whether intentionally or not, are transformed into caricatures of themselves? As I noted at the outset, the slogan "ice age, decline and destruction" is currently being shouted from every street corner, or at least from every *feuilleton*. As indicated before, the entire complex is not without its own prehistory. Limits of space prevent me from offering a full examination of this prehistory, that comes to the fore with Max Dauthendey's short epic *Die Untergangsstunde der 'Titanic'* ("The *Titanic's* Hour of Doom") of 1913 and Kafka's stories *Der Kübelreiter* ("The Bucket Rider") and *Ein Landarzt* ("A Country Doctor") of 1916-17, but extends well back into the nineteenth century. Instead, I will pick out Friedrich Dürrenmatt's "Comedy in Two Acts" of 1962, *Die Physiker* ("The Physicists"). It is no accident that Dürrenmatt's notes to the drama, "21 Points to *The Physicists,"* contain the apodictic sentence: "A story has been thought to its conclusion when it has taken its worst possible turn."[34] Actually, it would seem that the "story"—which is also our history—already had taken its "worst possible turn" five years previously. I am referring, of course, to Beckett's *Endgame* that premiered in London in 1957. No words need be wasted recounting the content of this play, for it is all too obvious that here the final days have already arrived. The total catastrophe, atomic or otherwise, has either long since taken place or else continues unabated. Or could it be that both of these possibilities are equally true? In any case, one should mention in this connection Theodor W. Adorno's long and influential essay, *Versuch, das Endspiel zu verstehen* ("An Attempt to Understand the Endgame"), an essay that both deals with and is dedicated to Samuel Beckett. Adorno not only makes continual reference to Kafka, he also proclaims the "permanent catastrophe," a catastrophe that in no way excludes an "additional chain of catastrophes caused by human beings."[35] This same twofold and highly pessimistic concept of catastrophe is presented by Friedrich Dürrenmatt, a writer fascinated by decline and destruction, indeed by the destruction of the world. His play *Porträt eines Planeten* ("Portrait of a Planet") first concerns itself with the catastrophic conditions on Earth and then culminates with the "cosmic" or "world catastrophe," the destruction of our planet that will occur when the sun swells into a supernova and finally explodes with unimaginable force ("although," as Dürrenmatt bitterly adds in his foreword, "it is, to an improbable degree, altogether more probable that mankind will destroy itself.")[36]

"Friedrich Dürrenmatt's Endgame": this title, analogous to that of the volume devoted to Müller, could quite justifiably be given to *Porträt eines Planeten.* Moreover, the global destruction that is presented in this play of 1970 corresponds exactly to the universal freezing one encounters in Bernhard's bleak chronicle, *Frost,* the work that, back in 1963, signaled the beginning of the latest phase in the history of the motif. Ice and annihilation, as noted at the beginning, or final and permanent catastrophe, as I feel entitled to state now, are the distinguishing characteristics of its subsequent development. The imagination of contemporary writers is no longer ignited by the threat of a nuclear holocaust;[37] rather, it is increasingly haunted by the vision of a sinking ship or an ice age. Such visions derive, I believe, both from the spreading popularity of the "spaceship Earth" concept and from the closely related development of an acute ecological consciousness, that is to say, an insight into the gradual and seemingly inexorable destruction of the world by mankind. Furthermore, it is no accident that the already mythic sinking of the "Titanic" by a "monstrous" iceberg of "unprecedented" immensity and coldness[38] has been vividly represented not just by Enzensberger and that, finally, as in the case of the *Hamletmaschine,* "the depths of the ocean" and "the ice age" collide and merge with one another. It seems clear that these twin images of catastrophe are actually different facets of a single vision, a vision in which a desperate sense of societal and interpersonal alienation continues to manifest itself. The first type of alienation, that of the societal variety, is clearly exemplified by East German writers such as Müller and Wolf. It can hardly be denied that in the GDR metaphorical concepts such as "ice age" and "freezing" possess a highly concrete political dimension insofar as they represent a reversal of the proverbial though brief "thaw" with its both concrete and metaphorical dimension. This is not to imply that in West Germany, in the aftermath of the turbulence that marked the late sixties and early seventies, the political climate has not turned considerably cooler. However, in the West German context this chill seems somewhat less deadening and paralyzing than east of the Elbe. Whatever the exact level of societal frost in the Federal Republic, there can be no doubt that it possesses a superabundance of individual coldness, an iciness in interpersonal relationships that, though it is experienced separately by each person, is ultimately a function of society as a whole. The extent to which the coldness has crept into the family, a sphere previously regarded as a primary source of security and warmth, is presented with impressive vividness in one of the most recent works that deal with this theme, a work which also offers a new and truly original variation of the basic motif: Helga M. Novak's somber reminiscence, *Die Eisheiligen* ("The Ice Saints") of 1979.[39] "One easily feels chilled while reading this book," was the lapidary comment offered by one reviewer. He went on to note that the chill did not necessarily derive from the fact that Novak's account of a childhood contains numerous references to "coldness, snow, biting wind, numb feet": "Those are only the external, measurable correlatives of an iciness that has penetrated all family situations and expressions of feeling."[40]

The iciness is in fact universal and is spreading relentlessly. Its poetic correlatives are not just the coldness, the snow, and the biting wind one finds in Novak's book, the numbness within and between individuals, but rather, more generally, the ice age and the destruction of the world, the final days, and the endgame. That these correlatives are uttered and written, indeed proclaimed, most frequently in the Federal Republic is something that cannot be denied, just as one cannot deny the link that exists with the East German concept of "thaw." For example, Michael Krüger reviewed Nicolas Born's last novel[41] and gave his discussion the following title: "War in Lebanon—German Ice Age." Krüger reports that, on the one hand, Born's protagonist is in a "state of iciness"; on the other, the novel as a whole is a "book about Germany, [a fact that] . . . explains the iciness."[42] In another review we are offered an explanation, not of the German iciness and ice age, but rather of the Austrian endgame—according to the title of the article, a "Double Endgame." The review focuses primarily on Ernst Jandl's two plays, *Die Humanisten* ("The Humanists") and *Aus der Fremde* ("From a Foreign Land"), both of which, according to the critic, are *bona fide* endgames. He is able to support this thesis with a statement made by Jandl himself: "I view *The Humanists* as a sort of endgame: nothing comes afterward."[43] Unfortunately, there *is* something that comes afterward, at least for us: our story takes Dürrenmatt's "worst possible turn" and leaves us in a new "Ice Age of Reason"—part of the title of yet another review. This phrase, clearly predestined to become a slogan, is particularly significant in that it catapults us into an entirely new area. The complete title of the review reads: "Does Konrad Lorenz Have to Become a Grey Goose? Magic, Ethnography, and Alternative Rationality. On the Eve of a New Ice Age of Reason." The author of this wide-ranging article is by no means satisfied with frozen reason; instead, he sees the approach of a general and all-pervasive "winter." Did not Baudelaire observe that one can appraise poets on the basis of their images, similes, and motifs? And is not this also true, perhaps to an even greater extent, for the swarms of less talented contemporaries, indeed for an era in its entirety? Admittedly, the present era appears to be just as strongly characterized by the almost manic way it seizes upon certain images and "signs" that it then, with startling celerity, proceeds to market, popularize, and, ultimately, devalue.

As regards the motifs of decline and destruction and the end of the world, it is only to be expected that the trend will continue and that with every new day and every new literary supplement the examples will keep piling up. We are witnessing the same process of marketing and popularization, the same rapid and massive devaluation. Yet all this does not simply negate the validity of the poets' visions. Even older texts that are typical of the 1950's and early 1960s, texts such as Marie Luise Kaschnitz's story *Der Tag X* ("Day X"), a deeply disturbing presentiment of nuclear annihilation,[44] have not lost any of their original intensity. However, in recent years the sinking ships have multiplied to the point where we are now confronted by vast fleets of them.[45] Brasch launched his pathetically unseaworthy "European Culture"; a year later, Enzensberger sent his own luxury liner plunging down into the depths of the ocean. More recently, these unfortunate hulks have been joined by a satirical journal that bears the name *Titanic,* as well as by an opera, Wilhelm Dieter Siebert's *Untergang der Titanic* ("The Sinking of the 'Titanic'"). Shipwrecks, wherever one looks! Or as Karl Krolow put it decades ago in the motto for one of his poems: "If one looks closely, every place is a shipwreck."[46] It can hardly come as a surprise when one reads that contemporary German film is increasingly filled with "melancholy apostrophes to death and the final days." At any rate, Enzensberger's epic of a doomed ship and a doomed world certainly is no longer the only one of its kind—and Brasch's *Kargo* is by no means its only companion. One wonders, then, if it was the desire to re-establish an equilibrium that led the indefatigable Enzensberger to produce a series of songs of catastrophe? And is this why they evoked among critics the image of "a ship slowly heeling over or at least a ship with a bad list"?[47] Whatever the answers to these questions, the fact is that in 1979 there appeared a record album entitled *Der Abendstern* ("The Evening Star") sung by Ingrid Caven, with music by Peer Raben; two-thirds of the songs on this record—eight altogether—featured lyrics written by Hans Magnus Enzensberger. One of these songs, *In zehn Minuten ist alles vorbei* ("In Ten Minutes It Will All Be Over"), contains the following lines:

Attention! Attention! This is the management speaking.
There will be no survivors.[48]

Macabre and melancholy statements of this sort are, the critics inform us, "often announced in these songs." However, they also insist that what one encounters here tend to be distinctly "cheerful cataclysms." We are even told that the singer Caven "merrily" warbles these apocalyptic ditties.

In all respects, Enzensberger's *Abendstern* songs clearly represent the current highpoint of the popularization trend. Yet at the same time it seems that we are confronted here by a genuine and serious paradox. One critic noted that in these songs "defiance and resistance repeatedly assert themselves." The same critic writes about Enzensberger's end-of-the-world poetry in general:

> Instead of losing themselves in strident gallows humor, these songs encourage us to not allow ourselves to be dragged down, not even by the acute popular melancholy, and to remain wide awake; and rather than wallowing in nostalgia and decadence and escapism and narcissistic posturing, they propagate critical reflection, analytical confrontation, hope, and, how awful, humor.[49]

Are we to believe this critic? Could it be that despite all the weeping and moaning there still exists humor and even confidence? Could it be that at the end of this bleak path one finds a way back? It is not without reason that I pose these questions; for there is yet another book by the Swiss Meyer with the title *Die Rückfahrt* ("The Return Trip"). Published in 1977, it offers a treatment not only of all aspects of the themes of catastrophe and doom but also of the closely related present-day historical situation, a treatment that, in its soundness and scope, has yet to be surpassed in contemporary German-language literature. Meyer is equally familiar with the concept of "spaceship Earth" and with the ecological "apocalypse of a world without space, a world overfilled with human beings, on the verge of madness and insanity"; he deals both with the downfall of the individual and the "end of the world"; he writes of the "second . . . big bang," the final, man-made catastrophe, as well as the senseless and purely random, but nonetheless fatal car crash.[50] Meyer's visions of decline and destruction, death and annihilation finally culminate in a cosmic catastrophe, indeed in *the* catastrophe, something that leads not to an ice age but instead to a final, permanent and hence timeless "freezing" of the entire universe. Such freezing, Meyer mercilessly informs us, will have to result in "a condition of *eternal night,* of *absolute silence,* and an all-encompassing intergalactic *rigor mortis.*"[51]

And yet, despite everything, *Die Rückfahrt* attempts to articulate hope. Even the title is ambiguous. On the one hand, it refers to a thoroughly mundane car trip, while on the other it is connected to the protagonist's reminiscences and thus alludes to the notion that time itself can flow backwards—if one's conception of time differs from that which is commonly held. This "perpendicular" or "pendulum-like conception of time,"[52] a conception that allows time to change in the most literal sense, clashes with the familiar linear view of time as something totally irreversible as well as with the view, sporadically asserted ever since antiquity, of time as something cyclical or circular based on eternal repetition.[53] It is only in change and renewal and our ability to partake in them that we can attain hope—perhaps even salvation. Thus speculates Meyer's protagonist while driving with a companion. But in the midst of this line of thought the car goes into a skid, rolls down a steep embankment and comes to rest on its two occupants. The doubter survives, the man who saw hope is killed. *Die Rückfahrt* ends with this unexplained and inexplicable accident, the parabolic nature of which is both undeniable and highly ambiguous. Is it (to draw the bleakest possible conclusion) an image of the ineluctability of the catastrophe that will occur when we least expect it?

Whatever the answer, the closing words of the old man in the work with which we began, the play "Ice Age," apply to us as well. We, too, are still alive—for the time being.

Notes

*A shortened German version of this essay entitled, "The Ice Age Cometh: Skizzenhaftes zu einem Motivkomplex in der deutschen Gegenwartsliteratur, " appeared in *Festschrift for E. W. Herd,* ed. August Obermayer (Dunedin, New Zealand: Department of German, University of Otago, 1980), pp. 78–85. Another German version, "Eiszeit und Untergang: Zu einem Motivkomplex in der deutschen Gegenwartsliteratur," was published in *Monashefte*, 73 (1981), 155-86.

1. Tankred Dorst, *Eiszeit: Ein Stück* (Frankfurt: Suhrkamp, 1973 [first published in 1972]), p. 120.
2. Ibid., p. 74.
3. Ibid., pp. 119–20.
4. Bernhard Sorg, *Thomas Bernhard* (Munich: Beck/Edition Text + Kritik, 1977), pp. 71, 64.
5. Sorg goes so far as to speak of *Frost* in terms of the *Entwicklungsroman,* albeit with certain limitations.
6. Thomas Bernhard, *Frost* (Frankfurt: Suhrkamp, 1972 [first published in 1963]), pp. 247, 41, 153.
7. Ibid., p. 301.
8. Ibid., p. 152 (Bernhard's emphasis).
9. Ibid., p. 38.
10. See Wolf Donner, "Berichte zur Lage der Nation: Ingrid Caven singt Lieder von Hans Magnus Enzensberger," *Der Spiegel,* 15 October 1979, p. 245.
11. E. Y. Meyer, *In Trubschachen: Roman* (Frankfurt: Suhrkamp, 1979 [first published in 1973]); see especially pp. 200, *et passim.*

12. For a differing interpretation, see Richard Weber, "'Ich war, ich bin, ich werde sein!' Versuch, die politische Dimension der HAMLETMASCHINE zu orten," *Die Hamletmaschine, Heiner Müllers Endspiel,* ed. Theo Girshausen (Cologne: Prometh Verlag, 1978), pp. 86–97, 165–67.

13. Heiner Müller, *Geschichten aus der Produktion 1: Stücke. Prosa. Gedichte. Protokolle* (Berlin: Rotbuch Verlag, 1974), p. 134.

14. Heiner Müller, *Mauser* (Berlin: Wagenbach, 1978), p. 97.

15. Ibid.

16. Weber, p. 97; concerning Müller's statement, see Weber, p. 167.

17. In a letter to me dated 2 June 1979, Günter Kunert spoke of this "relevance of classic authors," a relevance that he described as being present in Kleist "in an unexpected and even shocking manner." In the same connection he considered (as a possible title) the phrase, "The Presence of the Past" ("Die Gegenwart der Vergangenheit").

18. Christa Wolf, *Kein Ort. Nirgends* (Darmstadt and Neuwied: Luchterhand, 1979), pp. 133–34, 148, 151. The East German edition was published by Aufbau Verlag (Berlin and Weimar).

19. For an elaboration of this idea, see my earlier study "Bewusstsein als Verhängnis: Über Gottfried Benns Weg in die Kunst," *Die Kunst im Schatten des Gottes: Für und wider Gottfried Benn,* ed. Reinhold Grimm and Wolf-Dieter Marsch (Göttingen: Sachse und Pohl, 1962), pp. 40–84.

20. Thomas Brasch, *Kargo: 32. Versuch auf einem untergehenden Schiff aus der eigenen Haut zu kommen* (Frankfurt: Suhrkamp, 1979 [first published in 1977]), p. 61.

21. Hans Magnus Enzensberger, *Der Untergang der Titanic: Eine Komödie* (Frankfurt: Suhrkamp, 1978), pp. 15, 115.

22. Ibid., p. 17.

23. Ibid., p. 54.

24. Ibid., e.g. pp. 14, 20, 22.

25. Ibid., pp. 53, 56.

26. Ibid., 115.

27. Brasch, p. 147.

28. Meyer, *In Trubschachen,* pp. 125 *et passim.*

29. For example, Achternbusch's 'novel' *Die Stunde des Todes* ("The Hour of Death"; Frankfurt: Suhrkamp, 1975), a volume that contains numerous pictures, shows the author kneeling or wading in snow. The photograph in question appears three times: on the front and back cover as well as in the text, where it takes up two pages. The caption speaks of a "Katastrofe" [sic].

30. Herbert Achternbusch, *Die Atlantikschwimmer* (Frankfurt: Suhrkamp, 1978), pp. 299, 325.

31. Ibid., p. 303; for the two subsequent quotes, see pp. 310, 322.

32. Ibid., p. 323.

33. Heinrich Heine, *Sämtliche Werke,* ed. Ernst Elster (Leipzig and Vienna: Bibliographisches Institut, n.d.), I, 78. See also the translation of the poem by Aaron Kramer, *The Poetry and Prose of Heinrich Heine,* ed. Frederic Ewen (New York: The Citadel Press, 1969), p. 74.

34. Friedrich Dürrenmatt, *Die Physiker: Eine Komödie in zwei Akten* (Zurich: Verlag der Arche, 1962), p. 70. See also *The Physicists,* trans. James Kirkup (New York: Grove Press, 1964), p. 95.

35. Theodor W. Adorno, *Noten zur Literatur II* (Frankfurt: Suhrkamp, 1961), pp. 188–236; here p. 193.

36. Friedrich Dürrenmatt, *Porträt eines Planeten* (Zurich: Verlag der Arche, 1971), p. 7.
37. See my essay "Ein Menschenalter danach: Über das zweistrophige Gedicht 'Hiroshima' von Marie Luise Kaschnitz," *Monatshefte,* 71 (1979), 5-18.
38. Enzensberger, *Der Untergang der Titanic,* pp. 28, 17. It should be noted that Enzensberger has produced one of the most important analyses of the ecology problem and the ecology movement. See Hans Magnus Enzensberger, "Zur Kritik der politischen Ökologie," *Kursbuch,* 33 (October 1973), 1-42; reprinted in: Hans Magnus Enzensberger, *Palaver: Politische Überlegungen (1967-1973)* (Frankfurt: Suhrkamp, 1974), pp. 169-232.
39. Helga M. Novak, *Die Eisheiligen* (Darmstadt and Neuwied: Luchterhand, 1979).
40. Gert Ueding, "Fotoalbum mit verzerrten Gesichtern," *Frankfurter Allgemeine Zeitung,* 22 September 1979, supplement.
41. Nicolas Born, *Die Fälschung: Roman* (Reinbek: Rowohlt, 1979).
42. Michael Krüger, "Krieg in Libanon—deutsche Eiszeit," *Die Zeit,* 26 October 1979, p. 24.
43. Helmut Schödel, "Doppeltes Endspiel," *Die Zeit,* 26 October 1979, p. 21; the Jandl quote is also found here.
44. Marie Luise Kaschnitz, "Der Tag X," *Eisbären: Ausgewählte Erzählungen* (Frankfurt: Insel Verlag, 1972); see also Anita Baus, *Standortbestimmung als Prozess: Eine Untersuchung zur Prosa von Marie Luise Kaschnitz* (Bonn: Bouvier Verlag, 1974), pp. 215-16.
45. Concerning the following, see the *Spiegel* article by Donner mentioned in n. 10, above.
46. Karl Krolow, *Die Zeichen der Welt: Neue Gedichte* (Stuttgart: Deutsche Verlags-Anstalt, 1952), p. 41. As Krolow notes, the quote is taken from Petronius; the title of the Krolow poem in question is "Verlassene Küste."
47. Manfred Sack, "Lieder vom Dichter," *Die Zeit,* 9 November 1979, p. 9.
48. Quoted in Donner, n. 10, above.
49. Donner.
50. E. Y. Meyer, *Die Rückfahrt: Roman* (Frankfurt: Suhrkamp, 1977), pp. 355, 351-52, 70, 426.
51. Ibid., p. 131 (Meyer's emphasis); I would like to emphasize that I have allowed myself here to use the terms "ice age" and "freezing" in a metaphorical sense.
52. Ibid., pp. 426, 69-70, and especially 424, where one reads: "The art of having time run *backwards* is based . . . on a totally different concept of time, a conception in which time swings back and forth like a pendulum: time there is not a line and neither is it a cycle but rather an oscillation, that is to say a rocking or a swinging" (Meyer's emphasis).
53. Ibid.

Günter Grass in Search of
a Literary Theory

Peter Demetz

German writers who returned to literature from World War II often share a distrust of literary theory that distinctly separates them from the younger generation who came to literature through the doors of the advanced university seminar on Theodor Adorno and Walter Benjamin. Grass is one of those writers who, in matters of theory, have shown an attitude of "without me" (*ohne mich*) that was characteristic of the returning soldier or *Landser*. Such an attitude was programmatically strengthened by the Group 47 whose members preferred practical criticism in shirt-sleeves to ritual quotations from the classics of whatever sort. But practical performances imply their own theory, however inarticulate, and it is not unfair to say that Grass from his days in Paris (where he learned more about surrealism and the absurd theater than we usually want to acknowledge) until the early sixties preferred an eclectic *menu* of antimimetic strategies concocted from narrative and poetological possibilities preceding and following the age of middle-class realism. He wanted to do anything, provided it did not read like a nineteenth-century novel or look like a realistic painting, and his imaginative energies were so restive that even the picaresque patterns emerging from *The Tin Drum* (1959) and *Dog Years* (1963) were countered by abrupt changes of narrative perspective and disturbing verbal exercises in surrealist image making. Yet in the late sixties, beginning with *Local Anaesthetic* (1969), his narrative prose distinctly changes, and critics in Germany and elsewhere often were wont to complain about the whimsical games of an undisciplined author rather than to recognize the radical transformations of his narrative assumptions and the necessity to use other norms when judging his prose. I relate the incisive change in narrative articulation to Grass's willingness to engage with Alfred Döblin's

(1878–1957) theory and practice; while Grass usually plays his cards close to his chest and only fleetingly suggests that he has learned something from Apollinaire or Herman Melville, his essay "About my Teacher Döblin," first presented as a lecture at the Berlin Akademie der Künste in 1967, constitutes a theoretical and confessional text of far-reaching implications (AL, 67–91). It is Grass's own attention to Döblin's "futurism" that compels me to ask whether Grass, as a new disciple of Döblin, does not write closer to the Italian futurists, and to some of F. T. Marinetti's ideas, than we are willing to believe. The socialist Grass and Marinetti, alternating between being Mussolini's ally or adversary on the right, may be worlds apart in their political concepts but the question remains whether they do not, with Döblin as their intellectual mediator, agree on some conceptual issues of writing antimimetic prose.

Grass's relationship to Döblin is one of the imagination rather than a matter of historical encounters. Grass never met Döblin personally, and though he often argues against people who prefer books to experience (especially when he turns against the radical students), he admits that his thankful enthusiasm for Döblin is a totally bookish affair. Many of Grass's formulations in his 1967 Berlin Academy address derive from the edition of Döblin's works that was begun by Walter Muschg in 1960 and has been largely ignored by German readers—"the edition lies like a lead weight on the publisher's shelf," Grass remarked (AL, 68). Hence it is essential to see that Grass prefers to concentrate on Döblin's theory and practice from 1912 to 1940 and to disregard his later works. Like most West German intellectuals, he refuses to find himself involved with Döblin, the aging catholic, but closely discusses Döblin's view of Marinetti and analyses his novels from *Die drei Sprünge des Wang-lun* ("The Three Leaps of Wang-lun"; 1915) to *Berge, Meere und Giganten* ("Mountains, Seas and Giants"; 1924) in terms of narrative experimentation. Further, Grass states that he could not speak about his own work without thinking of "the futurist process of production" (AL, 91) in the prose of his teacher. My argument hinges, of course, on Döblin's view and use of Marinetti, and I am fully aware that I have to touch, at least briefly, on a much-discussed issue of Döblin criticism. It was Armin Arnold who, some time ago, made the most enthusiastic case for Döblin as an early and enthusiastic disciple of Marinetti.[1] But not everybody wants to take his or her cue from Arnold's impressive textual comparisons between some of Marinetti's and Döblin's prose pieces. I believe that much depends on how we read and interpret Döblin's "Open Letter to Marinetti," first published in the expressionist periodical *Der Sturm* (March 1913).[2] Grass would agree with Arnold, I suspect, that the belligerent tone of Döblin's critical proclamation against Marinetti should not be taken as a final argument without qualifications; if we read the open letter carefully and in context with Döblin's enthusiastic

communications about futurist paintings that he published in the same avant-
garde periodical in May 1912, we come to see that Döblin, in trying to decide
whether he should condemn or respect Marinetti, makes a sharp distinction
between futurist painting and Marinetti's early futurist novel *Mafarka le Futuriste* (1909) on the one hand, and both his "Technical Manifesto of Futurist
Literature" (11 May 1912) and the experimental text entitled "The Battle" on
the other. That text was to illustrate by onomatopoeia and other devices what
Marinetti had in mind when compiling his stringent catalogue of rules about
verbs, nouns, infinitives, and the destruction of syntax. Döblin has no doubts
whatsoever about the emancipatory force of futurist painting, its *Intensität*
and *Ursprünglichkeit* ("intensity" and "originality"; Döblin, 9), praises Marinetti's prose narrative *Mafarka le Futuriste,* published long before the literary manifestoes, for its massive passion and yet *Sachlichkeit* ("objectivity";
Döblin, 9), and concentrates his attack on the antigrammatical rules that
Marinetti had announced in the most intolerant way. In an often quoted line,
he tells Marinetti to cultivate his futurism while he would go on cultivating his
own *Döblinism* (Döblin, 15), and yet it is another question entirely in what
way *Döblinism* was disguising and preserving essential characteristics of futurist poetics. While we have yet to discover by close analysis of Döblin's
novels in what way he uses and transforms Marinetti's concepts, Grass, at
least in his Berlin Academy speech, has made up his mind and clearly says
that he is deeply in debt to the futurist practice of Döblin's prose.

Grass is attracted to Döblin by his belligerent aversion to the limitations
of the realistic narrative, that is, inherited psychology, the reductive mon-
otony of established forms, and the use of the linear plot that repressed the
manifold and energetic fullness of the world; when Grass praises Döblin for
setting in motion people and natural forces together—"the elements are
storming along," he writes (AL, 71)—he sounds exactly like Döblin praising
Marinetti for the explosive virtues of *Mafarka* in which mountains and
masses are moved as lightly as feathers. I would be inclined to say that
Döblin, in his theory and practice, held to a tectonic concept of prose writing
dominated by gaps, eruptions, quick changes of materials and massive, occa-
sionally brutal effects rather than pristine *finesse.* Döblin demanded, at least
in his early years, a narrative that would not speak about but hold up to us the
total world in cosmological flux; deriding the French preference for the lean
and clean narrative, he called for a *Kinostil* ("cinematic style") of rapid montage, the abrupt use of many elements, "the phantastic, epic, enhanced, the
fairy- talelike, the burlesque . . . the relaxed game" (Döblin, 43)—a "built"
epic style of expansive and contradictory gestures, a narrative generated by
"stacking, heaping, shifting, and pushing" (Döblin, 20) rather than by merely satisfying the demands for a simple plot, usually preferred by readers whose
sensibilities had been paralysed by the simplifications of the newspapers. But

it is in his programmatic recommendations for a particular syntax that allows the writer to combine the *Nebeneinander* of complexities with their *Hintereinander* or juxtaposition with linearity (Döblin, 17) that Döblin comes closest to the central futurist principle of synchrony or *simultaneitá*. I think we have not sufficiently noticed that Grass particularly praises the *grosse gleichzeitige Bewegung* or "great synchronic motion" (AL, 74) in Döblin's narratives and quotes individual sentences that distinctly try to account for the simultaneity of what is being told. Reading these sentences out of context (AL, 74), we may have great trouble to decide whether they are taken from Döblin's *Wallenstein* or from one of the historic episodes in *The Flounder:* "An abbot bit off the leg of his capon, estimated, while it cracked, the value of the silver platter from the Palatinate, left [by the Protestants] and handed over to him by pious Walloons."[3] Is the passage taken from Döblin or Grass? It was penned by Döblin.

It is essential to consider Grass's concern with Döblin's theory and practice because the idea of a tectonic narrative built of disparate materials and energetically trying to articulate the *simultaneitá* of many events if not history itself, may help us to deal fairly with his major writings of the sixties and after, especially *The Flounder* (1977). Critics on both sides of the Atlantic have been at odds how to deal with a novel that adamantly refuses to be a novel, at least in the manner of the nineteenth century; American readers had the meager choice of agreeing with those who, like Morris Dickstein, praise Grass for having written "a monotonous miscellany in the guise of narrative fiction"[4] or with someone like Nigel Dennis who complained in a rather finicky way about the "endlessness of contents, the lack of elegance and a disturbing flabbiness" that prevents the narrative from really "cutting deep."[5] It is, of course, true that we are disturbed and often frustrated when perusing *The Flounder* after reading a novel by Jane Austen, Theodor Fontane, or Iris Murdoch, but we may train for feeling the philological and constructive pleasures of the later Grass by reading Thomas Pynchon or Gabriel García Márquez. Unfortunately, Grass's pastiche and language parodies come in entire avalanches that first overwhelm us by their mass; in our first confusion we underrate the marvelous precision of linguistic collages (dialect versus literary language) or the Joycean language games. For example, the fat abbess who likes to pluck goose feathers develops a staccato style while Amanda Woyke, who endlessly peels potatoes, has a more long-winded way of telling her stories. Grass himself ironically characterizes something of his own procedures when he describes Margarete Rusch's table conversations or rather monologues as "a subliminal mumbling with subplots as intricate as the politics of her time" (F, 194), and praises her, Gargantua's German sister, for her wonderful ability to reel off several stories and instructive disquisitions at once without dropping a single thread (F, 193). Margarete does by epic instinct what Grass wants to do by seizing on Döblin's futurist ideas about the novel—that is, to create a narrative order sustained by the idea of synchrony of all events in our mind, and the subsequent necessity to counteract all linearity and mere sequence by strategies and ploys that arrest or at least substantially diminish time. History may be organized by the principle of *Zeitweil* ("changing time phases"), or the revealing moment, but characters tend to return if not reincarnate in these different and yet analogous moments. The narrator himself identifies with nearly all eligible males throughout the Kashubian and Danzig vicissitudes, and all the female tribal cooks, whether of the Stone Age or of later time phases, are present once again as members of the Women's Tribunal. Thus Ms. Schönherr corresponds to Awa, Helga Paasch to Wigga, Ruth Simoneit to Mestwina, and so on.[6] Characteristic gestures and everyday actions of seemingly little import, at least at first reading, hold back the flow of time: women and men always dig their teeth into crackling apples—an act suggesting their love for each other, as the historical catalogue demonstrates (F, 416–17); sceptical women always keep their heads tilted when feeling amused by boundless male enthusiasm, as the examples from the Stone Age to modern Poland show (F, 504–505); when pregnant but imprudent Ilsebill jumps over a ditch and falls, fortunately without hurting herself, we are not spared a list of similar incidents that happened in earlier times (F, 335). Speaking about a Polish fellow artist, the narrator suggests that they have much in common: "On our paper most things take place simultaneously" (F, 123), insisting, in his later book *Kopfgeburten* (1980) or *Headbirths* (1982) , that epic time is really constituted by the fourth realm of *die Vergegenkunft* (KG, 130) that, here defined in a Joycean pun, effectively combines past (*Ver/gangenheit*), present (*Gegen/wart*), and future (*Zu/kunft*).

In some contrast to his younger contemporaries, Grass may be an amateur of literary theory, but in engaging Döblin, he has lost his theoretical innocence, and I would suggest that we should read his remarks on "The Reading Worker," offered in 1974 on the occasion of the one hundredth anniversary of the founding of the Gutenberg literary guild (Büchergilde Gutenberg), as his most advanced, thoughtful, and articulate theoretical statement, well worth being considered in its substantial implications. It is a polemical piece addressed to those who believe that working people cannot but read the most simple kind of literature (left-wing pulp, so to speak), and Grass defines his argument by a striking futurist analogy between the complexities of the technological process of industrial production and the complications of modern writing. Using Döblin's if not Marinetti's terms, he offers us a statement about his recent writings, conceptually clearer than ever before. He says that people in factories are better qualified than others to read difficult narratives because they know their assumptions from their own daily experience, "this simultaneity of events, the recurrent overlapping of consciousness, the chorus of inarticulate internal monologues" (DZ, 204). The aesthetics of new writing closely correspond to these experiences of material production; it explodes, Grass says (using one of Döblin's favorite terms), all linear agreements and chronologies and actually reflects the structure of technological production in its "thrusts, bottlenecks, discharges" (DZ, 204). These ideas are not irrelevant for our reading of *The Flounder,* for the narrator repeats the argument within the novel itself (F, 429–30) and insists on the key concept of *Überlappen* ("overlapping"). Actually, Grass quotes himself here owing to the fact that he had used this concept in his 1974 speech at Büchergilde Gutenberg (DZ, 204; F, 429); once again, when he discusses his writing with workers in a Kiel factory, he argues in favor of technological synchrony and tectonic construction (F, 429–30). Perhaps we should think twice before we decide whether to read the later Grass as an experimenting pioneer or a late heir to futurist tradition, transmitted to him by his teacher Döblin. Maybe he is both, and a pioneer precisely because he is so close to our restive grandfathers of 1909.

Notes

1. Armin Arnold, *Die Literatur des Expressionismus* (Stuttgart: Kohlhammer, 1966), pp. 69–106.
2. Alfred Döblin, *Aufsätze zur Literatur* (Olten: Walter, 1963), pp. 9–15. Subsequently cited as Döblin with page reference.
3. Alfred Döblin. *Wallenstein. Roman* (Olten: Walter, 1965), pp. 10–11.
4. Morris Dickstein, "An Epic Ribald Miscellany," pp. 12, 60. See also Sigrid Mayer, "The Critical Reception of *The Flounder* in the United States: Epic and Graphic Aspects," below, pp. 179–195.
5. Nigel Dennis, "The One That Got Away," pp. 22–23.
6. See Structural Diagram, below, pp. 198–199.

"I, Down Through the Ages": Reflections on the Poetics of Günter Grass*

Ruprecht Wimmer

TRANSLATED BY SUSAN C. ANDERSON

I

In his narrative *The Meeting at Telgte* Günter Grass poses a riddle to his readers—a riddle that critics conceived of as a problem either to be solved or simply to be accepted as a matter of course. On the one hand, one has sought to attribute the "I" that haunts the text to Grass and, by using analogy to leap the bounds of time, to a single one of the Baroque authors who are convening in a little Westphalian place of pilgrimage. These authors, so to speak in spiritual range of Münster, where negotiations are underway to end the Thirty Years' War, would like to have a say in what is taking place there politically. On the other hand, in light of the preceding novel *The Flounder,* critics felt justified in assigning this "I" to Grass's newly practiced omniscient perspective; by dismissing more specific attempts at identification, these critics assigned the "I" to all figures simultaneously and none exclusively.

"Who was I? Neither Logau nor Gelnhausen. Still others might have been invited—Neumark, for instance, but he stayed in Königsberg; or Tscherning, whose absence was especially deplored by Buchner. Whoever I may have been, I knew . . ." (MT, 84).

Before we can lay aside the riddle that is so explicitly posed by the author, we have to at least begin to puzzle through it. The narrative begins with

25

an epic *Gestus* that appears to be a mixture of the conventional frame narrative and elements of a perplexing game. The introductory, paradoxical aphorism sets a time-carousel in motion: "The thing that hath been tomorrow is that which shall be yesterday. Our stories of today need not have taken place in the present" (MT, 3). Then, the omniscient narrator fades in with a phrase promising suspense: "This one began more than three hundred years ago. . . . If I am writing down what happened in Telgte, it is because . . ." (MT, 3). Yet, the time-paradox is still there: the person addressed, the seventy-year-old birthday boy Hans Werner Richter, had "gathered his fellow writers around him" in 1947; at the same time, like his fellow writers and the author, he is much older and has "grown hoary white" (MT, 3). Is this a frame narrator setting himself on par with the author and, with respect to a friend who is going to be honored, telling a centuries-old, yet timeless story that is relevant to the present? For a while, it seems so. The meeting in Oesede of the invited writers who arrived first, the unsuccessful quest for lodgings there, the arrival of the Nuremberg colleagues along with the happy-go-lucky Gelnhausen, his proposal to go to Telgte, the way there, and the stop at the Telgte Bridge Tavern of Gelnhausen's old friend Libuschka, the nocturnal concerns and scheming thoughts of the organizer Simon Dach, his letter to his wife at home in Königsberg—all that could just as easily have been related in a nineteenth-century *Novelle*. One becomes accustomed to seeing the "I" of the introduction as necessary and fitting there and only there. When this "I" speaks up again, toward the end of the plot-section that was just outlined above, with clearly omniscient ambition, the reader will accept this as a conventionally possible interruption of the frame structure: "What more Simon Dach wrote to his Regina I shall leave to the two of them. Only his last, sleep-bringing thoughts are still within my reach . . . . I shall put them in order" (MT, 16). There is soon an end to this one-dimensionality. After Dach had greeted the gathering in the early afternoon of the following day and had commemorated the dead, after the first dispute had erupted at the mention of the Jesuit Spee and turned to pleasant chatter, the hitherto harmless and inconspicuous "I" literally explodes in the texture of the inner narration: "Then there was talk of student years in Leiden: Gryphius and Hofmannswaldau, Zesen and young Scheffler had been fed wild visionary ideas there. Someone (I?) asked why, in honoring the dead, Dach had neglected to mention the 'Görlitz shoemaker,' since after all, the followers of Böhme were here represented" (MT, 21).

The narrator resumes what he was saying in the beginning with surprising radicality; like his friend and his group he has "grown hoary white . . . since those olden times" (MT, 3) and can be present at a centuries-old literary discussion. It is not symptomatic for the further development of the narrative that the first-person narrator brings his Baroque extension only vaguely into the picture and does not know, or does not want to know, whether he was really the one who had asked the question. Before the narrator condescends to register the confusion of the reader, he does his utmost to increase it. In the succession of the following readings, meals, and evening discussions up to the final burning of the Bridge Tavern, the "I" appears in the number of those present as if it belonged there: "Obviously, we could never have come to any agreement as to whether to write '*teutsch*' or '*deutsch*,' but any praise of the German language gave us a lift" (MT, 27). Or: "Heinrich Schütz, who had attended the debate as though absent, answered the question: For the sake of the written words, which poets alone had the power to write in accordance with the dictates of art. And also to wrest from helplessness—he knew it well—a faint 'and yet.' With that we could agree" (MT, 68–69).

On the other hand, the "I" presents itself—even though always *ex negativo*—as a distinct *persona*. It suggests its specific presence which is not the presence of another; as, for example, at the first evening discussion that degenerates into general obscenities but results in silence when the suffering of Magdeburg is mentioned: "And I had joined in the laughter, I had let stories occur to me, I had started the trouble, and—once it was started—I had willingly sat in the seat of the scornful" (MT, 39–40).

Czepko, the innkeeper Libuschka, Gelnhausen, Gryphius, Moscherosch, Weckherlin, Logau, sometimes Paul Gerhardt, Hofmannswaldau, Schneuber, Lauremberg, Harsdörffer, Rist, and Dach had participated in the round. Birken, Greflinger, and Scheffler most certainly had not since they were rolling in the hay with Libuschka's maidservants. Shall we begin to eliminate those persons who are spatially separated from the "I" and assume that it is either identifiable with one of the rest or belongs to a further Baroque poet who is intentionally not named? In any case, the author would like to lure us in this direction by not identifying a number of persons; at the beginning, for example, some "other Silesians" (MT, 3) are mentioned in addition to those whose names are given. Further, the author provides other opportunities for eliminating possible candidates. When Paul Gerhardt, without mincing words, would like to contradict the composer Heinrich Schütz after his critique of Gryph's tragedy, it is time to eat lunch: "But Gerhardt was not given leave just yet. Neither Rist nor Zesen, both of whom were perishing to answer, obtained permission. (Nor did I, full as I was of ready words.) . . . Simon Dach adjourned the session . . .. Harsdörffer inquired whether Gelnhausen was back . . ." (MT, 62–63). Thus, in addition to those who have already departed, as mentioned above (Birken, Greflinger, Scheffler), Gerhardt, Rist, Zesen, Harsdörffer, and Gelnhausen are now discarded. We forego collecting further, often quite well-hidden indications of this sort, particularly since the author does not pursue his course of eliminating possible candidates to be identified with the "I"; there is more than one remaining.

However, he keeps the reader's desire for association awake with other techniques; he lets his "I" not only linger with one or several groups at specific places, but almost pedantically assigns him a place at the table at the big feast: "For now Birken . . . stood up, half concealed from me by the child-size Apollo . . . to pronounce an out-and-out Protestant grace" (MT, 84). Not only does the author have the "I" record events; he also has the "I" participate in them: "With some difficulty I restrained Zesen from going to the Ems . . ." (MT, 92).

However, the author finally disavows identifications, or rather eliminations, of the aforesaid kind when he attributes pronouncements he made in the past—in the meantime, they have become canonical—to the "I" or puts them unexpectedly in the mouths of other characters. Grass's skepticism—that of the sculptor versus the writer—is commonly known from his early years with Group 47: "The atmosphere was rather unpleasant to me in the beginning. There were people, some of them my age, who spoke in an exceedingly poised manner; hardly had they heard something before they had an opinion on it. . . ."[1] He says about Rist—of course it cannot be decided whether it is from the perspective of the Baroque "I" or from that of the initial narrator—that he "had an opinion about everything" (MT, 75). Yet, pious Paul Gerhardt, whom even the most broad-minded might have difficulty envisioning as a Baroque analogy to Grass, has a similar reservation: "All that, the glib talk and perpetual know-it-allness of the literati, so repelled him that he . . . longed to go home" (MT, 48). In addition, programmatic statements by various figures such as Schütz's short speech cited above (MT, 68-69), Logau's reprimand concerning the diplomatic mendacity of the manifesto draft (MT, 122–23), and, of course, Gelnhausen's farewell address that turns into a poetological program (MT, 109-13), directly reflect Grass's commitment. What is even more difficult to ascertain and, indeed, requires a specialist, is the fusing of the character of Gelnhausen with that of the author-narrator by means of astrological elements. Very quickly after the narrative appeared, Klaus Haberkamm was able to prove that Grass, by employing astrology, not only endowed this character with gestures and words, which he perceives and recognizes as his own, but that, so to speak, he also expresses his solidarity with Gelnhausen, who thinks and writes like him. One might even go so far as to say that Grass, using epic-fantastic license, identifies with Gelnhausen.[2] And yet, because of the seemingly or deceptively logical signals in the narrative—they were explained above—we do not really wish to speak, as Haberkamm does, of "the approximate equivalence of the observer in the narrative, who represents him [Grass], with the character Gelnhausen—an equivalence that is achieved especially by means of astrological narrative ingredients."[3] Rather, it appears that the author knows that he is sufficiently safe from discovery toward the end of the text when he creates a proud distance from the reader and interpreter and announces: "I know who I was then" (MT, 132). Is it his aim to help his public guess and yet keep it from figuring out the problem, guard it from the solution? Indeed, that does not mean that the book is concerned only with the intrinsic value of the procedure, with a permanent questioning whose answer has to be foregone. Perhaps the answer to the omnipresent question about the "I" is contained not so much in a "solution," but can be extracted from what Grass has tried to determine in the course of his development as the possible result and effect of writing in always novel approaches.

II

An "I" that, so to speak, repeatedly takes off and touches down in different places; moreover, an "I" that travels through time—the immediate recourse is to *The Flounder*. Nevertheless, let us undertake a quick expedition through the stages of Grass's epic works, beginning with *The Tin Drum*. This, his first novel, has invited interpretation from the very start, mostly concerning its protagonist. The contradictory interpretations of the character Oskar depict him and his function, as is well known, as a protestor, who is standing at a distance; as the hero of a negative *Bildungsroman*, as an antirealistic artist figure; indeed, as a personified structural principle, which exists only on narrative-technical grounds.[4] In fact, one does not lack evidence for any of these theses. Particularly the last-mentioned thesis, which endeavors to reconcile the character's contradictions and those of his perspectives, seeks to justify, on the basis of the dominance of things that Oskar represents and denotes, that the retrospectively narrating subject Oskar fails to establish the drummer's relationship to his particular milieu. In keeping with our interest, we want to try to briefly grasp the plurality of the protagonist in the following manner: Oskar appears to be almost an omniscient witness, a conscious critic, both in retrospect and in the original situation, a motivator of plot and fate—and occasionally a consolidation of the conditions around him in an allegorical way. He is also present as a witness where this is difficult to motivate within a realistic narrative, for instance, when Greff, the spartanlike-homophile greengrocer, swims in the icy Baltic: "Don't ask me, please, how I know. Oskar knew just about everything in those days" (TD, 294). It has already been indicated that the "I" of *The Meeting at Telgte* both betrays and stylizes the author-narrator's bad conscience about his fictional omnipresence. The correlation of both texts cannot be doubted because of the resumption of the above formulation that borders on Grass quoting Grass: "How do I know all this? I was sitting in their midst, I was there" (MT, 83–84).

Oskar's presence at all the events that he deems essential empowers him in principle to provide evaluations. However, he does not constantly assume this stance, not even indirectly through the child's perspective that appears unbiased only to the superficial observer. The author lets the retrospective narrator oscillate between accounts in which the narrator is subordinated to the events, unmasking incomprehension, and intentional criticism. The various perspectives—they cannot be pinned down entirely—are assigned to both the narrating and "narrated" Oskar. However, beyond that, from case to case, the hero refutes the thesis that he is nothing but a personified narrative technique; he does so by acting and generating events and, further, by assuming the role of fate for other characters. Suffice it to refer to Oskar's disruption of a Nazi demonstration by means of a waltz, to his causing the deaths of both of his fathers, and to the dwarf's career as gangleader. One may consider Oskar's outlined positions of witness, critic, and acting figure of fate as essentially one, and interpret them as generating each other and merging with each other. However, Oskar's fourth position, that tending toward the allegorical, is a partially passive one in contrast to his other functions. The novel begins with Oskar's resolution that transcends realism: he refuses to grow up and remains outside of the petit-bourgeois world that is degenerating into Nazism. He remains outside in order to record that world and work into it in a different way. However, when he gives up his "dwarfness"—again through sheer willpower—in order to grow, his former smallness appears to be not only an act of protest, but also an adequate form of existence under the prevailing social and political circumstances. Oskar begins to grow when he turns twenty-one; moreover, he begins to grow in the year 1945 and after the death of his second father, the Nazi sympathizer Alfred Matzerath. Oskar wants and is allowed to grow up in the period of reconstruction. Through this, he reflects not only the surrounding conditions, but appears as their exponent. He seems to become a complete allegory, when, after his move to the newly established Federal Republic, his growth degenerates into a deformation that occurs independently of his will (see TD, 356). Oskar's changing attitudes towards drumming parallel in part his growth that turns into deformation and, in addition, his fairy-talelike, magical ability to break glass by singing, as well as his equally fairy-talelike loss of that ability. These abilities support the reader's allegorical speculation, but without letting him arrive at a solution. After all, these activities Oskar engages in contain, like Oskar himself, elements of witnessing, assessment, and action in a like and yet contradictory manner.

The subject matter of *The Tin Drum* was not exhausted after its appearance owing to the fact that Grass continued to develop the fictional realm delineated in the novel. Grass himself repeatedly reproached Germanists for not recognizing the relation of *Cat and Mouse* and *Dog Years* to his first novel.[5]

Meanwhile, there have been attempts to understand the close relationship of the three fictional works. We believe that the manner in which the author reflects upon himself in the novel—as is evident in the character of the drummer—constitutes such a specific unifying element. Each of the two following books shares with *The Tin Drum* not only the scenario of Danzig and the estuary of the Vistula, the period covering the Third Reich and its German successor states, and, finally, the character Oskar, who dimly appears in the background of both *Cat and Mouse* and *Dog Years.* The three works also exhibit their relationship through the problematic narrative perspectives to be found in them. These narrative perspectives address the almost identical material in different ways. Whether or not one ought to designate the entire complex as a trilogy (as has been the practice of bookstores lately), is a diverting and simplistic question. It forces the interpreter to respond quite unequivocally—from which nothing is gained. When John Reddick demands that the three works be characterized as a trilogy, he bases this on a "unity of place and time" on the one hand, and on the common denominator of "suffering" on the other. The conformity of the narrative structures in the three prose works—he adds *Local Anaesthetic* to them—as well as a "dualistic-dialectic principle" that evolved consistently in the three early works and beyond them, appear as detrimental factors to him.[6] Thus Reddick defines—actually, contrary to his own intent—two essential features of Grass's novelistic work: The calculated coherence of a group of novels on the one hand and an express transmission of relationships beyond the three initial works on the other. Both features shall be briefly discussed as far as they are relevant to our topic.

Within the first three works, the narrators turn the narration into an arduous, demanding experiment. They are the sanatorium patient Oskar in *The Tin Drum,* who conjures up the past by drumming but is constantly changing both as narrating and narrated "I"; the author collective of *Dog Years,* whose members successively almost force each other to narrate stories that both run parallel to each other and contradict each other; Pilenz in *Cat and Mouse,* who, as narrator, expressly admits that he could be an invention just like his hero: "And now it is up to me . . . to write. Even if we were both invented, I should have to write. The fellow who invented us because it's his business to invent people obliges me" (CM, 8). In this text Grass establishes—as far as we know, for the first time in his epic work—a definite relation of the narrating subject to the author and addresses the author's narrative work, his narrative risk.[7]

To be sure, the reader is irritated by the subjunctive of the one sentence ("even if *we were* both *invented*") and the affirmative *Gestus* of the other (the fellow who *invented* us); that which is at first assumed appears as fact without any transition. There is a compulsion towards confession and profession, which lets the invented and the real mingle. Thus we find in *Cat and Mouse* the beginnings of the author Grass's poetics that will assume more clearly defined contours in his later works. As always, the subject matter is a necessary component of these poetics; it causes the narrative fragility, the epic scruples. The prewar time, World War II, the ensuing reconstruction—the two great novels traverse these three "periods" in parallel fashion. The novella *Cat and Mouse* at least evokes all of them, even if its inner story is limited to World War II. The author launches all the narrators into a constellation in which they incur guilt and have to come to terms with it. On one side, they grapple with the subject matter that has been imposed upon them; on the other, they themselves embody the second stage, that of coming to terms with guilt, in their narrative function. They write: "For you can't keep such things to yourself" (CM, 76). The narrators' always new and always problematic approaches, set in juxtaposition, impede every precept of how to come to terms with guilt; in addition, they deny art one of its functions, that is, mastering life. The relation of the narrated material to its narrators does not add up. We do not need to go into any detail to prove this. Suffice it to mention the contradictory moral judgments that critics and scholars alike have pronounced on the narrator figures in their function of narrated figures. For example, Oskar appears as a clearsighted nonconformist as well as a pathological liar and multiple murderer. Matern in *Dog Years* is interpreted as both a "frustrated, brutal fairweather-friend" and a "basically good-hearted, upright character."[8] On the one hand, Pilenz in *Cat and Mouse* is supposed to exhibit traitorous features, on the other, his ambivalence is reduced to his hesitant following of Mahlke—although Pilenz's following does not extend to offering Mahlke assistance at the decisive moment. It did not require Grass's express confirmation of the thesis that all narrators perceive guilt as the motivating force of their writing. However, Grass establishes their points of view within the framework of events they narrate in only a precarious and approximate fashion. This is especially true of the narrators' relationship to their antagonists in *Cat and Mouse* and *Dog Years*.

The narrative stance connects *The Tin Drum, Cat and Mouse,* and *Dog Years;* moreover, the narrative stance to be encountered in this triad is also to be found in Grass's subsequent prose works, albeit in different constellations. Beyond a doubt, there is a caesura after the "trilogy." There are constants, albeit meager ones, from the previous works to be found in *Local Anaesthetic.* Again, there is a narrator who is deceptive in his conflicting nature and induces questions. *Studienrat* Eberhard Starusch also does not fit into a system of moral coordinates because he provoked contrary critical evaluations. For some he is the negative version of the Matern figure, for others, he is the author's mouthpiece, broadcasting the necessity of coming to terms with guilt.[9] However, the following shift in emphasis is essential: although Starusch traverses in his mind basically the same timespan as the narrators of the earlier novels and projects the Third Reich and the post-World War II period into the 1960s, the action takes place exclusively in the present—that also provides the perspective. Starusch reflects on the past as he sits in front of the T.V. screen at the dentist's office, which is either blank or produces associative images. There are two conclusions to be drawn from this shift in emphasis: first, Starusch's observation of the past proceeds from the point of view of analogy or of what is characteristically different from the present; second, precepts for the present are given—if formulated with hesitation. One may evaluate Starusch as he will—he embodies pedagogical impetus not only by virtue of his profession, the character of Starusch tries to affect the present by cogitating on his own phases of development. It is the activity of narrating and of synonymous invention that evolves from the "Danzig Trilogy" and is carried beyond it.

Thus Starusch finds his past as he invents it. However, at the same time he would like to utilize it. Until now, he has been the only character who appears equally determined by arduous narrative retrospective and present-oriented activity.

Invention and engagement overlap most clearly in *From the Diary of a Snail,* a work that one will hardly term a novel or *Novelle,* but that nonetheless is part of the chain of transmissions and intensifications that, in part, runs parallel to the process of poetological precision. The author discovers his past once more in Danzig by reinventing it; he accomplishes this by both creating and rejecting analogy and concretizes the past in the story of a man with the revealing name Doubt. Conversely, as far as the time level of the present in *Diary* is concerned, the author no longer retreats behind the different narrating figures that reflect or refract him. First of all, the author draws attention to himself by his choice of the title *Diary;* second, by his record of his election campaign trip on behalf of the Social Democratic Party; third, by incorporating his private family affairs, a thread of action that is fairly closely linked with both the story of Doubt and the election campaign. Grass places himself on the roster and "invents himself somewhere else." However, he gives unity to the different realms, which appear to be unrelated only at first sight, with a theoretical formula and an omnipresent complex of motifs. The project of the Dürer lecture to be held at Nuremberg emerges from the autobiographical stratum. The search for a third possibility between melancholy on the one hand and utopia on the other provides, as far as Grass is concerned, a surprisingly abstract pattern of thought. This pattern structures the events depicted and relates the narrative about Doubt and the recorded diary entries to each other. Thus, the image of the snail, which is stuck on the ground, constantly advancing, yet incapable of leaping or flying, is presented as an allegorising concrete detail. A political program of the "revisionist" Grass

emerges almost too clearly from all this and marks the temporary endpoint of
a line that begins with his reflection on the burden of Germany's past and ultimately leads to the author's political engagement, as Rothenberg was able to
demonstrate.[10] Individual aspects both supplement and relativize each other
in this many-layered reflection process. For our purpose it is critical that in
both *Local Anaesthetic* and *Diary*—to be sure, both are highly political
books—a technique emerges and is perfected that was to determine the unity
of Grass's further *oeuvre*. In the "Danzig Trilogy" a historical sequence of
events unfolds along disintegrating and reconstructed fictional byroads; these
events are surveyed from the vantage point of the preliminary goal—their relevance is made apparent by means of various refractions. Now, in *Diary,* the
historical finally becomes a stage where truth that is relevant to the present is
sought out, found, and invented. The narrative "I," which already hints at
its identity with the author in *Cat and Mouse* by attributing its compulsion to
narrate to the author, appears at least once—in *Diary*—explicitly as the "I"
of the contemporary author. In the same breath, though, it is projected back
on earlier planes of time.

Thus, *The Flounder* sketches early historical layers—they were presented
piecemeal in *The Tin Drum* and *Dog Years* and embedded in a successive narration—as stages whose sequence, on the one hand, is intended as the representation of a historical process, but, on the other, is to be understood as a
stratification of analogies. To be sure, in contrast to *Diary,* in *The Flounder*
the author does not use the purely autobiographical without a fictional qualification. Thus, the layer of the present is not strictly autobiographical, but includes the autobiographical as a fundamental possibility through its omnipresence. At any rate, the narrating "I" is more closely related to the author
than all previous narrating subjects. This author, only slightly disguised, can
spread over the times, linger in opposing figures in various time phases, balance and settle history from the earliest times to the present while he invents
as truth constellations between man and woman that are constantly changing
and oriented toward the future. Thus the both successive and simultaneous
process of masculine as well as feminine emancipation, which is both successful and unsuccessful, becomes a concert of invented truths.

III

We return to *The Meeting at Telgte.* Parenthetically we might add that
we do not want to be on the author's heels with our interpretation; hence we
are setting aside Grass's latest work *Kopfgeburten* (*Headbirths*) regardless of
whether it constitutes a new approach or a lightweight interlude. The chain of
transmission has not been broken between *The Flounder* and *The Meeting at
Telgte.* A close connection exists between the novel *The Flounder* and the pro-

se narrative *Telgte*—a connection that is comparable to that existing between the works of the "Danzig Trilogy." In the trilogy figures presented in one epic context had stimulated the growth of another one. The narrative function of one pluralistic figure in *The Tin Drum* had been transferred in *Cat and Mouse* to another, purportedly invented figure, that let the author, who was playing with his material, become intentionally visible; in *Dog Years* the narrative function had been distributed among several figures. In *Telgte* the belletristic layer from the anthropological mega-complex of *The Flounder* that had been embedded in the novel's emancipation chronicle, notably in the "Fourth Month," becomes independent. In *Telgte* the barely fictional "I," which lingers in various time-phases in *The Flounder,* "sits in" during a definite period of the past as the avowed "I" of the author. But one thing above all binds both works together: the truth, which is invented and, so to speak, taken care of by its inventor. "A good deal has been written about story-telling" is what it says in about the middle of *The Flounder.* "People want to hear the truth. But when truth is told, they say, 'Anyway, it's all made up.' Or, with a laugh, 'What that man won't think up next!'" (F, 290). If one observes the above cited maxim (given in abbreviated form) from the beginning of *Telgte* with the quotation from *The Flounder* in mind, then it becomes clear that just such a story, containing truth and yet usually dismissed as invention, is going to be told: "The thing that hath been tomorrow is that which shall be yesterday. Our stories of today need not have taken place in the present. This one began more than three hundred years ago. So did many other stories. Every story set in Germany goes back that far" (MT, 3).

We are not prepared to solve Grass's puzzle ("Who am I?"), nor to set it aside, but to recognize and describe it as a technique. The author of *The Flounder* had projected into men of all times, but at the same time into different men of one particular time-phase, an "I" that was barely distinct from himself, in an explicit, indeed, even demonstratively alogical manner. In *Telgte* he can use the freedom he claimed in *The Flounder* and find himself where truth "occurs"; that is, he sets out like an inventor on his journey through time and constructs and conveys truth as he writes it or copies it down. Yet, the result is not exhausted in our accepting the "I" merely as a changing identification of the author that always occurs wherever history and present are both signified, where history becomes transparent in stories of today that are not happening now or in stories that began more than three hundred years ago and are still continuing today. The authorial "I" dwells, to be sure, principally and sovereignly in the Baroque year preceding the German peace. It establishes history suitable for analogy, hence true history, in an extra-historical fashion. Yet, the author sees to it through special passages that the Baroque assembly does not merely serve as a prefiguration. We then, as readers as well as interpreters, do not take refuge in such self-satisfied state-

ments and perceptions maintaining that the task of the writer has been at all
times to speak out in the face of political events, to commit himself despite his
own shortcomings and the knowledge that his words will hardly be heeded.

With Gelnhausen, the author transfers a colleague from time immemorial to the Baroque convention, who clearly does not belong there, or at
least not yet. This procedure prohibits establishing an analogy with any author present at the gathering in 1947; only a qualified analogy is possible with
Günter Grass, who was not yet present at the first meeting of Group 47. It has
been mentioned above that an almost cryptical personal relationship exists
between Grass and Gelnhausen by means of astrology. However, this relationship between Gelnhausen and Grass's "I," which dwells in a different
time-phase, is destroyed by means of logic. The character of Gelnhausen
looms over the other poets; to be sure, both the "I's" identification with and
distanciation from each of these is possible but not demonstrated in any
decisive fashion.

Gelnhausen's first entrance gives us the key to his nature: "They [Hars-
dörffer and Birken] were accompanied by a red-bearded fellow who called
himself Christoffel Gelnhausen and whose gangling youthfulness . . . was
contradicted by his pockmarked face. In his green doublet and plumed hat
he looked like something out of a storybook [i.e., invented] . . . but Gelnhausen turned out to be more real than he looked" (MT, 6). Grass, an intimate of Grimmelshausen's work—he knows it better than that of all the other
Telgte poets—uses, not without justification, the wordpair "invented-real"
that is so central in his works. Thus he lets Gelnhausen appear as Grimmelshausen's character Simplicissimus, that is, in the clothing of the hunter from
Soest and with pockmarks acquired on his journey back from Paris. On the
other hand, he equips him with exact details of the author Grimmelshausen, a
biographically separate entity from his hero: "Moreover, he was serving as a
secretary at the headquarters of the Schauenburg regiment, then stationed in
Offenburg" (MT, 7). Yet, not only does the author Grass reinvent in the historical writer Grimmelshausen/Gelnhausen that author's own literary-con-
fessional character Simplicissimus, he also lets Gelnhausen begin to invent
himself in this figure. On the surface, he does this by having Gelnhausen confess his intention of becoming a writer. In the first scene Gelnhausen proclaims, not without second thoughts, that he himself "wielded the pen,
though for the present only in Colonel Schauenburg's regimental
chancellery" (MT, 8). Later on, he threatens Libuschka with his literary revenge (see MT, 101), but finally proclaims his intent in his surprising farewell
to the nonplused poets, of wanting to write "By Jupiter, Mercury, and Apollo" (MT, 113). Grass does this more convincingly when he likens
Gelnhausen's fabricated excuses—they are sometimes palliating, but always
stylized— to the creative act. When Gelnhausen is called to account by Hein-

rich Schütz at the feast because of food that he claims to have acquired legal-
ly, he replies, among other things, with a truth that every reader of Grimmelshausen's novel *Simplicissimus* can recognize as exclusively literary. Gelnhausen establishes an apparent parallel between the story of a family who had
fled into the forest during the foraging and his own biography: "Stoffel went
on to say that he knew a story that had had a similar sad beginning in the
Spessart Mountains. 'Paw and Maw' had perished miserably. But he was still
alive" (MT, 91). In reality, though, it is—with some inaccuracies—the
biography of his future hero that Gelnhausen presents as his own. The
character Gelnhausen, who wavers between a historical and literary silhouette
and reflects on his position between both, finally receives the almost official
assignment to become a writer from Heinrich Schütz, who belongs there just
as little as Gelnhausen. He, "a stranger though known to all" (MT, 49),
comes later and leaves earlier; he appears as the representative of the absolute
art of music; in fact, as the exponent of the artistic conscience: "It seems, as
Harsdörffer later reported, that he [Schütz] told the regimental secretary
never again to put his murderous fictions into practice, but to write them
down bravely, for life had given him lessons enough" (MT, 92). Thus what
Grass means by truth, that is, "the truth of art," crystallizes in the character
of Gelnhausen. Stoffel (the historical author Christoffel von Grimmelshausen), who is at the same time the Simpel (Grimmelshausen's fictive character
Simplicissimus), appears as a personified, poetological confession.

And exactly that places the character in the position of becoming a Baroque extension of the author, not as an observer, but as his helper. Since
Gelnhausen—here he is once again fundamentally different from the other
poets—appears in a fictionalized manner, his literary counterpart Courasche/
Libuschka can also come into play: billetting officer and innkeeper do not
spring from literary history that combines alexandrines and fantasy as do the
other poets gathered at Telgte; they are both in part and entirely literature.
They leave, for a time, their fictive biography to bring about the meeting's
fiction of truth. After they have accomplished what the author desired, they
disappear. Gelnhausen leaves with an unknown destination, a little like the
helpful spirit who leaves to itself what he has created; Libuschka assumes
again her literary silhouette. She rides away on her donkey into the title engraving of Grimmelshausen's *Courasche,* back to the band of gypsies waiting
at Klatenberg. According to Grimmelshausen, she has been their queen since
the battle of Herbsthausen and will remain so until after the peace treaty.[11] A
half-fictional and a fictional character, secretive, bound "with special glue,"
help the author achieve a Pan-hour of truth as they bring their fictional existence to a halt. However, this truth, for the very reason that its creators point
out its artistic formation and decay, encompasses more than the mere adage
of the necessity and frailty of the poet's word in troubled times.

Notes

*This article is the slightly expanded version of my inaugural lecture at the University of Münster on 11 November 1980.

1. See the interview of Grass by Nicole Casanova, *Atelier des métamorphoses.* Quoted from the partial reprint in *Der Spiegel,* "Am liebsten lüge ich gedruckt," p. 221.
2. See Klaus Haberkamm, "Mit allen Weisheiten Saturns geschlagen," pp. 67–78.
3. Ibid., p. 73.
4. See, for example, Hans Magnus Enzensberger, "Wilhelm Meister, auf Blech getrommelt," pp. 8–12; Gerhart Mayer, "Zum deutschen Antibildungsroman," pp. 55–64; Jürgen Rothenberg, *Günter Grass. Das Chaos in verbesserter Ausführung,* pp. 9–32.
5. See Rothenberg, *Günter Grass,* p. 59.
6. John Reddick, "Ein epische Trilogie des Leidens? *Die Blechtrommel, Katz und Maus, Hundejahre,"* TuK, pp. 60–73.
7. See the interpretation by Gerhard Kaiser, *Günter Grass. Katz und Maus.*
8. See Wilhelm Johannes Schwarz, *Der Erzähler Günter Grass,* p. 51, and Reddick, "Eine epische Trilogie des Leidens?," p. 64.
9. See Heinz Ludwig Arnold, "Zeitroman mit Auslegern: Günter Grass' *Örtlich betäubt,"* Grass, ed. Jurgensen, pp. 97–102, especially pp. 100–101.
10. Rothenberg, *Günter Grass,* pp. 113–60.
11. H. J. C. von Grimmelshausen, *Courage, the Adventuress and The False Messiah,* trans. and introd. Hans Speier (Princeton: Princeton University Press, 1964), p. 220.

Beyond *The Flounder:* Narrative Dialectic in *The Meeting at Telgte*

Judith Ryan

I

"Present only in retrospect"

It has been said of Grass that all his fat novels contain a slim masterpiece struggling to get out.[1] In two instances, the short work had in fact managed to escape from the longer one: *Cat and Mouse* was originally conceived as part of *Dog Years,* and *The Meeting at Telgte* is manifestly a byproduct of *The Flounder.*[2] But the relation between the two later works is more complex than the image of the perennial dieter suggests. To begin with, *The Flounder* contains a critique of the central idea of *Telgte,* with its whimsical but largely hermetic account of a fictive meeting of Baroque writers. Ilsebill, *The Flounder's* representative of the present in its orientation towards the future, expresses a view not far removed from that of some critics of *Telgte:* "You and your blasted idyll! . . . You and your baroque escapism. Wouldn't it just suit you" (F, 94).[3] Is *Telgte* just an escape from the political demands of today? Are we to see it, as certain reviewers have done, as the resignatory conclusion to Günter Grass's long struggle with the problem of writing as a form of engagement?[4] Ilsebill's reproach recurs throughout *The Flounder,* linking narration with lying, retrospection with escapism: "You with your historical evasions and your stories that are all lies!"[5] Repeatedly, she questions the narrative stance on which both *The Flounder* and *Telgte* are based. The issue be-

39

comes even more pointed in connection with the "gourd-vine arbor," a motif that forms one of the clearest links between the two novels. The reference here is to an image used by the Baroque poets who figure in the "Fourth Month" of *The Flounder* as well as in *Telgte*. For them, the metaphorical sanctuary was also a vantage-point from which to voice their invectives on seventeenth-century society. In keeping with the history of vegetables sketched out in *The Flounder,* the narrator decides relatively early on to grow a similar gourd-vine arbor in the garden of his house: "And in the garden (next to the graveyard) I'll grow a gourd-vine arbor for us, like the one that throve for three summers during the Thirty Years' War on Königsberg's Pregel Island, across the way from the tavern" (F, 92).

On the one hand, the arbor will be a place of escape from reality, a shelter sufficient unto itself: "A gourd–vine arbor would give us and our little boy when he gets here a place to think in without having to travel, because a gourd-vine arbor would be just perfect for you and me" (F, 93). On the other hand, like its Baroque predecessor,[6] it will also provide the ideal critical vantage-point, since, while it "doesn't amount to much," it is nonetheless a "fit place from which to see the world as a whole with all its changing horrors" (F, 93). But if this sounds suspiciously tantamount to the view that social criticism can best be performed from the shelter and security of a literary idyll, it is almost immediately counteracted by the sceptical Ilsebill, whose ready wit and sharp tongue promptly equate the gourd-vine arbor with the chamberpot of the fairy tale "The Fisherman and his Wife": "Gourd-vine arbor? Why not say 'pisspot,' like in the fairy tale?" (F, 95). Yet despite her scathing remarks about gourd vines, Ilsebill herself has a hidden affinity with the plant: "Even the past will cast shadows as the plant shoots up, so that, while you are bourgeoning along with the gourds, I shall able to tell you about Awa Wigga Mestwina . . ." (F, 93).

The physical similarity between Ilsebill's pregnant body and the rapidly swelling pumpkins is only superficially the point at issue; more significant is her perceived relationship to time. Although she thinks of herself as fully anchored in the present, her pregnancy automatically connects her with the future and draws the narrator's attention to the passing of time itself. The reenactment of human history in the gestation of the unborn child is one of the many ways in which the past throws its shadow in this novel. And the issue it most urgently raises is one familiar to readers of Grass, the question of what he called in his anniversary lecture on Albrecht Dürer "stasis in progress."[7] Does history simply involve the recurrence of the same? Do we always end up back in the same chamber pot where we started out?

These are questions that Grass answers one way in *The Flounder,* another way in *Telgte.* I shall be arguing that he answers it more cogently and more effectively in the slim novel than in the fat one. In thinking about this problem, it is important to see how time (or history) and narration are intertwined in the two works. I shall begin with *The Flounder;* a more detailed study of *Telgte* will be undertaken in part two of this paper. Towards the end of *The Flounder* the narrator seems to come down in favor of historical recurrence: "At last it was all confirmed. Fairy tales only stop for a time, or they start up again after the end. The truth is told, in a different way each time" (F, 545). This formulation implies that narration is only a surface phenomenon, an apparent variable that in fact conceals the actual identity of the various historical phases it treats. The narrative posture throughout the book seems to confirm this view. The narrator does not simply identify himself imaginatively with various figures from the past, he claims actually to have been those figures. From the relatively undifferentiated Edek of primitive times to the very Grass-like narrator of today, the storyteller undergoes multiple transformations. Even within a given historical period, his identity is not necessarily restricted to a single person: in the "Fourth Month," for example, he is Martin Opitz and the painter Möller interchangeably. On the very first page of the novel, he makes clear that, in one form or another, he has always been present: "I, down through the ages, have been I" (F, 3). But from the beginning it is also clear that there are two ways of looking at the narrator's (and Ilsebill's) perennial presence: "In those days Ilsebill's name was Awa. I, too, had a different name. But the idea of having been Awa doesn't appeal to Ilsebill" (F, 4).

It is not insignificant for the novel's examination of feminism that the basically male narrator is more willing to accept historical recurrence than is his female counterpart and critic. To be sure, the narrator is not as exclusively male as his overt identifications make him seem. The female cooks, representatives of their time and the real makers of history, are also in a sense part of him: "And so she sits inside me and writes her story," he says of Margarete Rusch (F, 212). But the basic dialogue between man and woman on which the narrative is based cannot afford to take this idea too far. Despite all the metamorphoses from period to period, Grass never seems to have entertained the notion of a metamorphosis from one sex to the other—on the model of Virginia Woolf's *Orlando,* for example. In fact, a transsexual metamorphosis would run counter to the central thesis of the novel, that male and female differ from each other largely by virtue of their temporal orientation, the woman looking always forwards, the man perennially backwards:

Ah Ilsebill! I dreamed the Flounder was talking to you. I heard the two of you, laughing. Smooth was the sea. And there you were, working out the future. I was sitting far away; I'd been written off. Present only in retrospect. A man and his story: Once upon a time . . . . (F, 453)

The judgment passed on the male and female roles thus becomes quite complex. To be sure women are seen as being, in a rather underhand way, the most decisive actors in the progression of history, whose movement is defined in terms of the introduction of different gastronomical delights and of whose existence people are simply not aware "between hunger and hunger" (F, 11). Women are the makers of the future (as evidenced by their ability to bear children), while the men sit ineffectually and wistfully reflecting on the past. Yet however "far away" and "written off," it is the man who controls the narrative as a whole.

More than this, the novel subscribes quite aggressively to a belief in the primacy of narrative. At one point it is even suggested that the young Grimmelshausen, perched safely in a tree, compared the Thirty Years' War with battle scenes familiar from literature, "so demonstrating once again that nothing happens but what has first been prefigured by the written word" (F, 255). Literature virtually lays down the law to reality, which can do little more than what is prescribed for it in print. This gives writing, for all its nostalgic backward-looking, a remarkable potency. Yet at the beginning of the novel, Ilsebill makes it clear that the conception of the child should have priority over the narrator's wish to recount their prehistory (F, 4), and at the end, Ilsebill runs on ahead, leaving the narrator desperately trying to catch up. Such paradoxes lie at the very heart of the novel's exploration of the relative importance (and strange interlacing) of physical and artistic creation.

The problematic relationship between the narration and time is only partially resolved by the use of a narrator who slips in and out of personalities and epochs because he is essentially a projection made possible by the author's creative imagination. The trouble with such a technique is that it emphasizes recurrence at the expense of historical change; were it not for basic similarities between the present and the past, the imaginative identification of the modern writer with his various past selves would simply not be possible. This has important consequences, however, for writing that also seeks to be politically effective.

Can fundamental relationships such as those explored in *The Flounder* really be changed in any significant way over the course of time? What influence can writers have on the course of history if they themselves, to judge by this particular narrator, remain essentially the same? Can writing ever amount to anything other than a perennial plaint about this "vale of tears" (F, 93)?

The Flounder left Grass with two problems that could not be resolved within its narrative framework. First, its concern with feminist issues and its concomitant restriction of the writer to predominantly one side of the debate stranded him in a rather desolate view of the function and potential of writing. Second, his conception of the narrator in terms of constant metamorphoses through time brought with it a perception of history as more or less unchanging.[8] In *Telgte* Grass wrestles again with these problems in an attempt to provide a corrective to those tendencies in *The Flounder* that speak against his own hope of playing a meaningful role in contemporary political life. The adjustments needed were relatively minor, as we shall see, but they nonetheless salvaged Grass's reflections of writing and history from the dead end they had entered in the earlier novel.

Two aspects of *Telgte* are important here: its new conception of the narrator and its rethinking of the narrative presentation of the past. Though apparently originating in the Opitz chapter of *The Flounder* ("The Fourth Month"), *Telgte* also takes up an idea developed in the section of *The Flounder* that deals explicitly with its fairy-tale model ("The Sixth Month"). Here Grass imagines a conference of Romantic writers that evidently prefigures the conference of Baroque writers in *Telgte*. Though most of the details are fictive, the historical basis for the meeting is stronger than in the case of the Baroque poets. The Romantics did in fact collaborate and discuss their work together, and the idea of a conference in 1807 is not at all implausible. All the same, Grass takes care to modernize the idea somewhat, as he does also in *Telgte*, by approximating the meeting more closely to modern writers' conferences. The choice of words in his introductory sentence makes this plain; the Romantics have met "to discuss a publishing venture and exchange ideas" (F, 345).[9] The anachronism "publishing venture" or *verlegerisch tätig sein* (B, 438), has precisely the same effect as similar tricks of style in *Telgte*. Altogether, this section reads like a five-finger exercise for *Telgte*: "Two days later, the painter Philip Otto Runge and Clemens Brentano's sister arrived, he from Hamburg via Stettin, she from Berlin" (F, 345). More significant, though, is the avowed purpose of the conference, one that would doubtless have been quite far from the thoughts of the actual Romantic poets and artists who come together here:

> Since the general misery brought on by the war increased people's need for sweet-sounding words, and since fear sought refuge in fairy tales, they had come to this quiet spot, far from the city's bustle and from the political quarrels that had become the stuff of daily life, to compile a second and third volume [besides *The Boy's Magic Horn*] from their still-unsorted hoard of rare treasures, hoping at long last, after so much cold Enlightenment and classical rigor, to give their people some consolation, if only the consolation of escape. (F, 345)

The Romantics' efforts are thus placed directly in a political context. Their collections of ballads and fairy tales are seen as a counterweight to the ravages of the Napoleonic wars, and the forester's house in the Oliva woods functions as a Romantic version of the Baroque "gourd-vine arbor," sheltering the poets and the artists from direct exposure to the irritations of daily politics. Surrounded by nature and "as though outside of time" (F, 346), they find themselves confronted nonetheless with political issues. The painter Runge, explicitly said to be "aloof from the happenings of the day" (F, 346), is the one who brings to the group the fairy tale of the Flounder, and he brings it in two versions whose contrasting positions touch off the debate on male chauvinism between Bettina and Clemens Brentano. The second version of the tale presents the wife as modest, the husband as ambitious and demanding, until with his final wish to fly beyond the stars to heaven the whole scheme collapses and he finds himself back in a second Ice Age (F, 349).[10] Runge reports that his source for the tale, an old woman from an island in the north, had claimed both versions to be equally true: "The one and the other" (F, 349). What hinders the Grimms from accepting both versions is, in the last analysis, Bettina's own inner conflict between her engagement for women's rights and her admiration of Napoleon. Wilhelm Grimm identifies the ambitious fisherman with Napoleon, claiming that the tale prophesies the eventual catastrophic outcome of the latter's imperialistic strivings. But in the final discussion of the two versions the Romantics decide against the use of the second as a moralistic polemic against Napoleon (though Jakob at first suggests using it this way); in the end, mild-mannered Runge pleads for withholding the tale on account of its disturbingly "apocalyptic tone" (F, 353): "'It would seem,' said the painter with some bitterness, 'that we humans can tolerate the one truth and never the other'" (F, 353).

The cook Sophie Rotzoll protests in vain that only the second version is true, that all evil in the world is the fault of men. Their discussion is interrupted by the appearance of a typically Romantic moon, and Runge takes advantage of the poets' inspired ecstasy to burn the antimale version of the fairy tale. Young Wilhelm Grimm is aghast. But the manuscript is in ashes, and the Romantic company can do no more but return to the shelter of the forester's hut.

Precisely this constellation of events is taken up again by Grass in *The Meeting at Telgte* and made more explicit. Now it is the Baroque writers' manifesto against the Thirty Years' War that goes up in flames; but like the Romantics in *The Flounder,* they too are unable to engage effectively with the politics of their day. The changes Grass makes in *Telgte* are more telling than this similarity, however. Most important is his invention of a conference that bears a distinct resemblance to the meetings of Group 47. By taking a Baroque conference as his central metaphor, Grass draws our attention even more clearly to the fictive nature of his invention. The Romantics, after all, often did work together as a group. And by restricting himself to a single instance of the past-present comparison, he leaves the way open for a more dialectical exploration of this relationship than is possible in *The Flounder.* Thus he shifts the emphasis from continuity to discontinuity, and gives a new answer to the question whether truth always remains the same, told "in a different way each time."

Thus Grass makes *Telgte* an indirect critique of its predecessor, *The Flounder.* By moving beyond analogy to a more dialectical understanding of the past-present relation, *Telgte* exemplifies what Grass calls "progress in stasis" and restores the future-directedness that in *The Flounder* was separated from the reflections on the past by the sceptical figure of Ilsebill. In so doing, it demonstrates that what Grass calls in his most recent novel the "plufuturepresent" or *Vergegenkunft* (KG, 130) cannot, properly speaking, be conceived as a simultaneity, but as an intricate dialectical interplay.

The Meeting at Telgte can be seen as an end point in a line of development begun in *Local Anaesthetic* and continued in *From the Diary of a Snail*—two attempts to set present problems in perspective by relating them to events of the past. But in both those novels, the second of which is more overtly autobiographical than the first, the problems of the two temporal levels and the points of view from which they are shown are quite incommensurate. *The Flounder,* with its metamorphosing narrator, sets out to resolve this dilemma by taking more equivalent time-blocks, but its whimsical mode does little to undercut its essentially analogical conception. Not until *Telgte* does Grass, through an amusing narrative innovation, create a more appropriate model for thinking about the relationship between present and past.

II

"The thing that hath been tomorrow is that which shall be yesterday"

Underlying *The Meeting at Telgte* is a strategy much akin to the narrative technique of a detective story. Two puzzles emerge from the novel and urge the reader to resolve them. One is the mysterious arson of the inn at the end of the novel; the other is the very perpetration of the narrative itself. And in both instances, the book provides no answer. The overt puzzle it offers us, the identity of the arsonist, is just a "cover" for the more profound puzzle, the identity of the narrator. The concluding sentences of the novel indicate the two levels on which Grass integrates these puzzles into the narrative strategies of his tale: "I know who I was then. I know even more. But who set the Bridge Tavern on fire I don't know, I don't know . . ." (MT, 132). This sends us back to a rereading of the book; but the novel persistently resists revealing the two identities.

Reviewers of *The Meeting at Telgte* have generally seen it as a *roman à clef* in which the members of Group 47 can be identified in the various Ba-

roque poets who gather for the fictive meeting in Telgte. These identifications, in contrast to that of the arsonist and the narrator, are readily uncovered. The master poet, Simon Dach, is clearly Hans Werner Richter; the
young Grimmelshausen, known as Gelnhausen, bears some similarity to
Grass himself; and critical cunning rests reasonably content with a number of
other more or less convincing identifications: "One wonders whether
[Marcel] Reich-Ranicki is concealed in the gruff master Buchner and whether
the sensitive Birken is [Martin] Walser or [Hans Magnus] Enzensberger. Gryphius, also known as Gryf, [seems to be] an alias for [Heinrich] Böll. But
Georg Greflinger, the former diligent composer of Alexandrines who moves
to Hamburg to put out a weekly news magazine, is indisputably Rudolf Aug-
stein, one of the guests of Group 47."[11] All this is very amusing, and certainly
in tune with Grass's playful conception of the novel. That Grass evidently
identifies with Gelnhausen—the one character in the book who is most clearly
profiled and the most sympathetically presented—does not necessarily mean,
however, that this character must be the narrator. The difficulty lies in the
narrator's claim to have been a witness to every event described; yet there is
no single character so constantly present. Gelnhausen, in any event, spends a
good deal of the central portion of the narrative "requisitioning" supplies;
and Scheffler, whose fixation on the Virgin Mary reminds us of the protagonist in *Cat and Mouse*, is also absent for a significant part of the action. And
although the novel is evidently a spin-off from that section of *The Flounder*
where the narrator impersonated Martin Opitz, he is evidently not Opitz in
Telgte, the action of which takes place after Opitz's death in 1639. Grass has
cunningly woven into the story a series of circumstantial proofs against each
of the other figures as well—they are either demonstrably absent from pro-
ceedings the narrator claims to have witnessed in person, or they are explicitly
said to have been standing next to the narrator at a specific point in the discussion. One by one, the reader-detective is forced to eliminate the named
and identifiable characters as the narrator.[12]

   And yet the narrator is the very model of fictional impersonation. While
he perceives his world in acceptably Baroque terms, he is no mere embodiment of what one might term the "spirit of Baroque poetry."[13] On the contrary, he is very conscious of himself as a person, and his sense of self strongly
pervades the entire narrative. Indeed, he is quite annoyingly self-confident.
"I saw it," and "I know it," he iterates unceasingly, lauding himself over the
other characters whose point of view is more restricted. He says, for example:
"no wonder that the bedfellows failed to hear what else happened that early
morning. But I know" (MT, 45).

   "How do I know all this?" he asks another time, "I was sitting in their
midst, I was there" (MT, 83-84). He perceives what no one else can: "I alone
saw the three maids load one mule" (MT, 131); he describes what no one else

hears: "No one heard his lamentations," he says of Lauremberg after the fire (MT, 131). The resolution of the puzzle is simple: we are confronted here with none other than that familiar personage, the omniscient narrator.

The secret of Grass's playful irony lies in the fact that this is no conventional omniscient narrator, but rather the omniscient narrator personified. Never before, to the best of my knowledge, has the "omniscient narrator" spoken in so personal a tone. In fact, the very essence of the omniscient narrator consists in the fact that he is not conceived as a person at all, but rather as a construct hypothesized by the reader to explain the phenomenon of a narrative that purports to be able to supply us with complete information about its characters, their doings and their motivation. But Grass's narrator is simultaneously nobody and a very distinct somebody: "Someone (I?)" (MT, 21). He expresses specific opinions in the debate on the function of poetry, he identifies himself with the younger poets (MT, 119), he presents himself as having stood beside specific members of the group (TT, 41; MT, 29, has incorrect translation) or having had a particular response to the speeches (e.g, MT, 62), and otherwise behaves in every way like a separate individual and a real participant in the action. But paradoxically, he is also everywhere simultaneously and has complete knowledge about everything that occurs. He is a charming individual rooted in his own time and place, and—at the very same time—a narrative construct both omniscient and omnipresent.

The question arises why Grass should wish to play this game with his readers. I believe this has to do with his attempt to resolve some of the problems posed by the narrative strategy of *The Flounder.* The care with which Grass elaborates his displacement of Group 47 into the Baroque period suggests that more is meant than a mere equivalency between the two. The novel is more than just the "melancholy allegory"[14] by means of which it connects the two time periods—that is, the conclusion that the politicial import of Group 47 was no more significant than the politico-poetic manifesto of the fictive Baroque meeting, which ultimately goes up in flames, never to be salvaged. To read the story this way is to perceive only the "stasis" in the perennial "progression."[15] Thus we must ask more probingly what purpose underlies the dual–period construction of *Telgte.*

If we compare the novel with other examples of fiction in which past and present are (explicitly or implicitly) played off against one another—such as Uwe Johnson's *Anniversaries* or Christa Wolf's *No Place. Nowhere*—we immediately observe a striking difference. In such novels, the past functions either as a critical contrast to the present (as in *Anniversaries,* where the reflections on the Third Reich bring the problems of the early seventies into sharper focus) or as an allegory of the present (as in *No Place. Nowhere,* which posits an analogy between the position of the writer in the nineteenth century and The GDR). But Grass takes a rather different tack. After all, the meeting in

Telgte never did take place, the debates between the poets were more frequently written than spoken ones, their relationship in many cases literary,
not personal. The actuality of history is not Grass's starting point. "Everything is authentic," writes Raddatz in an early review of the novel, "every line
from Paul Gerhardt . . . is accurate, every sentence from Gryphius
correct,"[16] and yet, as he too realizes, "the reality was different." The meeting exists primarily as a backward projection of Group 47. Why should a writer displace the present into the past and distort the past itself into a fiction?

Raddatz's ingenious formulation of this technique, "not a keyhole, but
a telescope—into the present" is not really helpful.[17] After all, the perspective
of this novel (as opposed to its predominant narrative voice, which belongs to
the past) is clearly modified by knowledge of the present day. And even as it
draws connections with the past, the present perspective firmly closes off the
events of the past from us. Within the novel itself this is marked by an insistence on discontinuity of character: the narrator continually emphasizes that we
are not what we once were. Many of the figures appear under unfamiliar, earlier names: Gelnhausen, later Grimmelshausen; Scheffler, later Silesius; Libuschka, later Mother Courage. The final conflagration puts an end to the
convivial debate; it destroys the manifesto and with it the poets' hope of political influence in Germany; it marks the end of an epoch in which the meeting in Telgte stands unmatched: "But during that century no one assembled
us again at Telgte or anywhere else. I know how much further meetings would
have meant to us" (MT, 132). To be sure, this discontinuity corresponds to a
discontinuity of Grass's own time—the difference between his political position in 1947 and his stand in 1979. But the more significant disjunction is that
between the Baroque period and the post-1945 period, a disjunction that reveals itself despite all apparent similarities. Through the gap that opens between the Baroque impersonations and their present-day equivalents, between the Baroque voice of the narrator and the present relevance of his concern, between an irrevocable burning of a political manifesto and the hope
that the present has not forgotten its political mission, between the evident
fiction and the present-day reality to which it refers—through these gaps we
gradually discern the other face of the stasis the book apparently confirms.

The poets' sense of security as a collective counterforce to the troubled
times in which they live is subjected to a subtle play of irony. Though Albert
regards his gourd–vine arbor and Dach his leadership at the meeting as a shelter against the Thirty Years' War, it is precisely in the attic (*unter dem Dach*)
of the inn where they convene that the fire of the novel's conclusion is said to
have started. The comparison between Dach and the biblical Jonah is a thoroughly ironic one: "Just as Jona under his biblical gourd threatened sinful
Nineveh with God's wrath, so Dach admonishes his tripartite Königsberg"
(MT, 120). Yet it is he himself who is ultimately struck by the wrath of God,

through the fire and its destruction of the manifesto whose formulation has been the chief purpose of the conference. Similarly, Gryphius' attack on Dach is an indirect parody of the Bible story:

> You pen three hundred verses before my three I write,
> A laurel tree grows slowly, a cucumber overnight. (MT, 121)

The reference is not merely to Dach's prolific output (MT, 121) but to the gourd plant in the legend of Jonah that grew overnight while he was awaiting the destruction of Nineveh (which, having in the meantime repented, was therefore saved). The critical sense of Gryphius' verses implies the withering of the rapidly–growing gourd plant, whose protective shade was correspondingly short-lived; at the same time, the destruction of Dach's complacency is adumbrated in advance. By this comparison the narrator allows us to know more than do the characters themselves—we have moved outside the time-frame of the book's actual action and beyond the stasis of its actors' self-complacency.

When Gryphius casts to the ground the thistle plant selected by the poets to symbolize Germany, the pot breaks, but the plant itself remains intact. Yet this proclaimed "miracle," intended to evoke in the reader's awareness not merely Gryphius' Germany but also the divided Germany of our own time, is almost immediately undercut by the total destruction of the manifesto. The two incidents are related side by side (in chapters 21 and 23), separated only by the "fish dinner" of chapter 22, whose conciliatory and triumphant nature is thus proved to be a delusion. And then again—another turn of the screw!—the reader knows that despite the destruction of the fictive manifesto and the dispersal of the fictive meeting, peace really did come to Germany the very next year, and the Thirty Years' War was over. Here is yet another disjunction—once again the reader has been impelled to step outside the time-frame of the fiction and to view its action from a distance.

The novel's ironic comparisons are not restricted, however, to the rather dubious likeness between the "torn Germany" of Simon Dach's day and the "divided Germany" of our own. Grass also takes issue with yet another theory about Germany. Insofar as the manifesto says anything at all significant, it makes the claim that the poets themselves constitute the only real Germany in this troubled time: "The poets alone, so said the appeal, still knew what deserved the name of German. With many 'ardent sighs and tears' they had knitted the German language as the last bond; they were the other, the true Germany" (MT, 67). The formulation "the other Germany" has clear echoes for anyone familiar with what became known as the "two Germanies" debate amongst German writers who went into exile during World War II. Adherents of this theory posited the existence of a morally better Germany, not amongst poets, to be sure, but amongst those people whose impulse to protest had been effectively suppressed by the Nazi régime.

The argument of the fictive Baroque meeting that the poets represent the "true Germany," with its apparent absolution of them from guilt, is taken up again at a later point when the ineffectuality of the manifesto has become increasingly evident. Gryphius puts the counterargument categorically: "Everyone wallowed in sin. Everyone was burdened with guilt" (MT, 95). Again the reference to arguments made during the reflection on Nazism is unmistakeable. The narrator does recognize the weakness of this argument when he has Dach object to Gryphius' charge that "this verdict of universal guilt amounted to a universal acquittal" (MT, 95). The guilt of the writer is more complex than can be expressed either by the "one Germany" theory (essentially that espoused by Gryphius, that guilt weighs on all) or the "two Germanies" theory (that formulated primarily by Moscherosch and Rist in the manifesto, distinguishing the protesting poets from those who were content to go along with the war). Guiltless and guilty, individual and collective, the politically conscious writer inhabits a domain exasperatingly difficult to map out.

In the midst of this discussion Thomas Mann is indirectly invoked. Mann's position in the "two Germanies" debate is especially hard to assess; of all the participants, Mann was perhaps the most torn between the two sides of the argument.[18] His attempt to mediate between them in *Doctor Faustus* is only partially successful, and the latter chapters of the novel are marked by the rifts caused by his vacillating perception of his problem. Irony, the paramount method of Thomas Mann, is denounced in the Telgte debate (in an attack on Logau by Rist and Zesen) as "French [*welsch*] and therefore diabolical" (MT, 88). Obviously, the narrator does not identify himself with Rist and Zesen, but he clearly wishes to have the irony put to the critical test in the course of the fictive debate. What are we to make, then, of the fictional structure of *Telgte* itself?

A closer look reveals that the use of irony by Mann and Grass is radically different. Whereas Mann uses his displacement of pre–Hitlerian Germany into the period of the Faust book more to draw the parallels than to emphasize the differences (thought of course he also does this), Grass establishes similarities between Group 47 and the Baroque poets in order, ultimately, to undermine these very similarities. Nowhere is this difference between the two writers more evident than in the point of reference they choose for their dual-level tales: with Mann, a partial analogy between the two periods is drawn by the use of myth: with Grass, an idiosyncratic combination of history and fiction points up the unreliability of whatever parallels seem at first glance to be made. Mann's irony is a resignatory hovering between denial and recognition of an apparent historical recurrence; Grass's irony is a more provocative question of historical analogies and equivalences.

The Meeting at Telgte is not, therefore, a melancholy confession of "the total irrelevance of literary activity in our time."[19] Rather, it provides, less equivocally than *Doctor Faustus,* a critique of a still fashionable type of thought that all too unreflectingly draws analogies between two historical periods. The simplistic equivalences drawn at the beginning of the novel come to seem increasingly questionable. The story opens with correspondences: Richter, the friend turning seventy, is said to be "older, much older . . . and we, his present–day friends, have all grown hoary white with him since those olden times," and present events are said to have their origins in past ones: "Our stories of today need not have taken place in the present. This one began more than three hundred years ago" (MT, 3). But this strategy changes in the course of the book. Is it right to see the present as merely a repetition of the past? Although the narrator claims not to be any wiser than he was before (MT, 40), he gradually ceases to confound the various time planes. "I know who I was then" (MT, 132) clearly indicates this awareness of difference between past and present.

Furthermore, *Telgte* presupposes some knowledge on our part of what became of its Baroque figures in the years that follow its conclusion. We know that Gelnhausen became the famous novelist Grimmelshausen and Scheffler the poet Angelus Silesius; we know that Libuschka, the hospitable innkeeper, played another role later on as Mother Courage. These implicit references anticipate a future in which, by becoming something different from what they once were, the individual characters arrive at a goal which in the fiction itself cannot be reached. *Telgte* is thus a substitute for the destroyed manifesto, about which the narrator comments: "What would in any case not have been heard, remained unsaid" (MT, 131). The novel's impact lies not in allegorical equivalences, but in differentiation and estrangement.

More effectively than the analogically structured *The Flounder, Telgte* uses the discrepancies between the real present and an essentially fictive past to call for a rethinking of what writers can do to influence politics. What emerges is not a mere critique of Group 47, but an injunction to look beyond the perennial aspect of the relationship between literature and politics and to take into account its specific nature at any given historical moment. The personified omniscient narrator mediates between these two ways of seeing the problem—as recurrence and as difference—and asks us to seek a resolution not directly presented in the narrative as such.

In this context, the last words of the novel become significant. Only one small detail lies outside the knowledge of the otherwise omniscient and omnipresent narrator. As mentioned before, he claims ignorance as to who set the Bridge Tavern on fire: "I don't know, I don't know" (MT, 132). But if the narrator is to be identified as a person who is simultaneously a narrative technique, so the mysterious arsonist may similarly be a person who is also a component of plot. It is a *deus ex machina* that, while apparently destructive in its effects, nonetheless makes clear to the reader that there is more left to be done. By locating the blame in an unidentified person rather than, for example, in blind fate, the narrator steps outside the bounds of his Baroque world-view into the modern conception of individual responsibility. This final estrangement effect provokes in the reader a revaluation of the novel's conceptual framework. Together with the other paradoxes of its narrative and temporal structures, it forms an effective counter to those currently fashionable works that see the present as merely a subtle variant of the past.[20] By dislocating the present into a partly fictive and not entirely commensurate past, Grass shows his sceptical view of historical recurrence. Just as Brecht asks his audience to reject the essential passivity of characters like Mother Courage, so Grass makes his readers call into question his narrator's conclusion that writing inevitably remains politically ineffective.[21] A text that seemed to be a more or less private reflection on its author and his contemporaries has burst its boundaries and become an important statement on the dialectics of history and narration.

Notes

1. D. J. Enright, "Casting Out Demons," pp. 8-10.
2. Nigel Dennis, "The One That Got Away," pp. 18-19.
3. Manheim's translation of the passage (B, 119; F, 94) does not reproduce the echoes that are important for my comparison with *Telgte*. This could scarcely be expected, since the passage in question relies on a double entendre whose significance would not emerge until the publication of the German original of *Telgte* (1979).
4. Typical of reviewers who saw *Telgte* as basically resignatory in its message is Rolf Schneider, "Eine barocke Gruppe 47," pp. 217-19.
5. I have again slightly altered the passage (F, 168) to bring out the element of escapism suggested in the original.
6. The biblical aspect of this reference will be taken up in part II of this essay.
7. See the appendix to *Diary*: "On Stasis in Progress. Variations on Albrecht Dürer's Engraving *Melencolia I*."
8. See Peter Demetz, "Günter Grass in Search of a Literary Theory," above, pp. 19-24, who treats a number of characteristic gestures and everyday actions that "hold back the flow of time."
9. See also Siegfried Mews, "The 'Professorial' Flounder: Reflections on Grass's Use of Literary History," below, pp. 163-178.
10. See Reinhold Grimm, "'The Ice Age Cometh': A Motif in Modern German Literature," above, pp. 1-17.
11. Schneider, "Eine barocke Gruppe 47," p. 219. For thumbnail sketches of the Baroque poets, see "Dramatis Personae" and "Literary Societies" (MT, 137-47).
12. See also Ruprecht Wimmer, "'I, Down Through the Ages': Reflections on the Poetics of Günter Grass," above, pp. 25-38.

13. I differ here somewhat from Werner Hoffmeister, who described the narrator as a Thomas Mannian "Geist der Erzählung," in "Dach, Distel und die Dichter: Günter Grass' *Das Treffen in Telgte*," p. 283. Hoffmeister (p. 284) is doubtless right in identifying Mann's *The Holy Sinner* as Grass' most immediate literary model for the narrative technique of *Telgte:* but Grass goes further than Mann, who still retains a formal differentiation between the narrating monk and the bellringing spirit of narration.

14. Schneider, "Eine barocke Gruppe 47," p. 219.

15. Cf. the Dürer anniversary lecture appended to *Diary* (n. 7, above).

16. Fritz J. Raddatz, "Kein Treffen in Telgte," p. 13.

17. Ibid.

18. Hans Rudolf Vaget, "Kaisersaschern als geistige Lebensform. Zur Konzeption der deutschen Geschichte in Thomas Manns *Doktor Faustus*," *Der deutsche Roman und seine historischen und politischen Bedingungen,* ed. Wolfgang Paulsen (Bern and Munich: Francke, 1977), pp. 200-235.

19. Schneider, "Eine barocke Gruppe 47," p. 217.

20. Novels of this type were the subject of two papers presented at the MLA meeting, December 1980: Monika Totten, "Zur Romantik-Rezeption in der DDR: Christa Wolf und Karoline von Günderode"; Lieselotte Weingant, "Bei schwebendem Verfahren: Peter Roseis Variante zu Kafkas *Prozess*."

21. Theodor Verweyen and Gunther Witting, "Polyhistors neues Glück. Zu Günter Grass' Erzählung 'Das Treffen in Telgte' und ihrer Kritik," pp. 451-65, but especially p. 460, also stress the provocative nature of *Telgte*, which they regard as an implicit critique of the "new subjectivity" in recent German literature; but they do not develop this idea further.

The Prismatic Narrator:
Postulate and Practice

Gertrud Bauer Pickar

From the beginning, Günter Grass's prose works have been marked by experimentation with narrative perspective, exploration of the ambiguities and potentials inherent in a protagonist-narrator, and interaction of the projected and the experienced realities thus engendered. In *The Flounder*, Grass has broadened the protagonist-narrator duality by creating a complex of interrelated narrator figures. The narrative that results is rich in its diversity of perspective and kaleidoscopic in the illuminated fragments of existence proffered by the novel, which extends in time from a mythologically conceived early Stone Age to the present. The variant narrative perspectives that characterize the text of the novel, although intertwined and interacting, are both distinct and distinguishable. Furthermore, they are identifiable and attributable to specific protagonists with their own historical contexts and frames of reference, to the protagonist of the novel's fictional present, and to a personalized authorial voice that intrudes from a temporal level postdating the novel's fictional time frame. Yet this apparent multiplicity of narrative perspectives, like the spectrum cast by the light passing through a prism, is the manifestation of but a single, narrative consciousness, itself projected within the novel and contained by it; and the multiple narrator-protagonists are but the refracted personalities of that single narrative consciousness. The unique structuring of narrative perspective that Grass has effected in this novel, one for which I would offer the term "prismatic narrator," is the subject of this paper. In the discussion emphasis will be placed on the opening two chapters of the novel, where the concept and its narrative potential are first presented and where, once operational, its manifestations in the text and its ramifications for the narrative can be observed.

The opening chapter of the novel, which is largely introductory in nature, provides an explication of the novel's intent, defines the parameters of its interest, and indicates the structure for its presentation. It reveals the innate and tight interdependence of the work's thematic concerns and its narrative configuration and their entwined interaction. In this chapter, the concept of the multiple yet unified narrator is initially presented, its context and dimensions outlined and defined, its potential for narrative development indicated, and its projected uses sketched. Indeed, the structuring of narrative perspective, the assumptions upon which it is based, and its ramifications for the novel's plot development are postulated in the opening paragraphs. The novel begins in the fictive present in narrative tone: "Ilsebill put on more salt" (F,4)—a sentence that, in its terseness, sets the tone for a less than harmonious relationship between Ilsebill and her husband, the cook, and initiates the major subject of the novel, food. The second sentence, which incorporated the evening's menu and thus reenforces cooking and eating as primary concerns,[1] is followed by her question that posits the thematic lines of the novel's fictional present—procreation and narration: "Should we go to bed right away, or do you first want to tell me how when where our story began?" (F, 4). The following line—"I, down through the ages, have been I"—by shifting from the narrative preterite of the very beginning thrusts the narrative out of the established fictional framework and confronts the reader with a new temporal dimension.

The line, in addition, not only personalizes the work's narrative consciousness and provides the identification with Ilsebill's spouse, but also indicates the refraction of that narrative consciousness into previous existences dating back to the beginning of humankind. Following lines both indicate the narrator's perception of Ilsebill as the eternal female, existing as he has, through all of time, and posit the quarrel as the typical expression of the male-female relationship: "I remember our first quarrel, toward the end of the Neolithic... And just as, today,...we quarreled..., so then, ...we quarreled to the best of our neolithic vocabulary..." (F, 4).

In addition, a fictive level, other than the one just established by the narrative, intrudes later in the text with phrases such as "to this day" (F, 108). Such phrases, though not explicitly so attributed, appear to be identified by context with the protagonist-narrator. Subsequently, however, this tentative identification becomes suspect, and an additional layer, still identifiable in part with the protagonist-narrator, yet separate from and removed from the fictional present of the novel's frame, emerges to become ultimately clarified as the expression of an authorial consciousness that, though still personalized, postdates the events of that frame and is not encompassed by it.

The chapter establishes the temporal boundaries for the work's thematic dimensions from the mythological prehistory of the matriarchy of the
threebreasted Awa to the reassertion of the female will at the Women's Tribunal set in the novel's fictive present. Its limits extend from the first time
the Flounder was caught by the protagonist-narrator as a Stone Age fisherman around 3000 BC and initiated his role as an advisor to man to the second time the Flounder, now disillusioned and refusing the male of the
species further assistance, was caught by three Lesbians in a new attempt to
aid the cause of woman. It even encompasses the novel's protean antecedent, the fairy tale "The Fisherman and His Wife," its modern-day cast of
parallel characters and its self-avowed intent to present the alternative version to that Grimm tale.[2] The chapter traces the multiple existences of the
protagonist-narrator from a Neolithic Edek (the name is Grass's own invention) to the beleaguered and philandering spouse of a present-day Ilsebill,
while maintaining for the reader both an awareness of the continuous
nature, and the continuing presence, of the narrating consciousness in the
text and an awareness of the narrative situation, the Scheherazade motif of
the novel.[3] Furthermore, it incorporates in sequence, the series of cooks
whose stories are to be presented in greater length and detail in the subsequent chapters. These female figures exist not only as projections of the
protagonist-narrator's fantasy—"for I can speak only of cooks who are inside me and want to come out" (F, 9)—but also as manifestations of the
narrating consciousness, characters with whom the narrator in one of his
historical or contemporary embodiments, in one capacity or another, shares
bed and board: from the Stone Age Awa to the protagonist's twentieth-
century contemporaries, Sibylle Miehlau and Maria Kuczorra.[4]

The first chapter also initiates the various interwining story lines. On
the level of the fictional present, it records developments in those two activities mentioned in the opening paragraph, procreation and artistic creation,
whose very pairing underscores at this point the duality of the protagonist-
narrator. The interaction and the confluency of the subsequent pregnancy
and the protagonist-narrator's own literary task are reiterated in the closing
paragraphs of the chapter's opening segment: "And after the shoulder of
mutton with string beans and pears, she gave me nine months' time to
deliver myself of my cooks. When it comes to deadlines, we have equal
rights" (F, 8). The marital relationship between the protagonist and Ilsebill,
the progress of her pregnancy, the evoking of artistic fantasy and tale-
telling itself, and the task of creating a novel remain continuing concerns of
the fictive present throughout the novel. Indeed, the pregnancy is used to
provide the rationale for the internal division of the novel into nine segments and furnishes the titles of those chapters, beginning with the opening,

"The First Month." It establishes the temporal boundaries of the fictional present and furnishes both the scale for measuring progress in all the other activities set within the fictive present and the frame for encompassing the tales of the various cooks and man's history over some 5000 odd years. It thereby maintains the primacy of procreation over artistic creation implied by the initial, sequential ranking of those activities in response to Ilsebill's provocative question mentioned above, a primacy that continues to be reenforced as well by the choices the protagonist-narrator makes throughout his multiple-identity existence.[5]

Also introduced in the first chapter is the Flounder, who has been called both a "piscine Mephistopheles"[6] and "a sort of Kissinger."[7] His existence parallels that of the protagonist-narrator, and, like him, he plays out his role both in the fictive present of the frame and in the contained tales. He advises the protagonist-narrator in the latter's role as husband, suggesting on one occasion that he help his wife Ilsebill with the dishes; he advises him as author as well, recommending for example that the treatment of the various cooks be presented in chronological order—a recommendation in keeping with his own depiction in earlier times as the one who gave man a sense of history, of the passing of time, and of progress itself—and later even insists the work be named after him. Like the protagonist-narrator, he, too, exists through time and is shown on various occasions advising the various incarnations of the protagonist-narrator. (He even, at times, interacts with the woman of that particular era—it is he, who is responsible for the curious twist in Dorothea's mouth and who brings laughter to Maria in the closing passage of the novel.) The open chapter not only indicates the continuing and recurrent presence of the Flounder, but also records the tale of his capture a few months earlier by Siggie, Frankie, and Maxie, their decision to try the Flounder for his complicity in establishing and maintaining the historical domination of the male, and the opening of that trial in a converted movie theater in Berlin which begins "in mid-October, shortly after we ate mutton with beans and pears, begot, and conceived" (F, 43). The deliberations of that Women's Tribunal and the prosecution of the Flounder are thus presented as concurrent with the other strands of the fictive present, Ilsebill's pregnancy and the protagonist-narrator's literary project, and ultimately the verdict in his trial coincides with the resolution in those plotlines as well.

In addition to the initiation of the interplay of these contemporary fictive lines, the chapter also presents the first of the protagonist-narrator's tales of the nine (or eleven) cooks,[8] and with it also the first of the series of historical protagonist-narrators, resulting from the refraction of the narrative consciousness. These begin with his identity as an Edek, one of the Stone Age men, whose relatively undifferentiated personality and frequent use of the plural "we" reflect the commonality of male experience in that era under the rule of Awa.[9] His multiple and sequential existence over centuries is treated essentially as a continuum and a unicum, indicating the uniformity of existence and the lack of any significant change or development, until that day in the twelfth century BC when as a fisherman he catches the loquacious and edifying Flounder and with his help initiates the advent of history, progress, and male consciousness, and ushers man into the Iron Age. Scarcely more differentiated is the extension of his Edek experiences as a charcoal burner for Wigga, during whose reign the mythological third breast disappears, so that his continued experience can be summarized in a half sentence: "centuries went by without noticeable change. Only the weather varied" (F, 81). Change does come under the rule of the "third" cook—Mestwina, whom the protagonist-narrator serves in two identities— that of the simple shepherd and servant and as Bishop Adalbert, her would-be converter, dinner guest, eventual bedfellow, and ultimate victim.[10] This first of several subsequent dual existences is addressed directly by the narrator, who states unequivocally: "Shepherd and bishop—for the first time I sojourned doubly; I was split, and yet wholly the pagan shepherd and wholly the Christian zealot." He explains: "Life was no longer as simple as under Awa's care or in Wigga's shadow. Never again, except in relation to Dorothea or to Amanda Woyke the farm cook, neither of whom allowed of ambiguities, have I been able to wear myself out so completely at one with myself: unsplit and for life" (F, 104). This explanation serves as an example of the intrusion of the narrative consciousness into a passage whose perspective is otherwise restrained by its historical context. The identification with the bishop is frequently underscored and a few passages, like the one below, even indicate insight into the figure: "But as a bishop with a desperate craving for blows, I let myself be murdered without resistance, for even as a choirboy I had often confessed the wish to die a martyr's death and be canonized later on" (F, 104). Yet his existence as bishop is presented essentially in the third person, and the experiential level of the protagonist-narrator as shepherd is dominant.

Variations of multiple and simultaneous experiences are presented in subsequent chapters, in which dual identities existing within a specific time frame, such as those of the painter Möller and the poet Opitz are more evenly weighted: "For Agnes Kurbiella loved me without reserve, me Möller the town painter and me Opitz the poet and diplomat" (F, 265-66). Both Opitz and Möller shared Agnes—as a muse though with less than anticipated and predicted success, as a cook with doubled delight, and as bedmate with limited results, since each succeeded in fathering but one child, and each time only a girl. As a result of this dual relationship, however, their experiences are expressed jointly, in mutual terms: "What drew *us* to Agnes was her allegorical

emptiness" (F, 277; my italics).[11] In the case of Sophie Rotzoll, the protagonist-narrator is presented in a triple identity. He is thus able to present
fragments of his life as Pastor Blech, the former teacher of the young
Friedrich Bartholdy and employer of Sophie—"who was me in my
Napoleonic time-phase" (F, 362), as her subsequent employer and military
antagonist General Rapp—"who, however, was also me" (F, 364), and as
that hapless revolutionary Bartholdy himself.[12] With an assumed omniscience
born of his narrator role, the narrative consciousnes is also able to conclude
categorically, "But Sophie, whom I loved as Pastor Blech and as Governor
Rapp, loved only and undividedly me, her Fritz, who spent his life in fortress
arrest, faraway and unerodable" (F, 365). In yet another chapter, more numerous identities for the protagonist-narrator are cited, though these multiple personalities are not developed. Thus he claims for himself "Blacksmith
Rusch, Franciscan monk Stanislaus, Preacher Hegge, rich man Ferber, and
Abbot Jeschke" (F, 173), all of whom share a relationship with the central
cook Fat Gret. And, "If during the lifetime of the abbess Margarete I was
one and the other and successively this one and that one—her father, her
kitchen boy, her opponents and victims," he asks, why not add yet another
identity, albeit a more distant contemporary to that list—Vasco da Gama
(F, 173-74).[13] Further examples abound, yet those cited should suffice to indicate the virtually limitless variations permitted under the concept of the prismatic narrator and Grass's use of the device to create a kaleidoscopic and rich
diversity of perspective and narrative development.

A more detailed analysis of the second chapter reveals, in practice, the
enormous complexity and varied potentials of the concept that was delineated
and sketched in the preceding pages. There the multiplicity of narrator identity and its ramifications are explored, and the interaction of the time referen-
tials associated with the various protagonist-narrators and the consequences
for plot development, characterization and theme are probed and demonstrated.

The multiple levels established in the first chapter are retained and developed. The protagonist-narrator of the fictive present, married to Ilsebill, contends with her willful behavior, part of which he, as narrator, graciously attributes to her pregnancy, and part of which he assigns to her sexual identity.
He assumes a role as a protagonist in his own right in an identity that playful-
ly draws upon Grass's own activities,[14] that of a West German author, working with a film crew in Gdańsk while struggling with his own manuscript that
when completed, the reader is expected to believe, will be identical with the
book itself. Furthermore, his fictional present is congruent with that of the
Flounder's trial in Berlin, permitting him as the protagonist (a man, an
"enlightened" husband, and an author) to participate as an observer in that
trial and to interact, both as the protagonist and as an embodiment of the
narrative consciousness, with the participants in that trial. He thus both en-

joys a personal relationship with the plaintiff Sieglinde Huntscha and with
the other participants in that trial—"I had dealings with them all" (F, 380),
he remarks—and, in his function as narrator, establishes their relationship to
the nine cooks who live "within him."[15]

The initial subchapter of "The Second Month"—"How we became city
dwellers"—opens with a sentence demonstrating the narrative richness that
can be achieved by a refracted narrative stance. First it manifests the historical perspective provided by a knowledgeable narrative consciousness—"At
the time when Mestwina, drunk but with unerring aim, struck down Bishop
Adalbert" (F, 107)—in which the protagonist-narrator's co-identity with the
now murdered Adalbert is not disclosed. However, it also encompasses the
collective conscience of the multiple narrator-protagonists, as revealed by the
recurrent use of the term "us" that demonstrates the kinship between the narrator and the original inhabitants of that region. The "us" here is identifiable
with the shared Kashubian heritage, and not just expressive of the communality of the male experience continued from the Neolithic Edeks. It is a
heritage that is consistently asserted and maintained, even on those occasions
when the protagonist-narrator assumes a variant historical identity, either as
Bishop Adalbert, a complete outsider sent to convert and baptize the heathen
natives, or as Albrecht Slichting, the son of the swordsmith Kunrad Slichting,
one of the "new settlers" from Lower Saxony. The objective narrative tone,
endorsed by the third-person narration and the implied historical perspective,
thus mingles with the subjective, experiential tone manifested by the use of
the word "us" with its implication of a participatory protagonist role. It also
undergirds the association between the protagonist-narrator of the novel's
fictive present, the ostensible originator of the tales encompassed by the
novel, and the manifestation of an authorial consciousness no longer contained by the nine-months frame. In the former case, he shares his racial
heritage both with his ancestors in the biological sense, albeit as a character
with the work, and with his antecedents, as stipulated by the narrative intent
behind his assertion of multiple historial existences. In the latter case it is a
textual element, like the recurrent "today" or "nowadays" that is identifiable as the expression of the subjective presence of a personalized narrative
consciousness manifesting itself within the projected text of that consciousness, the narrative itself.

As the narrative proceeds, the protagonist-narrator of the novel's fictional present thrusts himself into the contemporary version of the commu-
nally shared and multiply experienced city of Gdańsk, together with his various
embodiments and their concerns, interests, memories or pseudo-memories,
with both his traveling and his intellectual baggage: "gaps in my manuscript,
still-undocumented assertions about my earlier life in the days of the High
Gothic Lenten Cook Dorothea of Montau, and advertisements requesting in-

formation about the curly-headed kitchenmaid Agnes Kurbiella and mentioning Baroque allegories in which she figures. Objections on the part of the Flounder. My Ilsebill's wishes" (F, 110). Just as with the filming, in which everything became "two-dimensionally present" (F, 110), so too in the narration, past and present, the projected and the actual, the learned and the experienced, sweeping generalities and specific details, are presented in a printed simultaneity, the one-dimensional feature of a related tale. Though the imagination may rove through time and space, the tale itself is related in a sequence dictated by the narrative intent, though often under the guise of involuntary reflection or thought association.

The fact that all time exists on one plane, that the historicity of sequence is suspended by the creative fantasy, is evidenced in the text itself. Thus the narrator exploits a pause in the television filming of reconstructed Gdańsk to descend historically into the seventeenth century and enter into the relationships of that day. Noting that Opitz's view of the Long Market was identical with that of the painter Möller, preserved in his painting being used in the television broadcast as a basis for presenting the renovation of the now Polish city, he leaves to follow Agnes (whom he had loved both as Opitz and as Möller and who, like Ilsebill, is also pregnant). Agnes is at that moment passing the courthouse, the very courthouse, he then notes, having already joined her in the seventeenth century, where he and the film crew would wait "three centuries later" for the house electrician. Finding the shift in month, from August to January difficult to explain but taking the shift in centuries for granted, the narrator in the next paragraph (by this time the electrician had arrived), is able to leave the seventeenth century (as well as the twentieth) and lurch another three hundred years back in time to witness the execution of sixteen knights. This interplay between the fictional present and fictional pasts is not an isolated phenomenon but rather a central feature of the narrative. Thus the protagonist-narrator asks the young man in charge of the Gdańsk restoration program to help him, the present-time commentator of the television film, to find the construction site of the new home and business that he, the fourteenth-century swordsmith was building. Leaving his comrades to pack up the filming equipment, he seeks traces of his High Gothic wife "near one of the side doors of Saint Catherine's" (F, 120). As he watches the crew remove "inappropriate" bones from the rubble at the reconstruction site, he muses that it was "distinctly possible that the bones of my swordmaker father, Kunrad Slichting, were here in this heap with those of other once prosperous burghers" (F, 122).[16] Shifts in time are possible of course in both directions. Thus while the protagonist-narrator is awaiting the appearance of his High Gothic Dorothea on her shopping trip across the market square, he is surprised by the appearance of his contemporary Maria, who passed by carrying *her* shopping bag. The fluidity of time thus engendered by the roving protagonist-narrator and his multiple, near simultaneous identities, is a dominant characteristic of the prose throughout the novel, although the frequency level of the shifting varies from section to section, adding yet greater variety to the textual pattern.

Although, as indicated earlier, the narrative consciousness often assumes multiple personalities within a particular time frame, in the second chapter there is but one whose experiences are central. It is the swordsmith Slichting, in whose identity the narrative consciousness exists as a participant in the historical setting of fourteenth-century Danzig and from whose perspective the tale of the next cook, Dorothea von Montau, is told. Noting in the first-person narrative mode, "I often went to Montau," Slichting recalls his first encounter with her and admits, "I fell in love with the child Dorothea then and there" (F, 117). In part his perspective is presented directly, without additional internal or external illumination. No motivation, for example, is provided for his rejection of the proffered divorce from Dorothea in Einsiedeln (F, 154). In part his perspective is enhanced by knowledge that clearly postdates the Dorothea era of his experience—"In those days flagellation was pretty much what pot smoking is today" (F, 118). In part the historical experiences of all the previous incarnations of the protagonist-narrator appear to be incorporated by the narrative perspective, as if the protagonist-narrator shared the collected experiences, the collective memories, of his predecessors. His view of the flagellants—"Who do you thing [sic] brought us the plague!" (F, 118), while it still bears communality of experience, indicates a shared, and not just individual, experience of that time. On other occasions, such experiences are universalized to such an extent that the reader recognizes that the narrator is speaking from the personal, yet collected experience of his earlier, multitudinous past, or perhaps even from his contemporary position: "Women have always kept me on a short lead. I've always tied myself to some Ilsebill's apron strings" (F, 117). Similarly at a point in time only loosely identified as "later" (F, 130), the first-person narrator addresses the Flounder, discussing and lamenting his life with Dorothea. He recalls both the Flounder's advice that he marry her and the wedding feast itself and concludes, "I assure you, friend Flounder, it was no happy guffawing, but a tinny bleating, as if she had escaped from Satan's goat barn, that my Dorothea served up to the bewildered remnants of the wedding party for dessert. And later on they wanted to make a saint of that cold-blooded bitch. What a laugh!" (F, 132). In that remark, the perspective of the contemporary narrative consciousness is joined with the historical and emotional response of the participant in a reaction to the former's own creation, the figure Dorothea.

In the concluding section of the chapter, which is cast in the form of a letter, the contemporary identity of the protagonist-narrator of the frame merges with his assumed historical identity. In this letter, ostensibly addressed to the former's Latin teacher, Doctor Stachnik, the narrative consciousness of Slichting testifies to Dorothea's ability to hover above the ground (a phenomenon that lent support to the nomination of the historical Dorothea for sainthood); as the contemporary protagonist-narrator and husband of Ilsebill, he includes her greetings to the good doctor, and as the authorial voice, he admits to not truly knowing what Dorothea herself, as the fictional character, the historical figure, or the embodiment of the feminine consciousness, really sought in her life or what she (in any of those forms) was really like.

The interplay between the refracted narrators and the narrative consciousness, fostered by the prismatic narrator, not only affects the experiences of the protagonist-narrators and the manner in which they are perceived and presented, as the Slichting episodes indicate, but also other aspects of the novel as well. Indeed, the interplay affects directly the nature, dimensions and interaction of time and place. As a result of the narrative constellation, the city, like the narrator, Ilsebill, and the Flounder, exists in all time levels at once. The phenomenon is perhaps most succinctly depicted in the section discussed above, "How we became city dwellers." The city, as the narrative consciousness specifically notes, is at one and the same time "My Giotheschants, Gidanie, Gdancyk, Danczik, Dantzig, Danzig, Gdańsk" (F, 109).[17] With a technique made familiar by modern film, the city of the present merges with the city of the past, and, as the narrative consciousness moves freely from one era to another, it changes its appearance as easily as its name. It can shift from the fourteenth-century city—"The city was growing quickly, and wanted to be defended with handy two-handers" (F, 109)—to one of World War II destruction depicted in documentary photographs, to the Gdańsk of thirty years later, which is visited by the protagonist-narrator in the novel's fictive present in connection with the film project mentioned previously.[18] There is both a constancy inherent to the place—the initial settlement was built on swampy land and to this day the citizens have a problem with land subsidence (F, 121)—and an accompanying constancy in the patterns of human behavior, a consistency in societal interaction and personal experience. As the narrator notes ironically, "All the same, one thing has changed in Danzig or Gdańsk since 1378; today the patricians have a different name" (F, 120). Just as he both presents the historical perspective through his multiple personalities and in his role as narrator suspends time through his narrative consciousness, which not only encompasses but also disregards temporal dimension, the narrative too both underscores the historical aspect and calls into question its correlatives of change and progress.

Rather than denying the historical element, the novel includes the cyclical, repetitive nature of history itself as a thematic interest. It is introduced repeatedly by the narrator himself, who notes, for example, that the city was a "bone of contention from the very first" (F,109), or that there are "Unpaid bills wherever you go" (F, 112). It is stressed by the intentional juxtaposition of historical incidents against more recent ones, highlighting the parallelism of specific events and the recurrence of political or societal realities. Thus the narrator compares the revolt of May 1378 to that of December 1970 and notes that the confusion about the number of workers executed in the fourteenth century is repeated in the twentieth (F, 114). Here place is used in a clearly intentional manner in a supportive role: "In Gdańsk five or seven seem to have been killed outside the shipyard entrance on Jakobswall, where the shipyard already had its entrance in the old days" (F, 114-15). The narrative moves repeatedly back and forth between those events, underscoring the same uncertainty regarding the number of the victims and the same silence with which inquiries are met and in which the incident remains shrouded.

Repetition is not just a factor for society in general, but also for the individual experience as well, as demonstrated in particular with regard to the protagonist-narrator, and the narrative is marked by a repetition of situations, activities, relationships, and types.[19] There is, of course, a clear internal justification for that phenomenon as well: "I, down through the ages, have been I." The novel almost reverberates with repeated actions and relationships as, for example, the eating of apples (F, 416).[20] Similarly, the protagonist-narrator can lament, "So many of my children by Dorothea, Agnes, Amanda, died on me. I had so much suffering behind me" (F, 275). In all his manifestations, he also shares a central relationship with a woman, although it varies in its exclusivity and satisfaction, and with a male friend—"a truculent fellow who was to become my friend off and on in the course of my various time-phases. . . . Only recently Lud died again. How I miss him!" (F, 63-64). It is quite clear that, from the narrator's point of view, this relationship is more positive than any of the others. Some personal features are also recurrent; for example, the protagonist-narrators tend to be involved in some form of artistic activity, and they perceive themselves as inadequate, both sexually and existentially. Their essential sameness is summarized aptly by the Flounder, "In all his time-phases, . . . he was a failure" (F, 39).

The multiple refraction of the narrative consciousness into variant time spheres also offers the possibility for comparison between the experiences of the historical protagonist-narrators and those of the fictive present. Indeed, the possibilities for comparison provided by the simultaneity of historical and contemporary manifestations are exploited as a means of covert characterization, as comparisons are drawn between the current marital relationship shared with Ilsebill and those experienced in earlier configurations, and between Ilsebill and other female constellations.

The similarities and parallels range from the realm of minutiae—Awa and Ilsebill have the same number of posterior dimples (F, 28)—to behavioral patterns. Speaking of Wigga, the narrator notes: "Her vengeance was no brief outburst, but long-lived, though after each of my public self-criticism sessions she would say, like Ilsebill the other day on the telephone, 'Let's forget all about it. Water under the bridge''' (F, 102). Similarly, his present-day Ilsebill tends to merge with Dorothea. When his wife loses her temper, he can comment with assumed objectivity, "it seemed possible that Ilsebill's rage was High Gothic in origin" (F,129), and when she screams, he compares her to "that Dorothea who has been pressing against my gall bladder since the fourteenth century" (F, 129). He claims to have exchanged for a Venetian goblet Ilsebill's silver scourge—"a fine piece of swordmaker's craftsmanship" (F, 129)—the very instrument the reader had just learned that the child Dorothea "wheedled" Slichting into giving her (F, 117). He likewise is able to lump his wife Ilsebill, the plaintiff Sieglinde Huntscha, and his Gothic Dorothea into one—"it is always the same type that makes me weak and fluttery, that I fall for, that reduces me to strictly nothing" (F, 141). Noting that Sieglinde suddenly became quiet, he comments, "That is how it was when a gray veil cloaked Dorothea's eyes; and that's how it is when Ilsebill . . . suddenly . . . exchanges her optical organs for glass eyes" (F, 144). In his conversations with Ilsebill in the fictive present, he also interjects his "experiences" with the other, historical figures. Describing his life with Dorothea, he summarizes, "That, Ilsebill, is what love did to me " (F, 264); later he attempts to placate her anger and allay her suspicions by insisting that it is indeed the historical Agnes, "whom I also have in mind when I come to you and absent-mindedly—which always makes for a fight—call you Agnes" (F, 272).

The protagonist-narrator also uses his fictive experiences with these figures as a means for measuring the nature of Ilsebill's feelings, and reverence, towards him. He thus muses over Agnes's veneration of Opitz's quills, and wonders if Ilsebill would similarly honor his typewriter, were he to die (F, 266). There can be no question, that Ilsebill, considering the various projections of the protagonist-narrator in the past and in the present, comes off poorly. Her weaknesses, which do not become obvious in the description of the protagonist-narrator's relationship with her in the fictional present, are thus uncovered in the multiple comparisons with the entire array of female characters.

More significant, however, than the possibilities for characterization are the opportunities for narrative variation proffered by the constellation of a prismatic narrator. The limitations intrinsic to the concept of a protagonist-narrator are suspended here by the pervading presence of the narrative consciousness associated with him. Thus where a less sophisticated system would leave the numerous protagonist-narrator figures limited by what they had experienced, understood, and remembered, whether they were functioning in the novel's fictional present or on one of its historical planes, this format provides a structure for supplementing their experiences with a knowledge of his-

tory, of their subsequent experiences, and of the experiences of succesive protagonist-narrators, all well beyond their defined scope. Ultimately, as the
source of their existence, the narrative consciousness has, as an option, potential omniscience with regard to them. The selective employment of such
projected omniscience and its occasional deferment to the Flounder[21] provide
some of the narrative variants exhibited in the novel.

The narrative versatility offered by the prismatic narrator includes a
range of subjectivity attributable to and exhibited by the protagonist-narrator
in his multiple guises. It is, for example, dominant in his accounts as an Edek
and scant in the case of Bishop Adalbert. The degree to which personal experiences are transmitted varies greatly and on occasion is attributed to their
own decisions. Thus the protagonist-narrator as Friedrich Bartholdy, for example, notes that he never spoke to Sophie about his years of imprisonment,
despite her repeated questioning (F, 360), and, as if as a result of his reticence,
the reader, too, is kept uninformed about his experiences during those years.

In some cases, the multiple identities continue to battle for a more fa-
vored status long after their own episode has been presented. Thus, while the
protagonist-narrator chats in the fictive present with Ilsebill and Griselde, he
continues to struggle (parenthetically) with his earlier historical identities:
"(No, no! I don't want to have been her conspiratorial Fritz condemned to
life imprisonment in the fortress.) . . . (I'd rather be Governor Rapp, who sur-
vived the stuffed calf's head and kept order to the end.) . . . No, I don't want
to have been Rapp, either. I'd rather just be Sophie's fatherly friend" (F,
384-85).

At times the narrative consciousness intrudes to provide information beyond the immediate ken of the participants in the midst of their deliberations,
achieving thereby an ironic dispelling of the simulated reality.[22] When Jakob
Grimm deliberates whether he should accept an offer as private librarian, the
parenthetical comment "He did" (F, 440) is added; discussing Bettina Brentano's reaction to her brother's assertion that the Ilsebill of the fairy tale represented "the very essence of womanhood," it is noted, again in parenthe-
sis, that she would later become "a militant champion of women's rights" (F,
351). The attempt to relativize the fictional reality of the moment in this section, which deals, among others, with the authors Arnim and Brentano, might
be interpreted as an attempt to emulate romantic irony, and as such can also
be interpreted as an attempt to mold the language and the narrative mode to
reflect to some degree the literary style appropriate to the temporal reference.[23]

There are also times when the narrative consciousness insists on remaining bound to experiences of the historical identities and then pleads ignorance: "And then the third breast disappeared. I don't know the details—I
wasn't around just then . . ." (F, 68). Possible causes for its disappearance,
however, are suggested. The reaction to the loss suffered by the Edeks of that

time is presented directly and as personally experienced—"Gone was the third breast. . . . Unsuckled, we reached into the void from that day on"—and the consequence of that loss from the collective perspective is indicated: "After that we grew restless. Dissatisfaction set in" (F, 69).

In another play with feigned ignorance, the text first relays Pastor Blech's view that Sophie did indeed sleep with Governor Rapp, then questions that contention: "But maybe there's nothing in the whole story," and ultimately provides a rational explanation for her behavior, having assumed "probably Sophie never crawled into Rapp's French bed" (F, 376). At any rate, it was not her love for Fritz, but her German patriotism that kept her from succumbing to that temptation. The issue, however, is never definitely resolved, and the option of having the protagonist-narrator as Rapp himself clarify the question, which clearly lies within the narrative structure of the novel, is not exercised.

In other instances, narrative omniscience is employed without apology or explanation, and episodes are related in the text in which the protagonist-narrator is not present in any of his manifestations. For example, both Lena Stubbe's trip to the international conference in the seventh chapter and the "Father's Day" segment that constitutes the eighth chapter are presented without benefit of a participatory perspective.[24] In connection with the latter episode, the narrative constraints of the novel are sprung. There the attempt to attribute to the Lesbian Maxie, who had just raped the sleeping Billy, the memory of the experience of Axel Ludström, who, centuries earlier, had initiated the multiple rape of the maid Agnes, is without internal or structural justification. It may have been intended by Grass as a clever recreation of the Agnes-Axel relationship in the new constellation of Billy-Maxie, but it is not based upon any of the narrative options furnished within the novel and mars an otherwise complex, yet controlled narrative.

The interaction of the dual functions of the central figure, those of protagonist and narrator, is itself the subject of considerable thematic development within the novel. The protagonist-narrator lives, as it were, in two worlds, one of his imagination and one of prescribed connubial reality. He attempts to sketch his wife, and it is Sophie's face that looks up at him from his sketch pad (F, 357); he sits pensively, waiting for the door to open and wonders if it will be his wife—"The door is still holding. But when it crashes, you will bring me war or make me look for coins with your question, 'Got two mark-pieces for a slot machine?'"—or one of his fantasy figures: "But then the door opened gently and Agnes came in, bent over me and my scribble-scrabble, and said play words" (F, 278).

Waiting for Ilsebill to finish her shopping and left to his own devices for a few moments, he pursues his "obsessive daydream of having been Vasco da Gama" (F, 343). Then, having assumed that identity, he muses, "But when I was still Vasco da Gama, full of unrest and inwardly rich in figures . . ." (F, 344), only to regain his perspective and, attributing the evocation of the fantasy to the incense burning in the shop, returns to the reality of Ilsebill's purchase. Often his fantasy intrudes upon his interaction with others. Ilsebill complains, for example, "He's not here at all. He's miles away. He's always got company in the back of his mind" (F, 383), and during a dinner party, he is quick to find better company, drawing from his own fantasy: "I refilled glasses, dished out, and kept silent, busy with thoughts of Sophie . . ." (F, 386). When bad weather causes guests to cancel, he takes the opportunity to supply his own: "Thinking up guests: historical, contemporary, future" (F, 369).

Similarly at his intimate dinner, arranged at Ilsebill's insistence, the protagonist-narrator notes they were eating as three, and simultaneously "with many more" as well (F, 393). Present in the conversation, and in his own consciousness, and thus "in attendance" at the lavish meal he had prepared in honor of Griselde's visit, which the two women consume with more discussion than reverence, are all the women participants in the Tribunal. In addition, in the course of the meal he is visited by, or visits, the women of his historical pasts. Attributed in part to the addition of powdered, hallucinatory mushrooms, the protagonist-narrator then projects all into one expanded dinner party: "For in the meantime, thanks to the special ingredient, our meal for three had taken on a new dimension. Not only were the complete Flounder Party—so it seemed to me—and Schönherr, the personified authority of the Women's Tribunal, sitting at the table along with Paasch, Osslieb, and Witzlaff: in addition, Agnes Kurbiella and Amanda Woyke, Mother Rusch, Saint Dorothea, and Sophie Rotzoll had escaped from their time-phases. . . . All had their doubles and vice versa. The table had grown" (F, 394).

Frequently no clues are furnished, besides those provided by the context, for the immediate, projected identity of the narrator at any one point in the narrative. As a result, when a passage begins with a statement, such as, "After the soup the company was already in high spirits" (F, 376), the reader must continue in the text in order to determine whether it is a dinner being served in the fictional present involving the protagonist-narrator, whether it is a meal he has conjured up and is interjecting into a conversation set in the fictional present as part of his tale-telling function, whether it is a meal set in the fictional past, at which he is present in one of his historical identities (that may subsequently be described in either first or third person), or one that he, assuming the stance of omniscient narrator, knows about, but did not participate in.

One of the more interesting interactions of the fictionalized projections of the protagonist-narrator and the espoused reality of the fictive present occurs in the last chapters of the novel, where the multiple plot lines are brought into greater juncture with one another. Not only do the realities of his projected, earlier identities intrude into his present, but his contemporaries in that fictive time frame accuse *him* of the crimes of those earlier, projected figures. Thus Ilsebill and Griselde make him personally responsible for the death of "his" children born in earlier centuries by Amanda Woyke and illegitimately by Agnes Kurbiella (F, 388). In recounting the conversation and the list of their complaints against him, he also incorporates both the first and third person pronouns to illustrate his personal involvement in their third-person discussion of him. The topics range from his political work—"all the projects I (he) had bungled despite the best of intentions . . . since I (he) could never make up my (his) mind"—to those of "his (my) children" (F, 388).

Approximately halfway through the novel, an additional fictive level, which was discussed briefly earlier and which is related directly to the phenomenon of the prismatic narrator as developed and manifested in *The Flounder*, becomes evident. In the midst of a discussion of the life and problems of Agnes, including her pathetic attempts to feed her sickly infant with watered milk, gruel, and prechewed leftovers, the protagonist-narrator notes, "I, too, fed our child prechewed food—out of labeled jars, costing 1.50 to 1.80 marks apiece, with vacuum caps that go pop when you open them" (F, 273). The comment incorporates a clear attempt to show the similarity in diet, while contrasting the change in food processing brought about by technological advances in the intervening centuries. Of greater interest here, however, are the words, "in a later day, when my Ilsebill went off on a trip" (F, 273), which occur within the line quoted above. They insert for the first time a clear and unmistakable reference to a time frame, subsequent to and not prescribed by the fictional frame of the novel. The following pages of the novel provide further elaboration of the nature of the narrative voice that intrudes here. It is clearly identifiable with the protagonist-narrator, Ilsebill's spouse. Ilsebill, having given birth to their child, has left for a vacation on the Antilles, leaving the new father in charge of the infant and its feeding, the very infant, whose gestation period marked the temporal frame of the work. This narrative voice recounts the ingredients of the recommended diet, and the manner of their preparation, with as much attention to detail as the various protagonist-narrators exhibited in their description of dishes throughout the novel. As a result of this fictional association with the novel's protagonist-narrator, the authorial voice manifested in these pages is not evidence of an extra-textual authorial presence equatable with the author Günter Grass himself, but rather of the personalized authorial voice of the novel's narrative consciousness alluded to earlier. It represents the third level, however brief its materialization, of the manifestation of the prismatic narrator, one which is projected forward from the novel's temporal frame, but is thematically re-

lated to the events of the work and linked to the personality of its chief protagonist. With this, the full spectrum of the prismatic narrator, as postulated
and practiced within the novel, has been displayed.

The range of narrative possibilities offered by this constellation through
the fracturing of the narrative consciousness and its identification with the
novel's protagonist-narrator, the interaction of that protagonist-narrator
with his projected historical identities, and the occasional intrusion of the
personalized authorial voice, all combine to make *The Flounder*, as its nine
months and fifty centuries unfold, a rich and fascinating work. With it, Grass
has not only written a novel with the most complex narrative structure he has
yet undertaken, but he has also created a new narrative configuration, the
prismatic narrator.[25]

Notes

1. The topics are more grandiosely referred to by the protagonist-narrator himself
   later in the novel as questions of world hunger and of nutrition, an identification
   that Grass clearly seems to prefer. Cf. also Hansjoachim Bleyl, "Danziger
   Alchemie," p. 629.
2. Paralleling the espoused narrative intent of presenting an alternative to the male-
   oriented or biased tale of "The Fisherman and His Wife," the chapter posits
   against the male-centered myth of the theft of fire (the traditional legend of Prometheus and the gods), which the Flounder seeks to disseminate, a feminist myth
   of the matriarchal era, based on the superhuman feat of the primitive goddess
   Awa, who entered the heavens and stole the fire from the Sky Wolf. The tale of
   male martyrdom for humanity is thus replaced by one of woman's care for the
   world, to which, however, is attached as a by-product, a mythological basis for the
   sexual insatiability that the novel's protagonist-narrators habitually attribute to
   the female figures.
3. The narrative situation is repeatedly stressed in the text in a variety of ways. Two
   incidents should suffice as examples. The protagonist-narrator, having cited the
   Flounder's advice around 2000 BC that he, an Edek, should kill Awa and thereby
   end the matriarchy, interjects a comment addressed to his wife, as if in answer to
   one of her comments: "No, Ilsebill. I didn't do it. . . . I've always been faithful to
   Awa; I still am" (F, 27). On another occasion, Ilsebill's direct request, "I'd rather
   you told me about Sophie" (F,370), initiates another tale-telling session. For
   discussion of this archetypal narrative situation, cf. Patrick O'Neill, "The
   Scheherazade Syndrome: Günter Grass' Meganovel *Der Butt*," *AoF*, pp. 1-22.
4. The cooks may be "in him" as concepts, as figments of his creative imagination,
   but none of the tales are told from their perspective. The narrator's historical embodiments are exclusively male, and there is no attempt to relate, or relate to, a female experience. Cf. Ruth Angress, "*Der Butt*—A Feminist Perspective," *AoF*,
   pp. 43-50. See also Structural Diagram, below, pp. 198-199.
5. The priorities in the protagonist-narrator's life might be more accurately described
   as sexual gratification, rather than procreation, and its dominance over artistic creativity may also contain, at least in incipient form, a complaint against women and
   their demands.

6. John Updike, "Fish Story," p. 205.

7. John Leonard, "Books of The Times," Sec. C, p. 24.

8. For a discussion of the numbering of the cooks, see O'Neill, "The Scheherazade Syndrome," p. 5.

9. The communality of experience is greatest in the earliest periods of human history. There it is "we Edeks" against the Awas, "we" Awas and Edeks against the males of another primitive tribe, and later "we" men of both tribes against the coalition of the women and their demands.

10. "I was her (and the tribe's) head shepherd, and at the same time I was Bishop Adalbert" (F, 103).

11. Grass is quite willing to explore the variant possibilities of such a dual existence. Thus on one occasion, the protagonist-narrator notes, "Often she was there, but I noticed only myself, whereas someone else (Möller) noticed her even though she was with me," although his conclusion, "Her love was placeless" (F, 271), is an inadequate explanation for the phenomenon just described. Referring to the relationship with Agnes as "a classical triangle," the protagonist-narrator at one point offers a rationale for his double existence—"I wanted to be painter and poet at once" (F, 277)—leaving the situation open for speculation, that perhaps Grass was projecting a division of his own artistic talents between two figures, so that he could speak as graphic artist and as poet of one and the same muse.

12. The narrative consciousness also permits himself the right to assess, from his vantage point, the various roles. Thus he notes on one occasion, "When I think of myself today as Rapp, I cannot help agreeing with what I, as Pastor Blech, said about him" (F, 365).

13. In connection with his assumption of the identity of Vasco da Gama, the protagonist-narrator introduces another narrative configuration. Not only does he assume the historical identity of Vasco da Gama as a contemporary of the abbess, but he also brings that identity into the fictional present of the novel's frame by noting that he had decided "to travel unofficially as Vasco da Gama" as well. Furthermore he also perceives his present identity as author and lecturer, as a reincarnation of that historical personage—"After many rebirths, Vasco is now a writer. He is writing a book in which he exists down through the ages: the Stone Age, the Early Christian, High Gothic, Reformation, and Baroque eras, the age of the Enlightenment, et cetera" (F, 175).

14. Some of the aspects include the description of the protagonist-narrator's life as a renowned author, his reading tours, his trip to India, his involvement in the filming in Gdańsk, and the attributing of the authorship of *From the Diary of a Snail* to the novel's protagonist. Cf. O'Neill, "The Scheherazade Syndrome," p. 11.

15. The name chosen for the presiding officer at the Tribunal, Ms. Schönherr, seems to rest upon a word play implying dependence upon the male world and, in a variation of the tale of Adam's rib, suggests woman's identity as that of a "pretty" male being. I am indebted to Norbert Ysermann, a graduate student at the University of Houston, for a further reference to a German television personality, Mrs. Dietmar Schönherr (Vivi Bach), whose talk-shows featuring married couples are familiar to German television audiences. For a discussion of the pairing of the women figures, see also Anke Burkhardt, Ursula Tesch and Friedrich Voit, "Geschichten zur Geschichte. Zum neuen Roman von Günter Grass *Der Butt*," *AoF,* p. 89.

16. The need to alter evidence in a documentary film—"really you don't need bones in a documentary" (F, 122)—is presented with an irony that must be intentional. It

raises as well the question of the reliability of the documentary, versus the fiction-alized presentation of reality.

17. Space is posited as a unifying aspect of the novel by Guy Stern, *"Der Butt* as an Experiment in the Structure of the Novel," *AoF,* pp. 53–54.

18. The protagonist-narrator, in an aside to Ilsebill, not only reveals his own egocen-tricity, but also substantiates the domination of the personal, experiential level over the societal, historical perception: "You see, Ilsebill, I have a better memory for flights of stairs, kitchen smells, winding sheets hung out of windows, and per-sonal defeats than for places" (F, 116).

19. Cf. Friedrich Ulfers' discussion of the treatment of history in the novel as a "Teufelskreis" in his article, "Myth and History in Günter Grass' *Der Butt,*" *AoF,* pp. 35–36.

    Although the basic male-female relationships do not seem to develop or evolve through time, there is an increasing sophistication of the figures, both in character-ization and in individualization. More significant, however, is the progress, both in the art of cooking and in the development and refinement of the agricultural pro-ducts used, that stands in marked contrast to the lack of significant change in basic human relationships and, in addition, makes the presence of continuing world hunger a more serious moral issue.

20. Other repeated activities include hunting for mushrooms—when Sophie is de-picted hunting for mushrooms, the same activity with Ilsebill is also recalled (F, 356)—and more frequently, both preparing meals and dining. When the protagon-ist-narrator in the fictional present, for example, has dinner guests, the memory or thought of dinners of previous eras invariably intrudes: "Just as we invite people to dinner . . . , so in the late days of my neolithic time-phase we also had guests" (F, 59).

21. The study of the prismatic narrator would not be complete without a brief com-mentary on the Flounder's narrator role. He, too, is periodically assigned that function, although set within the body of the narrative, and in turn, informs, ca-joles, criticizes, and advises the protagonist-narrator, both in his historical repre-sentations and in the fictional present. His impact on the forward thrust of the narrative is not to be ignored. There is, however, a substantial variance in the de-gree of authority with which he speaks. As presented to the reader, he fluctuates between self-espoused omniscience and clearly limited insight, although occa-sionally it is not possible to determine with certainty whether his errors in percep-tion are intentional or only accidental on his part, whether he is consciously assigned such fallibility by the protagonist-narrator, or whether it is an oversight on Grass's part. In any case, the protagonist-narrator is prepared to deny the Flounder's om-niscience. Speaking of the experiences of the Edeks with an hallucinatory root, he refers to the Flounder as one "who had never heard of our primordial drug" (F, 69), and on another occasion mentions something, which "the Flounder doesn't know" (F, 99). His credibility is furthermore impugned by his own commentary, through which he is revealed at times to be prejudiced and deceitful, if not down-right malicious.

22. This is strikingly different from examples discussed earlier, where a participatory perspective is extended temporarily into the present, placed in an expanded frame-work, or interpreted by the narrative consciousness.

23. Further credence to the assumption of such a conscious narrative intent on Grass's part can be deduced from the playful passages in the novel itself, in which the nar-rative consciousness comments how much has been written "about storytelling

and narrative style" (F, 298) and then suggests that the activities of his cooks were the determining factors in the structure of their narrative style. (See especially F, 299–300). Cf. also Siegfried Mews, "Der Butt als Germanist: Zur Rolle der Literatur in Günter Grass' Roman," *AoF,* pp. 24–31.

24. The earlier comment regarding the recent Father's Day—"naturally I was there"—is either a reference to the narrative consciousness's preemptive right to have been everywhere and to have experienced everything depicted or presented in the novel (although there is no other example of such an assertion in the text), or it is a loose end, one of those passages that might have had validity in an earlier draft of the novel, but that Grass failed to delete after changing his plans in the course of his writing.

25. See also the essays, (this book) by Ruprecht Wimmer, "'I, Down Through the Ages': Reflections on the Poetics of Günter Grass," pp. 25-38, and Judith Ryan, "Beyond *The Flounder:* Narrative Dialectic in *The Meeting at Telgte,*" pp. 39-53.

Between Stone Age and Present or The Simultaneity of the Nonsimultaneous: The Time Structure

Helmut Koopmann

TRANSLATED BY STEVEN JOYCE AND MONIKA PITTL

I

It is evident from the beginning that *The Flounder* is a novel both simple and difficult to read, one that is continuously told while ignoring all possible limits. Although in an almost contradictory and completely unbelievable way it projects the Stone Age into the present, everything nonetheless becomes possible and no limits are placed on this epic, though obstacles obstructing comprehension arise everywhere. All this is recognized by the reader when it becomes clear that the "I," the narrator, has a fictive and yet real omnipresence in the novel, which therefore abrogates the traditional system of time, of past, present and future. Even if the reader should have overlooked the proclamation of the "I's" omnipresence in the sixth line of the book, in the second chapter or "Second Month" at the latest it will, unmistakably and finally, be pointed out to him that the traditional sequence of time in this novel is no longer valid, since, here, the end of the book is already indicated. And that is not because it is an old epic technique to anticipate *in nuce* the end at the beginning. Between these two passages it is made clear to the reader that the beginning and end of the story, at least in the narrator's consciousness, are not to be separated, since they are to a certain extent concomitantly present. Even though the first poem of the book, "what I write about" (F, 8–9) does nothing more than delineate the range of the narration and anticipate possible

individual parts of that which is to come, for example, about "on my way to
Calcutta," it is really in the second chapter, where what is to come is mentioned. With the report of "Nine and more cooks" the panorama of
characters is sketched and likewise the sequence of events is transferred to simultaneity: the first cook, the Stone Age Awa, appears unexpectedly to the
dockworkers at Danzig or Gdańsk who started the rebellion in December
1970. Only a narrator who does not think much of an epic sequence and who
seems to abrogate the older order of narration simply for fun can successfully
accomplish this juxtaposition. As everything is told already at the beginning
of the novel by way of suggestion, so are the later, more explicit accounts of
that which is already known a repetition of what has already been told or, at
least, been mentioned; these repetitions do not add anything essentially new.
In the subchapter dealing with "Nine and more cooks" the reader learns that
Billy, the tenth cook, dies in Berlin in the 1960s on Ascension Day. In the
same sentence we are told about Maria, the eleventh cook, whose fate the
reader learns about in the last chapter—although he has already been informed
about this before in the first subchapter of "The Second Month." This omnipresence of events corresponds to the omnipresence of characters. Dorothea,
the fourth cook, who was born in 1347, commands the "Second Month" but
is still present in the last chapter, if only through memory. In addition, the
story of the Flounder is not only a narrative model in its entirety but also in its
various stages. These various stages of the fairy tale are parodistically told as
bedtime stories in the "Father's Day" Chapter.The history of a pregnancy
does not only run through the entire novel but appears again in the poem
"Quarrel" (F, 127). Again and again, we encounter repetitions or foreshad-
owing of repetitions in the novel. Ilsebill is always present, at the same time
she is, by the various stories that are told, forced repeatedly into the background, although the single stories are anything but closed in themselves,
since they overlap each other. The chronological continuation of the story, in-
extricably bound to the development represented in it, since a process and a
development seem to call urgently for a narration in successive stages, is repeatedly interrupted by contrary depth perspectives. Hence the story can also
be told backwards. When the reporter is in Danzig, where he has just flown in
order to direct a television documentary, and pauses to think and reflect, the
story proceeds in a contrary manner like this: "When the electrician finally
arrived and our three lamps, plugged into an auxiliary line, were again shed-
ding light on the municipal conservatory and on Anton Möller's *Tribute
Money* scene on the Long Market, I had just left the seventeenth century with
its varied religions and was back in the early fourteenth century—May 17,
1308 to be precise—watching the execution of the sixteen Pomeranian
knights, all members of the widely ramified Swenzas family" (F, 113–14). But
this regression is stopped shortly after that when the narrating consciousness

makes the backwards-oriented memory turn around and passes over seven centuries by association towards present time, in order to refer to the homogeneity of past and present events—over a fragile intellectual bridge. The fourteenth century beside the twentieth—this is anything but a compelling parallel; but such parallel would already be imposing too much order upon a domain that can never tolerate a sequential order. We read:

> History, to be sure, tells us with chronological precision that on February 6, 1296, the Polish king Przemyslaw was murdered in Rogasen, but the figures for the mass slaughter remain crude guesswork; just as in recent times I was unable to find out by random questioning of resident Poles (which I kept up as long as we were shooting the television film) how many workers in the Lenin Shipyard in Gdańsk and how many shipyard workers and longshoremen in nearby Gdynia were shot in mid-December, when the police and army of the People's Republic of Poland were ordered to fire on the striking workers. (F, 114)

So possible perspectives are again and again crossed by other ones. Without hesitation the story is told, almost simultaneously, both forwards and backwards. History is brought into line in anything but a sensible fashion, but especially because of this there is nothing prior or later within the novel, but always a sudden simultaneity of the nonsimultaneous. The Polish dockworkers' resistance is mentioned several times in the novel until at the end that which is already known for some time is told explicitly. The short report ends: "Details were not discussed. The whole thing was subsumed and deplored under the head of 'December Events'" (F, 115). Immediately after that we read: "And the Teutonic Knights were also quick to proceed to the order of the day" (F, 115). Why "And"? What is the common denominator and what of it has become visible? One only recognizes an almost superficial similarity of events, the end of an affair then and now that had to happen sometime. The comparison does not amount to anything else but to the attempt, then as now, to observe the happenings from a new perspective. Consequently, there is at best, a vague, unspecific similarity of those events that took place at the beginning of the twelfth century with those that are related by the narrator in connection with the revolt of the dockworkers of Danzig. That now as well as then they pass over into the daily routine, that something appears to be finished and done, although it has not been done, that alone creates the connection and relation between the revolt of the workers and the events around 1300, or better, that does not create the relationship but would allow the succession of both statements to appear as a painstakingly induced, violently opportunistic historical parallel—if such a parallel was, indeed, intended. Since everything is simultaneously present, and therefore nothing exists that has not always existed and continues to exist, this bold jump from the end of the Danzig revolt to the Teutonic order is successful. What is here placed next to each other and what is connected and put in relation to each other by nothing but an extremely vague association, is nevertheless firmly established in the consciousness of the reader as a forceful coincidence. What is anything but obvious is placed next to each other as obvious; it can hardly be regarded as a biased historical account and is not even prefaced by a brief introduction. But something like that still insures the continuation of history that, in turn, becomes a step backwards from present time to the thirteenth century because in the following, the Danzig dockworker revolt is no longer the question as one would have expected after the jump from the thirteenth to the twentieth century. Rather the Polish king and the Brandenburgers are discussed again; the narrator has once again embarked on a course backwards. Even with this the meandering course of the narration is still incomplete. The new step backwards into history does not last long but returns on the following pages (that is, for the second time within a short period) to the progression of the narration and narrator's thought. This is a progression or, perhaps, regression when, first, the victims of the slaughter perpetrated by the Teutonic order are mentioned, and, immediately after that, once again the strike and revolt of the harbor and dockworkers in East Prussia. Present, past, present again, past again, finally the present for the third time—what does it mean at all, which level of narration is the actual one, which one is only quoted for comparison?

This clearly cannot be answered from the immediate context of the passage but possibly from the novel's superstructure according to which history, to state it cautiously, started sometime in the Stone Age and is told up to the present. But even such hypothesis is not compelling. Since the present is already prospectively embedded in the stories of the Stone Age, there is no continuous narration in the traditional epic sense. And because there is not the normal succession in the relation between past and present, everything, the prehistoric and the present, can suddenly appear next to each other. With regard to historical continuity or causality, that which is presented here in juxtaposition has nothing at all to do with each other; at most the stories about the Teutonic order and the revolt of the dockworkers in East Prussia take place in the same area, in the same city. The potential and very often actual omnipresence of the various parts of the narration throughout the entire novel, the juxtaposition of what does not belong together, and the anticipation of things to come, vice versa the return of something already dealt with in the narration—all that destroys the conventional structure that one might expect of such a novel so thoroughly that beginning and end are no longer beginning and end of the story. Rather, they are only narrative indications that are necessary, owing to the fact that a novel, despite the omnipresence of events, has to have a beginning and an end and because the narration *eo ipso* demands a succession. But since this succession is constantly impinged upon, since it is anticipated and brought back, since the story is simultaneously told forward and again backward, since the twentieth century is unexpectedly superimposed on the Stone Age, the Stone Age in turn appears gratuitously in the stories of the present, one cannot talk any more about a chronologically narrated story. Even when, seen from the outside, it is told as usual, that is, from the beginning to the end.

II

Therefore, Grass seems to deal uninhibitedly with the parts of his material.[1] That he reports of times and things no one has even the faintest idea of may be legitimized by the narrator's traditional freedom. That everything is more or less present at the same time, recollected or anticipated from memory by association looks like an arbitrarily proceeding narrative subjectivity that on occasion seems to be the offspring of an anarchic fantasy. Nevertheless, there are special structuring devices in the narrative continuum, even if they are not incorporated in the conventional schemata for the narration and suspend the usual succession of events. In this novel the narration also has a direction, even the epic report is not the constant advance towards something new and unknown; until at the end, the narrative frame has been fleshed out according to the initially stated theme. The segmented time of the prenatal history of Helena Grass belongs to these structuring devices, for the novel runs through the phases from her conception to her birth, that is, the time from October 1973 to the summer of 1974.[2] The nine months of the pregnancy also supply the nine chapters of the book. In the poem "What I write about," close to the beginning of the novel, the narrator programmatically and unambiguously states his intention to "write as long as it lasts" (F, 8). That the first-person narrator will write as long as the time of the pregnancy will last, allows us to perceive a second structuring device. The nine months through which the story is told are simultaneously the time of gestation of the "headbirth," that is, the time of the novel's origin. But these are not the only two systems imposing a structure on the narrated events. A third system exists parallel to the two time frames of nine months. In the "First Month," hence simultaneously with the beginning of the narration, the Flounder is caught and is subsequently put on trial for nine months. The trial ends with the sentence passed by the so-called "Womenal" and the Flounder's newly won freedom. The prenatal history of Helena Grass, the history of the "headbirth," the report of the trial run exactly parallel; moreover the nine months until Helena's birth, the nine months of the writing of the novel, the nine months of the feminist tribunal are constantly related to each other by association and the respective reports about it are so balanced that none of these perspectives can be dominant. In the story of the trial against the Flounder, however, a further dimension is embedded that allows an additional structuring device to become evident. The story of the Flounder starts already when the Flounder is first pulled from the sea by a " . . . neolithic dolt and mediocrity . . ." (F, 38)—that is, by the "I" that has existed since that time. There is, then, a fourth ordering system; the epic report runs at the same time, among everything else, through the time extending from the Neolithic Age up to the immediate present, the time from the beginning of the matriarchy via the "'gradual'—'evolutionary . . . liberation of men from the rule of women'" (F, 39) to the patriarchy, to the "male cause."This looks like a reference to the prehistoric ideas of Bachofen,[3] which furnish the background for the far-reaching historical account. To be sure, history occurs only paradigmatically in nine significant examples, but these reconstruct something like an *ersatz* history. The segmented cultural history of mankind, in which the Flounder appears as the omniscient teacher, occurs as the fourth entity in addition to the nine months of the "headbirth," the physical birth, and the trial. This actually belongs to the realm of abstruse fairy tales, in which the Flounder exists only as a fairy-tale reality. But since the Flounder, an animal symbol like the snail in *From the Diary of a Snail,* at the same time belongs to the story of the narrating "I," the border between fairy-tale fiction and the realistic description of the "I" is constantly violated. The prehistory of mankind is successively integrated in the history of the "I" and the other structuring devices. All these systems are time structures that, despite all the discontinuity of narration, make continuous writing possible; they all supply the texture for an end-oriented narration. Real birth, "headbirth," the end of the trial, and history finally come together. Thus the end of the novel is the goal of two very divergent developments, one of which extends from the Stone Age to the present, whereas the other one is only a nine-months history. Ultimately, it is only of secondary importance whether this story concerns the nine months of the physical birth, the "headbirth," or of the trial. Nevertheless, these elements do not remain unconnected: the history of mankind is repeatedly superimposed on the prenatal history; the history of mankind in turn supplies the material for the Flounder's trial that ends with him being sentenced to death and, at the same time, to a new life.

III

World history, history of the birth, history of the novel's origin, history of the trial; on these four planes the novel proceeds. Certainly, they are not exclusively entwined with each other by the author's intermittent narrative style. Grass's artful conception goes further and causes them to become levels that necessarily imply one another. The relation of the "headbirth," that is, the story and history of the novel's origin, to the other stories and histories is easiest to understand. It is, indeed, remembered only by way of suggestion but it is nevertheless the summation of the other stories. It became reality by putting the other stories on paper; the result of the history of the work's origin is the novel in which the story of its genesis was integrated. What also remains clear is the relation of the story of the trial to world history; not only do the activities of the "Womenal" become evident in the report of the trial, but also that which subsequently led to the trial, that is, the role that the Flounder played in the history of mankind. Since the Flounder, according to the fairy tale, is not only immortal and omniscient but, the narrated "I" informs us, serves also as his teacher and advisor, everything is mentioned in the trial that concerned the narrated "I" throughout the millennia. This offers possibilities of dove-tailing: the extended history of mankind from neolithic times (even Grass does not risk going back further) up to the present is somewhat plausibly incorporated into the story of the trial. To be sure, the trial inevitably becomes equivocal and constantly moves in two contray directions. It evolves through the nine months of the Women's Tribunal toward a juridical end, the sentence. But since the ancient history of the Flounder is explored during the trial, the narrative again descends deep into history. It is, at the same time, a criminal story and a detective story; by going backwards and detecting the prehistory in all its stages the criminal story moves forward toward the end of the nine-months period. It is in the trial, and not in the prenatal growth of a human being, where something like a phylogenesis takes place. This happens, at the same time, in the genesis of the novel that is inseparably connected with the stages of the trial by virtue of the fact that the story of the novel's origin is also the report of the trial. What is most obscure is the relation of the actual nine-months story to the other stories. Since this story is not burdened with phylogenetic meaning, it can only acquire meaning in a figurative sense. It is always the same history of mankind that actualizes itself again and again in conception, gestation and birth of the child in exemplary fashion. Without the story of the nine months there would not be that history of mankind subject to the Women's Tribunal. Thus, all the stories about births in which the narrating "I" was involved become present in all the other stories. In the constant cycle of birth and death, the true history of mankind, as it was made by women and mothers, appears as the actual, the true history of humanity. Grass unleashes an unremitting attack upon conventional historiography, as we all know it, that constantly falsifies true history. Yet world history, in a subliminal fashion, is directly connected with the nine-months history of gestation, since this story, the actual protohistory, is similar to the history of nutrition that is also created by women, but has likewise not been recorded.

IV

Nevertheless, all these stories would diverge and the narrative lines would become hopelessly entangled if they were not all brought together in the consciousness of the narrating "I." For beside the *narrated* "I" that already existed in the Stone Age, and has lived many lives, there is that all-embracing other "I," the *narrating* "I" that is omniscient and disposes, narrating and reflecting, of everything. If, on the one hand, the narrated "I" is subject to a categorical system of time and place, the narrating "I," on the other hand, permanently abrogates this system. This leads to a confusing dynamic opposition between a narrating "I" that is constantly present by means of its critical reflections and an ignorant and unenlightened "I" that follows all the clumsy turns of history. But the omniscience of the narrating "I" protects the other narrated "I" in this (hi)story just in the nick of time from the worst mistakes or, subsequently, brings it to some degree of self-recognition. Therefore, these two "I's" are not arbitrary but closely related to each other.[4] But it is this omniscient "I" that gives the novel its inner unity and not the stringency of the action or the homogeneity of the narrated world. But this does not make the novel easier to understand. The novel has, at first sight, all the characteristics of an autobiographical novel such as the extraction of the prehistoric events from the memory of the reporter, the commentary on that which is reported in retrospect by someone who knows how the story of his own life went, the intermingling of world history with private history, and the distance that inevitably results from the chronological remoteness of the reporter to the events.

At the same time, the novel is a parody of autobiography because the consciousness of the "I" is no longer identical with the history it experiences, but simply with world history. World history, to a certain extent, seems to be internalized. It is, therefore, incorporated into the biography of a single person, although not in a way that the stages of world history seem to be repeated in his own history, but rather in such a way that the "I" has, indeed, lived many times, yet remains immortal in its consciousness. This process is elucidated in the objective correlative of the Flounder, who likewise has his fairy-tale immortality and attendant agelessness and omniscience. That parts of Günter Grass's real autobiography are fused with the novel plays no role with regard to the narrative structure, but allows us to draw conclusions concerning the identity of the first-person narrator and the author. They are, however, of no import to the novel.

Hence, the "I" or rather a modern form of the Super Ego gives the novel its constructive unity, a unity that is identical to what is associated in the "I's" consciousness. Therefore, the associative parallelisms of diverse elements do not so much have the purpose of destroying the tectonics of the traditional novel, but rather of introducing the "I's" consciousness as one that is always both receptive and encompasing. Thus, the ubiquitous simultaneity of the unsimultaneous is an attempt to replace the unity of the story by the unity of consciousness rather than to write a novel that adheres to the conventional rules of the genre. The narrative consciousness, moreover, combines not only the temporally and spatially distant, it also justifies this combination. From this point of view the fairy-tale Flounder serves only to elucidate: he also is immortal like the first-person narrator's consciousness (or as the Hegelian would call it, the consciousness of the *Weltgeist*). This, of course, does not mean that Grass adopted this fairy-tale figure for his novel without qualification. What the Flounder in the novel has in common with the one in the fairy tale is his immortality; what separates them (because it is not transferred to the novel) is the omnipotence of the Flounder who can fulfill wishes and can therefore effortlessly change reality. In place of his omnipotence there is omniscience in the novel, and therefore, the eternal consciousness of the "I," a narrator who wants us to acknowledge that he has already existed in the Stone Age and that he, as an immortal, has preserved the knowledge from that time together with all other stages of human history.

As far as the author's purpose is concerned, this is anything but new. As early as the beginning of our century there were novels of consciousness. Joyce's *Ulysses* influenced this type of novel as well as Proust's *Remembrance of Things Past*. In the German-speaking countries, Arthur Schnitzler impressively demonstrated the simultaneity of successive happenings in the consciousness of Fräulein Else, the main character in a novella by that same name. Whereas in *Fräulein Else* it was only the totality of a private world in which the past had the same weight as the immediate present in Else's consciousness, in Proust the consciousness of the whole contemporary world was present; Joyce even attempted to capture within the consciousness of one single character the consciousness of other characters and, beyond that, of cultural history in general. That space and time are only categories of experience that do not impose limitations on consciousness was also shown by Grass's teacher, Alfred Döblin, in his novel *Berlin Alexanderplatz* as well as his philosophical works. Especially in the 1920s there was no dearth of attempts to trace in quasi-phylogenetic fashion cultural-historical developments in the consciousness of an individual. It is not coincidental that Grass refers to matriarchy and patriarchy; he is obviously following Bachofen's cultural-historical considerations. Bachofen was popularized in the 1920s through Bernoulli's edition of his works[5] and, with deleterious effect, by Alfred Baeumler.[6] Making the unconscious part of consciousness through the return to psychic experiences and pre-experiences, the conviction that the soul's memory is far more extensive than intellectual memory, the presence of remote, culturally significant experiences in the subconsciousness of the single,

late-born person are all part of Freud's influence. So pervasive was this influence in the 1920s that their transposition into novels was practically a matter of course. The presence of the Isis-Osiris mythologem in Musil's *The Man
without Qualities* is as characteristic as the inclusion of prehistoric, precul-
tural phenomena in Broch's mountain novel "The Tempter" (*Der
Versucher*). This is also self-evident in Thomas Mann's Joseph tetralogy in
which Joseph's consciousness is likewise open to the very depths of time. But
again this archaic consciousness is represented by means of the most advanced narrative techniques. Grass becomes part of this tradition even though his
novel seems to have been written in violation of these traditions. To be sure,
Thomas Mann in his Joseph novel presents the victory of the paternal world
and glorifies the significance of the paternal principle. Further, until approximately 1929, the year of his lecture on Lessing,[7] Mann apostrophizes ancient
time as mythical time, as the time of the patriarchs, whereas Grass glorifies
the matriarchy as the crucial, but later forgotten protoform. These differences are only those of a common, but reversed perspective. Both authors assume that from the consciousness of the present such an entering into the pre-
past is not only possible, but deserves to be told. Grass merely reversed
Thomas Mann's view of things in many respects. He followed Bachofen rather than the apologists of the patriarchy. Consequently, he initiates, in conjunction with the feminist movement, a new tendency in the evaluation of history. Both authors' basic consensus remains unchanged, however; that is,
that it is possible for the consciousness of a later narrating "I" to fictitiously
retrace the course of cultural history. It is then only of secondary importance
under which auspices the development of this cultural history is seen.

V

Therefore, Günter Grass's novel with regard to technique and intention
is not a new form at all, but it is in the tradition of similarly extensive narrative attempts of our century. Grass's novel also follows the narrative tradition
of his predecessors in other ways. That the unsimultaneousness is or may become simultaneous in the first-person narrator's consciousness does not
mean that Grass stops at a mere inventory of former events, at the omnipresence of history in the consciousness. The novel is, like its predecessors, at the
same time an attempt at enlightenment that embraces several hundred pages.
Thus, the simultaneity of the unsimultaneousness is not a formula for the
status of consciousness, but for the development of consciousness that the
first-person narrator experiences in the course of the novel and that he inevitably forces upon the reader. That the nine months of prenatal existence of a
human being are concomitantly the nine months of a trial makes it clear from

the onset that with the development of man up to our time, a historical process in the development of mankind has taken place. Owing to the fact that this process has been misunderstood for so long, the novel endeavors to enlighten the reader. The Women's Tribunal, the "Womenal," also constitutes a going back to the mothers. The process of narration, partially identical with the trial against the Flounder, does not amount to anything but the justification of hitherto unmentioned or unjustifiably underestimated life forces. Thomas Mann's Joseph novel was an attempt to enlighten on behalf of a male spirit with which he intended to oppose the cult of matriarchy of Baeumler and the shabby glorification of prehistory during his time. Conversely, Grass's novel is an attempt to write about the role of women that has been underestimated so often and so greatly by hero-oriented historiography, and about everything connected with women's role, but especially about the history of human nutrition. From that point of view, the novel is not only a tracing of the history of mankind in general, but an attack on the falsely depicted history of mankind, that is, patriarchically interpreted history. Behind the particular story of the nine cooks, the history of women in general becomes apparent. It is a history of oppression and injustice that is not reported in neutral fashion. The "Father's Day" chapter at the end of the novel demonstrates to which extent this oppression reaches up to the immediate present.

Grass records the history of an emancipation, tried over and over again, but repeatedly warns that this emancipation must not lead to an adaptation of masculine modes of behavior. In case that happens, renewed suppression is the deadly consequence of such a falsely understood emancipation, the "Father's Day" chapter implies. Hence, Grass reinterprets predominantly masculine history by substituting the history of feminine development. It is self-evident that such newly written history is not heroic history, but an "elemental" one in which even basic biological facts are not suppressed, but, on the contrary, fully described. Seen from such a perspective, the work is indeed an anti-novel written against the colossal figures of history like Georg Büchner's early nineteenth-century works, *Danton's Death*, *Woyzeck*, and *Lenz*. They were likewise written in opposition to the parade horses of history, although Büchner's contemporaries perceived only descriptions of pathological conditions in the works. Büchner, for his part, could likewise only describe attempts at emancipation as symptoms of a disease. If one accepts the gist of Grass's novel, one is bound to acknowledge that he prescribes a healing process that is indispensable for society. Such a history of emancipation is absolutely necessary although it has failed time and again and could not be described as a history of an individual or as the history of a human life embedded in the cultural-historical chain of development. Novels of enlightenment are always novels of consciousness and vice versa; they involve going beyond the individual history of a single person. In so far as that is concerned, Grass carefully follows the considerations in *From the Diary of a Snail* in which this process of enlightenment becomes recognizable as nothing more than an extremely attenuated movement of a snail. *The Flounder* directly follows *Diary* in that prehistory had been incorporated into the representation of the present in that work. However, what appeared in *Diary* to be a bifurcation of the novel that was subsequently disparaged by the critics, resulted in *The Flounder* in a unified representation of the entire cultural history of mankind. By means of this cultural history Grass pursues enlightenment that results from his knowledge of the real history of mankind, an enlightenment of consciousness that alone is able to explain a seemingly chaotic history and draw conclusions therefrom. That such enlightenment is both possible and achievable is the premise of the novel; for this purpose all of world history simultaneously converges in the consciousness of the interpreter of history. Masculine world history is mostly that of "run-of-the-mill heroes":

> Every revolutionary process known to us has served up orgiastic rites of death, massacres drawing their justification from some masculine purity-principle or other. The guillotine was celebrated as humanistic progress, the Stalinist show trials met with the blessing of the knowing and unknowing; in the Nazi concentration camps re-education for death ceased to be anything more than a bureaucratic, administrative measure—in every case it was men, males, who with cold passion sprung from faith, with devotion to a just cause, with eyes fixed on the ultimate goal, with the chilling single-mindedness of archangels have antedated the deaths of fellow humans—pious self-assured males, far from their wives and families, ..." (F, 520)

This is essentially the course of masculine history, refuted in the novel not only by the birth of Helena Grass, but also by the sentence carried out against the Flounder. The verdict is not death, but rather postulates the future freedom of women: "'Henceforth he shall be available to us alone. We shall call him. We'll call him, all right!'" (F, 533).

For Grass, world history as determined by women is the opposite of that course of history that always tends to end with fatal consequences. Such a view is less indicative of a fatalistic insight into the immutability of masculine history than of hope for a change of this history granting women a voice in determining its course. But the insight into the fatality of male-determined history and into the possibility of a more human history assumes precisely what the novel attempts to describe: the simultaneity of the unsimultaneous, the knowledge of the fatal course of mankind's history that is being rewritten here so that it may develop differently in the future. The simultaneity of the unsimultaneous is in the consciousness of the first-person narrator an irrevocable assumption for a future history of mankind that develops in a human way. Therefore, a process with an optimistic result is described in the novel despite all the fatal periods of masculine-determined history.

History is being rewritten in a feminine way. Real history, of course, does not change; it remains a history of suppression and aberrations, of lack of freedom and tyranny, an inhuman history through the millennia that is neither revocable nor changeable. Only its interpretation may be corrected; thus the novel has only one goal—to reinterpret conventional history by advancing its true version. History, as seen by women, has to be assessed differently, has to be newly read and written in a more discriminating way. That is all the novel demands; hence the legitimate references to ancient history as well as the radical re-evaluation of tradition. This achievement, however, is only possible for a perceiving consciousness, a narrating "I" that sees everything including itself and its own stages of development. The introduction of such a narrating consciousness amounts almost to a further fairy-tale motif that, however, is intended to bring the essential truth to light. Precisely the omniscient consciousness means the simultaneity of the unsimultaneous; association is its analytical instrument, the ever newly reflected memory is its field of action. Since the mere retelling of the story, the history of mankind is certainly not at stake, but rather, so to speak, the consciousness of the history of mankind that comes to its self-awareness, a chronologically well-organized narration is of no consequence. Nor should it be of any consequence lest it interfere with the associatively and analogously operating process of recognition. Nothing happens *de facto* simultaneously; but in the consciousness preserving that which has taken place there is the simultaneity of past and present, the suspension of time, and the coexistence of various trains of thought. Therefore, the various intersecting courses of time are not contradictions in the process of narration; rather, they are the inevitable and essential presuppositions of recognition that is only possible in a complex, many-layered memory. Precisely this process of recognition is the issue. It is, at the same time, the trial against the Flounder that, in biological terms, encompasses the nine months from nothingness to a viable human being, but, on a different level, passes through the immeasurable space of time, from the beginnings of the first thoughts and feelings up to the present, complex consciousness. The novel is then both the story of the "headbirth" and the history of mankind seen in a new and (as Grass thinks) correct way. Hence Grass provides a process of consciousness, a process of recognition, not a real one; the novel supplies a paraphrase of history, not real history. The "headbirth" is the most important event, even though it is placed in a neutral parallel to the real birth of a girl. The interlacing structures of time, the coexistence of successive events, the simultaneity of the unsimultaneous are the prerequisites that make recognition possible. This can only happen when chronology is abrogated so that the perceiving "I" can confirm: "I, down through the ages, have been I" (F, 3).

The "I's" omnipresence remains until the end of the novel, when some of the characters, long since dead, return once more from the past, varying C. F. Meyers' poem "Stapfen" (Steps):

> "Then slowly she came to meet her footprints. But it wasn't Maria who came back. It must be Dorothea, I thought with alarm. As step by step she grew larger, I began to hope for Agnes. That was not Sophie's walk. Is Billy, my poor Sibylle, coming back?
> Ilsebill came. She overlooked me, overstepped me." (F, 547)

Of course, they only return to where the process of the novel takes place, that is, in the retentive consciousness. In the penultimate sentence of the novel the simultaneity of the unsimultaneous concomitantly happens once more: the successive events are finally preserved in the recognizing consciousness. History, the real occurrences, have become a story in the true sense, a conscious, knowing retelling of that other history that can only be accomplished by someone who has been present "down through the ages," from the Stone Age to our time. Such is the prerogative of the omniscient narrator, who remarks: "On our paper most things happen simultaneously" (F, 123). This is like a fairy tale but, according to Grass, only in this way can reality appear and both real history and narrated stories can be written in the proper fashion.

Notes

1. See Fritz J. Raddatz, "Heute lüge ich lieber gedruckt. *Zeit*-Gespräch über den *Butt* mit Günter Grass," pp. 8-9. In this interview Grass claimed that he could not recall how he had come across the fairy tale "The Fisherman and His Wife." He further stated that he, as author, was the last person to be able to report on "such complicated matter as a creative process that lasted for years." For a general account on the fairy tale, see Heinz Rölleke, *Der wahre Butt. Die wundersamen Wandlungen des Märchens vom Fischer und seiner Frau.*
2. See Volker Neuhaus, *Günter Grass*, p. 134.
3. Johann Jakob Bachofen, *Urreligion und antike Symbole. Systematisch angeordnete Auswahl aus seinen Werken*, ed. Carl Albrecht Bernouilli. 3 vols. (Leipzig: Reclam, 1926).
4. In the interview with Raddatz (n. 1, above), Grass confirmed that the "I" of both author and narrator is present from the beginning but that this "I" becomes fictional as the novel unfolds. However, there is no transformation of one "I" into the other since the tension between narrating and narrated "I" is sustained throughout the novel.

5. See n. 3, above.

6. *Der Mythus von Orient und Occident. Eine Metaphysik der alten Welt.* Aus den Werken von J. J. Bachofen, introd. Alfred Baeumler, ed. Manfred Schroeter (Munich: Beck, 1926).

7. Thomas Mann, "Rede über Lessing," *Gesammelte Werke*, IX (Frankfurt am Main: S. Fischer, 1960), 229-45.

Raw and Cooked, Myth and *Märchen*

Edward Diller

"To eat is a necessity, but to eat intelligently is an art!" La Rochefoucauld

Creation begins with a story, with a mythology. It begins with a story of gods and goddesses, with a golden age of existence, and its ends with the Fall, with the dubious fate of its people, with the advent of common history. Mythologies convey their authority by no lesser means than the heroic adventures and sacred values of their early divinities, who by virtue of their character and achievements create the archetypal models that will identify the central concern and final destiny of the race. Myths are the essential stories of a culture forever after, for below the narration of their surface events lies always a system of elusive assumptions, predictions, and instructions to stimulate one's sense of longing and encourage future actions.

Mythologies also answer the larger questions about identity, purpose, and one's place in the universe; and so, here as in other novels, Günter Grass begins his narration of *The Flounder* with the searching question of origins, of primal myths and historical evolution, of present problems and past transgressions. Ilsebill, the eternally transforming spouse and feminine principle of *The Flounder* begins the novel by asking: "'Should we go to bed right away, or do you first want to tell me how when where our story began?'" (F, 3). So the perennial husband-narrator-protagonist begins like an oracle of old to reflect, cogitate, and return slowly in time to a period of time before time, to prehistory, to *illo tempore,* to that comfortable *Urzeit* when all life was still embraced by the fullness of nature and a sense of unity:

I, down through the ages, have been I. And Ilsebill, too, has been from the beginning. I remember our first quarrel, toward the end of the Neolithic, some

91

two thousand years before the incarnation of our Lord, when myths were beginning to distinguish between raw food and cooked food. . . . In those days
Ilsebill's name was Awa. (F, 3)

Turning first to aetiological mythogyms, Grass presents straight away
the main themes of the novel knotted together as a problem that will have to
be examined over and over again in the next 500 pages. The novel begins with
the preparation of food and eating before going to bed, with the "impregnation" of Ilsebill, with sex and story-telling, and with a pregnancy that sets the
schedule for the narration of an archetypal history of the race: its birth,
growth, struggles, victories, failures, and disintegration through recorded
time. However, it is Grass's intention not only to present the fundamental
mythology of his people but also to follow the misfortunes of the myth itself
when challenged by history and compelled to manifest its archaic demands in
the form of social dislocations and a perennial longing to replace by force
what was once lost by folly.

History may tell us something of the consequences of those efforts since
the Fall, but only our myths and the arts that preserve them give us a sense of
who we are (as Ilsebill inquires in the first paragraph), why we are as we are,
what happened to us along the way, and what it means to be human.

Henri Frankfort insists that without a sense of our mythology or a mini-
mal awareness of how the ancient archetypes still permeate our daily actions
and present-day institutions, "The spheres of metaphysics, politics, and eth-
ics are doomed to remain a convenience without any deep significance. For
the life of man and the function of the state are for mythopoeic thought im-
bedded in nature and the natural processes are affected by the acts of man, no
less than man's life depends on the harmonious integrations with nature."[1]
That concern, in brief, communicates something of the underlying assumption that the author of *The Flounder* wants to convey to his readers. But the
task is as large as it is complex, and to accomplish it fully Grass generously
offers up the history-embellishing ingredients of legend, folktale, cooking
recipes, poetry, and talking fish, the mythology of the tribe, the secret of how
fire was taken away from the Sky Wolf, and how the dominance of women in
society died out with the disappearance of their third breast.[2]

It is no small achievement, as we shall see in the following, for Grass to
create a cogent and convincing mythology that can set the scene for each subsequent period of history and persuasively present the separation between the
Raw and the Cooked, Man's separation from nature, and the necessary art
and ritual of cooking through the ages. Grass underscores and enlarges that
division with the aid of the pompus Flounder and a sexist fairy tale to oppose
the sovereignty of the myth and the domination of men by the women goddesses and the natural forces of nature. But man's efforts to overcome his

past and create his own history leads to a perplexing combination of burgeoning power and progressive discontentment. His technological progress and growing control of women and nature turn out to be mere Pyrrhic victories, leading with each apparent achievement only to new crises and cataclysms. But below the surface events of recorded history the fundamental powers of the goddesses continue to transform nature into nourishment, to sustain life, and provide sexual satisfaction. Man's obsession with progress persists in the twentieth century, but his sense of belonging and coherence has diminished beyond hope. The former conditions for easy survival have been violated and lost, the promise of a greater destiny unfulfilled, and the puzzling sense of his human comedy unresolved. And so the novel ends with the vision of Maria in the sea, the Flounder now in *her* arms, transforming her once again into Dorothea and then into other aspects of the ancient goddesses. For man, however, the male of the species, existence is bathed in doubts, emptiness, and resignation. The professorial and prophetic Flounder has abandoned him to the aimless movement and vacuous forms of a future history that is devoid now of that grand conception of the Mythos with which everything once began.

I

After a short digression on the interrelationship of good food, sex, and pregnancy throughout the ages, the novel begins with the primordial, nurturing goddess, who was at once herself and all women: "Awa Awa Awa . . . all alike in every way. And so were the Awas. One two three" (F, 5). All different and yet all the same with their three breasts and sexual satisfactions. Thus "the Mythos begins," the narrator proclaims,[3] with the power of women, the *Mutterrecht,* to create, sustain, and control man and society. True, Grass writes, there may have been a greater Earth Goddess before Awa, an *Ur-Super-Nährmutter,* an aboriginal Super-Nourishing-Mother-Goddess, but nevertheless, "Awa was a goddess later on and had her three tits certified in hand-size idols. But other goddesses—for example, the Indian Kali—had four or more arms. That made practical sense. The Greek mother goddesses—Demeter, Hera—were however normally endowed and managed to stay in business for thousands of years."[4]

With the transition from the three to the two bosomed goddess, time itself was transformed from the timeless time of superabundance to the beginning of measured time, a time of struggle, specific events, recorded myths, and of human history. Even with the advent of recorded time Grass continues to measure history in terms of food and sex (cooks and mistresses) rather than centuries, but the fundamental story of humankind is the story of survival and should be chronicled in terms of those elements that ensure survival. Beyond that, the histrionics of recorded history are merely the excrescence of the human need for food, sexuality, and security; but once the ideals of the historians gather authority, they become in the minds of men purposes for which one would fight and die.

There is little room for doubt about this proposition when Grass presents the reader with the significantly placed first poem of the novel whose title, he claims, promises to reveal "What I write about" (F, 8-9). Each of the seven stanzas contains a bizarre admixture of mythic allusions and historical narration of a mankind preoccupied for three thousand years with the pleasure and pain of eating. In the words of the poem, this novel is "About food . . . / about superabundance . . . /gluttons . . . /tables of the rich . . . / spirit . . . bitter as gall/ . . . the belly went insane." The novel will therefore be about "gluttony, which is only a form of fear/ . . . hunger,/ . . . Meat, raw and cooked,/ . . . dated history,/the slaughter at Tannenberg Wittstock Kolin" and the remnants of men as well as food. The author will also tell about the digestion, transformation, and degeneration of food, "About nausea," about time and curdling milk, and about "tomorrow . . . /after yesterday's leftovers have become today's petrifaction." And there will be stories about the travail and emotion surrounding the consumption of food: "Sorrow, . . . love, . . . the nail/and the rope,/about quarrels" over details and trivia, about too many words "in the soup." The author concludes that, as the result of all this human effort and energy over the millennia, a message will emerge, "about us all at a table eaten bare,/and about you and me and the fishbones in our throats" (F, 9). But the fishbones that stick in our throats today constitute for Grass a dramatic contrast to the softer and more compatible food of yesteryear. The fishbone today is the result of a disruption in the natural order of creation and the consequence of the human history that continues to choke us.

But once upon a time the food of the all-nourishing Earth Mother was different, flowing unobstructed as it did in mythological times from the third breast of her body through the gullet of all mankind. This mythic perspective echoes in the clarion of Erich Neumann, who traces her from her beginnings, various incarnations and archetypal patterns throughout history and observes how she continues to exert her eternal powers even in our time. Keeping in mind the evolution of Grass's "nine or more cooks in us" who were derived from the primeval providers of nature and remained from century to century to receive and transform food and semen into sustenance and new life, one begins to comprehend something of Grass's awe of the vast power and hidden mysteries that allow women to function so well in the real world while possessing the astonishing capacity to transform it. In their special province of sexuality, pregnancy, childbirth, baking, cooking, home-making, and mother-hood, women have continued in various ways to satisfy the basic demands of the early myth by reenacting birth and feeding in accordance with the sacred models of Awa and the Great Earth Mother before her.

The mysterious power of the Mother Goddess to transform herself and nature, Neumann continues, "is based on the profound identity between the food-giving and the food-transforming Feminine, . . . the transformative aspect of the oven, . . . the mystery of the uterus."[5] The equation of *oven* and *uterus* is of special interest to readers of *The Flounder,* where cooking and sexuality combine in Grass's primal myth as the woman's secret pocket for hiding fire, cooking, and sex. We recall that Awa steals the embers of fire from the Sky Wolf by putting them in her *Tasche* (her pocket, "vagina") and, as a result, she herself becomes cooked and scarred. Ever after she is then condemned to a sexual itch, to the burning sensation of the fire in her vagina, in her oven that henceforth embraces the immediate mysteries of conception and transformation. With time those mysteries become associated with specific places and functions, primarily in the home and around the hearth where the woman's power seems to dominate: "In Roman mythology, the oven goddess and her festival, the Fornacalia, play such an important role in the connection. . . . between the transformation, birth of the bread, nourishment, and the Feminine that an old proverb says: 'The oven is the mother.'"[6]

According to Neuman, such "primordial mysteries of the Feminine are connected . . . with the proximate realities of everyday life." The Feminine also eventually dominates the important enclosures of society such as the "dwelling, tent, house, storeroom, and temple." In consequence, "Her rule over food was largely based on the fact that the female group formed the center of the dwelling," and "at its center, the fireplace, the seat of warmth and food preparation . . . [which] now begins to be improved by frying, roasting, and boiling. . . . A later development is the bake oven," in which grains are transformed into (give birth to) breads and cakes in a mysterious fashion, and the raw foods of yesterday are transformed into a gourmet art and pleasurable delight.[7]

The analogies of vessel, oven, heat, and transformation are significantly present in *The Flounder* from the very start. In "short order" the story takes us from the stove, to food preparation, to the table, to bed, and to the conception of a child whose gestation period determines the narrative structure and time frame of this novel that creates itself in the telling of the story. Grass confirms what Neumann concluded decades before, that the woman's "belly is a symbol for everything that's roomy" (F, 7), but he adds as a secondary concession that "Men survive only in the written word" (F, 103). Perhaps

that is why men make and write history; because, unlike women who remain
part and parcel of nature, the male can only produce "written matter [that]
can stand up against nature" (F, 103).

The protagonist-narrator of *The Flounder,* like Grass himself, stands
somewhere between nature itself and history. His creation is a child of the
mind, a story that eschews the grandiose achievements of recorded history: "I
soon proved unequal to history. They could smash up Rome without me;
Wigga's dumplings of herring roe and herring milt meant more to me I
would never again aspire to conquer or die, that is, to make history" (F, 102).
He observes the relationship between the exaggerated struggle of men for
power to gain and preserve enough food for themselves after the Fall from
plentitude, a struggle that resulted in a world of increasing shortages and deprivation for most of its inhabitants: hunger, merely daily bread, and entrails!
Meat, raw and cooked; fear of hunger, diets of war and slaughter; disgusting
and spoiled foods, pitiful left-overs, putrified and hardened; but hunger does
not stop with food alone. It chews up love in the process, brings loneliness
and death, until nothing is left on the table, until all that is left anywhere (as
Grass insists in one place after another) are "the fishbones [stuck] in our
throats" (F, 9).

In the transition from the original fullness of creation to the process of
secular time, the initial sense of a unified continuum between humans and nature had been lost. With that, new problems, challenges, and struggles quickly multiplied as a progression of events that could be analyzed and recorded
in a rather interesting and objective manner. The result was something called
formal history, a story and a study that apparently replaced the ancient myths
by force of its verifiability; but even in the face of causal logic and factual
persuasion Grass continues to insist that the mysterious power of the original
myths persists and ultimately prevails in every age. As the cooks and spouses
march through the pages of Grass's novels, plays, and poetry, each of them
succeeds in one way or another in acting out the so-called Feminine Principle
of providing for and transforming the world through one or both of the dual
aspects of the ancient goddess Awa, or, more recently, Ilsebill. Even when denying their relationship to the earlier goddesses—"the idea of having been
Awa doesn't appeal to Ilsebill" (F, 4)—the women in Grass's writings reaf-
firm their traditional kinship. But whether the idea appeals to Ilsebill or not,
the mythopoeic quality of the sustaining and denying goddesses of old intrudes irresistibly on the character of Grass's women and on the imagination
of his readers.

II

Günter Grass introduces the clause "When the raw was separated from
the cooked in myths" in the second paragraph of *The Flounder,* therefore

borrowing not only the title of Claude Lévi-Strauss's book, *Le Cru et le Cuit* (1964),[8] but also his basic premise of separation between the primitive and the civilized, myth and history, man and nature. The theft of fire is the major event in the primal mythology of *The Flounder,* the great adventure of the goddess Awa that so clearly separated the raw and the cooked and led to the loss of a paradisiacal state, brought special advantages to some groups within the community but problems and complications of a different sort to all humanity. Not only the procedures of preparation and food gathering changed after the theft of fire but also the whole network of kinship relations, the social roles and responsibilities, and the acquisition of power on various levels of society. With separate tasks now and a greater sense of division between man and nature, male and female, past, present and future, a new awareness arose of possible shortages of food, of sexual deprivation, and therefore of a greater need for power to protect one's food sources and other means of satisfaction and security. Anxiety, insecurity, hunger, and longing are discovered; and, as a result, fire became a means not only of cooking but also of transforming the raw materials of nature into tools and weapons. With that came a whole technology of production and a need to organize, redefine, and control the members of the society in accordance with their special skills and talents. The roots of modern civilization and the consciousness of division and discontentment had taken hold.

Man had made his choice, rejected the Golden Age, and henceforth had to consume what he had cooked up—an irony that Grass does not fail to recognize in one episode after another. In his new urge to dominate and control and hunger for what had once been easy, accessible, and satisfying, man now continued to divide and dominate various aspects of his environment evermore. The division of labor and authority shifted dramatically between the sexes with men assuming the job of hunter, warrior, and organizer while the women were relegated to the position of food-gatherer, spouse, and cook. Grass points out, however, that over the ages men and women have often managed to acquire a sense of mutuality and satisfaction in the sharing of food and bodies; but with the passage of time the dominant role and the larger decisions of their shared fate fell to the male.

Thus, man's need for food and the new art of cooking created the bedrock of history and changed the dynamics of home and family in a most significant way. Beyond the walls of one's house lay the settlement, the community, the nation, other nations, the empire, and then the whole Earth. Food shared came to indicate membership in an extended family, in a community or political entity; and food taken or denied denoted hostility, strength, power over life, and therefore the power to rule.

Similar configurations of power continued to develop on a smaller scale within the family. At home, in the house, around the hearth, what was prepared with care and artfulness became more than a measure of nourishment.

It became a sign of care, concern, creativity—a special kind of power. In certain respects one came to depend as much on the preparer as on the provider, but more often than not the division of tasks led to various degrees of subordination of women as well as kindly worship from afar of those arts and processes that men could no longer fully understand. Food became a means of emotional communication and the invention of a recipe or the preparation of a fine meal often conveyed affection and tender feelings more effectively than abstract words or awkward gestures. But the satisfactions of women in the last analysis did depend on the willingness of the male to sense and acknowledge the achievements of his spouse and cook. The male achieved a dominant and controlling position, and he came by it through effort and the advice of the Flounder to keep his women "bed-warm" (F, 30) and busy at home.

The theme of sexual repression is significant in the novel; it is introduced at the outset by Ilsebill's carping demands and the early appearance of the three women's libbers: Siggie, Maxie, and Frankie. Ilsebill's demands for a dishwasher and other material items expressed a kind of power on her part, which is then demonstrated as a political movement by the militant feminists who no longer want to beg for the power and possessions that should rightfully be theirs. They reject the whole idea that it was ever right and natural for women to do the cooking, provide sex, rear children, and be at the service of the male. They contend with absolute conviction that brutal power has been exerted over them for centuries, imprisoning them in their separate roles, robbing them of their natural power and self-respect. With a fresh perspective on history and a sense of liberation within them, women now perceive a sinister and calculated strategy to dominate them that had in fact been introduced millennia before. Enraged and determined, the Women's Tribunal in Berlin therefore intends to prove now with the aid of a talking fish that they have indeed been the victims of an historical conspiracy.

"One cannot argue against justice," the narrator remarks, but then again if their claims prove to be true, how is one to reconcile such injustice with the embracing story of the ideal myth of mankind? After all, the ideals and origins of a people are to be taken seriously. They should carry religious significance for all and be rooted deeply in the soul of the folk, if not as absolute truth then at least as a desirable picture of truth and justice. "To tell a myth," writes Mircea Eliade, "to proclaim what happened *ab origine,*" to relate "*a primordial event that took place in illo tempore,* the recital of what the gods or the semidivine beings did at the beginning of time," constitutes a fundamental belief for a people, for "Once told, that is, revealed, the myth becomes apodictic truth; it establishes a truth that is absolute.'"[9]

At every turn, however, the Women's Tribunal is determined to show how much rhetorical assertions about higher authority and the imagery of folktales have depicted women as inferior and small-minded. Women have been manipulated and demeaned, the Tribunal asserts, and every effort should now be made to prove that the role of women in history and legend has been disgracefully and illegally cast as subservient.

With the appearance of the Women's Tribunal the basic question of the novel manifests itself in new perspective: How did the fullness and comfort of the primordial world (defined once as mythic unity) degenerate into a world of such opposition between the sexes, into such states of hostility, brutality, suffering, and hunger? Who was at fault? Who is to blame? Has the culprit been caught? Can the fish, the Flounder, the Women's Tribunal now set the record straight and put an end to the injustice of the ages? Hardly! For Grass simple answers and satisfying conclusions are never possible for problems of such complexity. There is an alter aspect to every question, and questions posed in the abstract can never be resolved fully in the concrete. Liberation, justice, equality, rights, and so on are eternally worth striving for; in their particular manifestations in history, politics, and social conflict, they demand and deserve one's full support. Worthy as the individual struggle against human evils may be, the struggle itself has too often caused only more brutality, injury, and pain. But even beyond that, Grass and his narrator, however tolerant and curious about new political possibilities and social justice they may be, remain preoccupied at bottom with the idea of a larger and lost unity that eludes logic but remains the major goal and artistic intention of Grass's literature.

III

The title of this novel, *The Flounder,* is, after all, derived from the folk tale of "The Fisherman and His Wife" (*Von dem Fischer un syner Fru*). According to the novel, it seems that there are two versions of the story, the first of which was destroyed in order to conceal the planned conspiracy of masculine superiority in society. The second version on the other hand, passed on by the Brothers Grimm, fostered discrimination and degraded the woman as "a quarrelsome bitch who wanted to have, to possess, to command more and more" (F, 20). This popular version perpetuated sexual bias by emphasizing the greed, the arrogant demands, the petty scorn of the fisherman's wife, Ilsebill, as a contrast to her husband who was conscientious, well-intending, and proverbially good-hearted.

Now, however, and with the Flounder's approval, the protagonist resolves to relate the original version of the story in order to set the record straight. The alternate version of the *Märchen* turns out to be much more than another account of lost wealth or a cute story about a talking fish. More than a slightly veiled moralizing fairy tale, the second version reveals the full personality and intelligence of the fish as unlimited in factual knowledge and professorial in tone. He imparts curiosity and valuable information to man and encourages the growth of his self-confidence and awareness (F, 32–33). The Flounder teaches man the use of fire as a forge, the techniques of tool–making and weaponry, and the various other tricks of technology. From the Flounder, so the story goes, man also learns the rudiments of counting, calculations, planning, organization, and consequently commerce, warfare, politics, and power. But regardless of the diversity of achievements that the Flounder extols, Grass continues to remind the reader in one way or another that the consequence of this pedagogy of the professorial fish was the Fall from paradise and the conscious division of the male and female principle. Under the guidance of the Flounder the male gained greater power and independence on the one hand but his progress was accompanied on the other hand by growing feelings of doubt, distance, and dissatisfaction.

Originally the Flounder spoke like "the serpent of Eden" about man's "state of infantilism" (F, 23) about his submissiveness and about the rights of "a *man* in quest of enduring, meaning-charged form," of "a sense of importance" (F, 24), and finally about a need in the world for the "well-matured decision of a masculine will" (F, 23). With each additional bit of knowledge, he continued, man could establish greater freedom from "Awa, the three-breasted paragon of historyless femininity, your all-devouring megacunt, in short your mother goddess" (F, 27). There were regrets of course, but as the narrator finally confides his contra-mythology ambitions to his wife: "So much ur-motherly loving care, even if it kept me warm and in innocence, was bound to become oppressive in the long run" (F, 30).

To free men from their bondage and to introduce history the academic Flounder informed the fisherman "how to keep the womenfolk supinely bed-warm and teach them how to suffer in cheerful silence" (F, 30). He also insisted that "Nature is sick of being submitted to with womanish passivity; it wants to be mastered by men" (F, 32–33). With that it becomes clear that the function of the Flounder is to oppose the static state of mythic unity by tantalizing man with fruit from the quickly growing tree of knowledge. Traditionally, it is with the growth of knowledge that the masculine urge for dominance begins and the story of his freedom and power, control of women and nature, and his particular destiny evolves. The talking fish, like the talking serpent of Paradise, serves again in his fairy-tale function to tempt man's secret wishes for independence, special knowledge, and a fate of his own.

The talking fish and the talking serpent, the male dominance that replaces matriarchal sovereignty, the knowledge and striving now prized above creaturely comforts and even survival—all convey a sense of the new myth that is to accompany the new era: Christianity. The sermons of the Flounder echo the text of the Bible, which is now completely compatible with the movement of history and progress. The Flounder's story begins with the goddesses but rapidly interlaces the episodes of missionaries who invade the primitive unity. They appear awkward, weak, incongruous, but eventually they communicate their messages of self-denial, abstract morality, material progress, sacred wars, and earthly conquests along with the lofty fantasies of future salvation. Their stories take hold, for the new religion is compatible with the values of advancing time. It is the sole purpose of this Christianity to abolish the old myths and to identify itself with historical evolution and the power of progress. And success comes for the church with Bishop Adalbert on 12 April 997, to be exact, who acts as the tribe's head shepherd but who was at the same time another missionary who had come to convert the heathens. Mestwina slew him with a cast-iron spoon, but the historical sources falsely gave the credit to the Prussians for the act. That, too, became history, and Christianity continued to profit from it. By the time Dorothea arrived, the next of the heroines and lovers, she could logically appear in the role of a religious fanatic. She believed the new fairy tale: "Had the Lord Jesus sent me? Had I brought her a message from sweet Jesus?" (F, 117). Dorothea dreamt her fantasy, flayed herself for purity, and introduced useless suffering for the sake of greater power and achievement. The new faith had made her merely psychological, ego-gratifying, and hungry for salvation.

The fairy tale, unlike the myth that is originally religious in nature, tends to gratify the listener and reader with fantasies of ego satisfaction, wish-fulfilling images, and imagined hopes. It appears to have emerged in popularity where harsh laws and immediate necessities prohibited easy access to personal gains and achievement. Appropriate to the genre therefore, the fairy tale about the Flounder establishes itself in this novel as the adversary to static satisfaction of a mere physical order as imposed on man by the matriarchal society and the sacred myth. As the tempter and teacher, it is the Flounder who precipitates the Fall from unity and the beginning of civilization. He is really the primary story-teller and the formal historian. It is the Flounder who initially analyzes and evaluates the social situation in which Edek, the male subject of Awa, finds himself; and it is of course the Flounder who instigates and sustains the process by which life may be lived differently, more "civilized," and in dramatic variance to the natural processes of creation.

More important from the Flounder's point of view than merely gratifying a few wishes is the desire to educate the male, to teach him to think analytically, to become the maker of tools and the father of the future. The loquacious Flounder therefore not only makes a strong appeal to the submerged wishes of the male but also furnishes the knowledge required to move beyond his comfortable, but mindless and primitive state. With that, the Flounder is established as the antagonist between male and female, myth and fairy tale. After all, it is the fable of the fish that invades the realm of the myth in order to impose the new vision of the future and to replay archetypically the temptation of knowledge as the fundamental sin against the unity and sanctity of nature. The surrender to the temptation is accompanied ever after with a sense of punishment and the new recognition of growing shortages, denials, and "the sweat on one's brow."

As the feeling of union with nature gives way to material struggle and acquisition, the power of the myth appears to collapse as the consciousness of mankind shifts largely from a sense of emotional cohesion to one of greedy pragmatism. Mankind is wrenched back and forth between involvement with the basic questions of survival and its memories of the earlier times of wholeness and ease. Seen in the overall context of the novel, therefore, the conflict of myth with fairy tale and their digression into history stands finally as the central conflict between faith and necessity, between ideal and reality, and (as depicted in all its variations ranging from kitchen and bedroom to international politics and human survival) as the embracing framework of the human tragicomedy that Grass wants to portray.

IV

Anaximander claimed that "Man was a fish in the beginning," and Grass concludes that the world has never been the same since the fish began to talk. His words split in two that original oceanic consciousness and left in its wake a narrow chronicle of provocative observations and logical conclusions. Once the fish began to talk and spew out one fact after another, the world became self-conscious, ego-centered, and concerned with its own achievements and history. Once the Flounder began to talk a new process of thinking and awareness became evident—historical thinking based on formal arrangement and factual analysis of conquests, heroic action, and of progress.

What Grass describes in his fiction, Susanne Langer succeeds most effectively in analyzing philosophically; that is, the significance of history as measured by its own standards and in comparison to other possible modes of "knowing":

> The historical mind . . . destroyed the mythical orientation of European culture; the historian, not the mathematician, introduced the "higher criticism," the standard of *actual fact*. It is he who is the real apostle of the realistic age. . . . Our increasing command of casual laws makes for more and more complicated activities; we have put many stages of artifice and device, of manufacture and alteration, between ourselves and the rest of nature. . . . But human power is knowledge, he knows that; the knowledge of natural *facts* and the scientific laws of their transformation. . . . But *between the facts* run the threads of unrecorded reality, momentarily recognized, wherever they come to the surface.[10]

Grass demonstrates precisely what Langer describes here by making the
Flounder with his scholastic precision, instructive homiletics, and complete
reliance on *actual facts* the historian of this novel. Superior in tone and as
literal-minded as possible, the Flounder's empirical disquisitions are more
concerned with the presenting of facts and arguments than with the personal
desires or the future welfare of human beings. Conversely, Günter Grass,
alert to both the limited ability of history to explain human existence and, at
the same time, the apparent authority it exerts over our thinking, questions
and exposes its formal depiction of human events by developing other kinds
of history: the history of food, starvation, sexuality, survival.

But the Flounder, powerful though he may be, is just one voice among
many in this novel. He bores us as he instructs, and though his speeches are
important, their effect produces little satisfaction and no love. And for all the
fish's verifiable success as the mentor of man's intellect, the reader and the
novelist himself seem compelled finally to move beyond the tedium of his
facts and single vision to ask the larger and more embracing questions of
meaning.

As in Grass's other major novels, a serious attempt has been made in *The
Flounder* to compound the personal stories, historical eras, and major motives of human existence into a single complexity that in some way may trans-
cend the apparent confusion as a kind of "grand simplification." By creating
first of all a backdrop of mythology and then confronting it with the analytical logic and practical ambition of human intelligence, Grass has in fact ex-
pounded his deepest urge to bestow shape and a measure of meaning on the
elusive movement of mankind in its evolution from the simplicity of nature to
the perplexities of a twentieth-century civilization turned against itself. In the
last analysis, therefore, Grass attempts to acquire something of an overview
by recasting the ingredients of mankind in a grand potage of eras that might
rekindle intellectual curiosity and a vague sense of one's former cohesion with
the world.

Theodore Ziolkowski observes that the greatest of artists and thinkers
are all in some measure mythopoets who hunger for a full sense of unity and
completeness with this world, much in the way that Einstein did when he dedicated himself to the discovery of a unified field theory, that is, an intuited
overall principle of creation:

> When Einstein, toward the end of his life, sought to bring all of his learning,
> his scientific rational theories, together into what he called a "Unified Field
> Theory," I think he was mythmaking. At that point he was trying for a grand
> synthesis that is somehow just a shade beyond what can be reduced to rational
> explanation. He wanted a grand simplification. Einstein needed that. I think
> that's an example of a modern myth.[11]

Grass's writings are similarly motivated by an intuition of that "grand synthesis." By weaving into the warp of daily necessities the weft of myth and history, he hopes to discover their common quality.

But yet, where can one possibly find a universal design, an ultimate substance, the embracing concept to reunite what has been so diversified and fragmented through the ages? Perhaps, ironically enough, in our eternal and shared need of food and our preoccupation for survival. That is certainly something that binds mankind together in a common purpose. Clifton Fadiman once claimed that "The alimentary canal contains the only stream that flows through all history and geography, leaving banks on which cluster those works that mark man as most civilized."[12] With a similar metaphor in mind Grass sets out to create an artistic unity that begins with the natural milk of Mother Nature and then observes it and its secondary effects as it flows through the alimentary canal of all humanity—digesting, sustaining, reducing, and indirectly producing that residue of outer events that we may then define as civilization and history.

V

Fadiman also remarked that "A man who is careful with his palate is not likely to be careless with his paragraphs,"[13] and Grass is no exception. One should not overlook the fact that Grass himself is finally the gourmand and the narrator of *The Flounder*. And he is also the cook who does in fact provide the reader with a coherent and spicy stew that simmers at length in the primal myth, boils over the heat of centuries, is stirred and peppered by the salty Flounder, spiced further by a controversy of elements, and served up finally as the kind of novel that Wellek and Warren describe as *mythic*, as a "composed story telling of origins and destinies; the explanations of . . . why the world is and why we do as we do, in pedagogic images of the nature and destiny of man."[14]

The last question posited in *The Flounder* about "future history" can certainly not be answered in logical terms, but the basic myth and the general framework of the novel point nevertheless to an interesting possibility for further conjecture. The realization of how far we have come and how little we still know may help us accept a more humble position in the scheme of things and await the next turn of events. But accompanied now by the imposing contrast of how things once were and how they are now, the readers of *The Flounder* might yet derive a fresh sense of common origins and the mutual need to share and survive this complex world less frantically, more simply. But there, too, Grass leaves openness and questions. He will not rationalize a conclusion if the fullness of his intention does not yield one up of its own accord: "Ah, Flounder!" the author and narrator sigh, "Where have you swum off to? It's so still, and nothing is decided. What's to become of us? We're worn out, our quarrel has dozed off, it's only talking in its sleep. Little words hang on. Apples of discord roll across the table" (F, 543); but, then again, the author continues, "Fairy tales only stop for a time, or they start up again after the end. The truth is told, in a different way each time" (F, 545).

Notes

1. H[enri] and H[enrietta] A. Frankfort, *Before Philosophy: The Intellectual Adventure of Ancient Man* (Baltimore: Penguin, 1971), p. 36.
2. Grass strives repeatedly for a quality of comprehensive realism that can be conveyed best by a variety of stylistic forms and literary inventions. What Grass once asserted about *The Tin Drum* now applies equally well to *The Flounder:* It is "first and foremost a realistic novel. The satire, the legend, the parable, the ghost story, in short, everything that is stupidly and simplistically stamped as surrealism nowadays, serve and belong to this realism." See Kurt Lothar Tank, *Günter Grass,* p. 57.
3. See B, 11; F, 5, fails to emphasize this announcement sufficiently.
4. B, 11; F, 5. For the theme of mythic goddesses in Grass's process of mythopoesis, see Edward Diller, *A Mythic Journey: Günter Grass's Tin Drum,* pp. 8–36.
5. Erich Neumann, *The Great Mother* (Princeton: Princeton University Press, 1970), pp. 281–88.
6. Ibid.
7. Ibid.
8. Claude Lévi-Strauss, *Mythologica I: Das Rohe und das Gekochte,* trans. Eva Moldenhauer (Frankfurt am Main: Suhrkamp, 1971). See also Scott H. Abbott, "The Raw and the Cooked: Claude Lévi-Strauss and Günter Grass," below, 107–120.
9. Mircea Eliade, *The Sacred and Profane,* trans. Willard R. Trask (New York: Harcourt Brace, 1959), pp. 68–72.
10. Susanne K. Langer, *Philosophy in a New Key* (Cambridge, Mass.: Harvard University Press, 1957), pp. 276–81.
11. Theodore Ziolkowski, "A Round-Table Discussion," *Myth and Reason: A Symposium,* ed. Walter D. Wetzels (Austin: University of Texas Press, 1973), p. 176.
12. Clifton Fadiman, Introd., *The Art of Eating,* by Mary F. K. Fisher (New York: Vintage, 1976), pp. xii–xiii.
13. Ibid.
14. Rene Wellek and Austin Warren, *Theory of Literature* (New York: Harcourt Brace, 1956), p. 190.

The Raw and the Cooked:
Claude Lévi-Strauss and Günter Grass

Scott H. Abbott

... it is through myths explaining the origin of fire, and thus of cooking, that we gain access to myths about man's loss of immortality; among the Apinaye, for instance, the origin of mortality is only one episode of the myths relating to the origin of fire. We thus begin to understand the truly essential place occupied by cooking in native thought: not only does cooking mark the transition from nature to culture, but through it and by means of it, the human state can be defined with all its attributes, even those that, like mortality, might seem to be the most unquestionably natural.

Claude Lévi-Strauss, *The Raw and the Cooked*

Near the beginning of Günter Grass's novel *The Flounder*, when the narrator says, in reflection, "I remember our first quarrel, toward the end of the Neolithic, some two thousand years before the incarnation of our Lord, when myths were beginning to distinguish between the raw and the cooked" (F,3), he makes a pointed intertextual reference, informing the reader that there is another text against which his work should be read. Implicit in the quotation is the promise of added intelligibility if we recognize and use the work cited in our reading of the novel. The reference, of course, is to *The Raw and the Cooked*, a work by Claude Lévi-Strauss dealing with myths of Amazonian Indians.[1] As we shall see, these myths concerning the origin of fire, with East European alterations, play an important role in *The Flounder*. In addition, the cooking fire, in its mediatory structural position as postulated by Lévi-Strauss, serves Grass as a metaphor with which to oppose the mythical machinations of the Flounder. If we know Lévi-Strauss's work, many otherwise opaque passages in the novel become transparent. First, then, a brief account of two of the aetiological myths cited by Lévi-Strauss (and three slight variations).

In the introduction to one of the myths of the origin of fire we read: "formerly, men did not know how to make fire. When they killed game, they cut the flesh into thin strips, which they laid out on stones to dry in the sun. They also ate rotten wood" (p. 67). A similar myth continues the account as a young Indian, Botoque, is left in a bird's nest on top of a steep rock. A jaguar passes by and invites him to come down:

Botoque was afraid and hesitated a long time; in the end he made up his mind, and the jaguar in friendly fashion, suggested that if he would sit astride its back, it would take him to its home to have a meal of grilled meat. But the young man did not understand the meaning of the word "grilled" because in those days, the Indians were unacquainted with fire and ate their meat raw.

At the jaguar's home Botoque eats his first meal of cooked meat, is adopted, despite the objections of the jaguar's wife, and then is mistreated by the wife while the jaguar is away:

The jaguar scolded the wife, but in vain. One day it gave Botoque a brand new bow and some arrows, taught him how to use them, and advised him to use them against the woman, should the need arise. Botoque killed her by shooting an arrow into her breast. He fled in terror, taking with him the weapons and a piece of grilled meat.

Botoque returns to his village, brings other Indians back and steals the fire, allowing the Indians to have light, cooked food, and warmth:

But the jaguar, incensed by the ingratitude of his adopted son, who had stolen 'fire and the secret of the bow and arrow,' was to remain full of hatred for all living creatures, especially human beings. Now only the reflection of fire could be seen in its eyes. It used its fangs for hunting and ate its meat raw, having solemnly renounced grilled meat. (pp. 66-67)

And finally, three variants that seem to have provided important images for the retelling of the myths in Grass's novel: (1) "it is because the hero refrains from mocking or deceiving the jaguar—and, more precisely because he refrains from laughing—that the jaguar does not eat him but *instructs* him in the arts of civilization" (p. 109); (2) the jaguar's wife is only wounded in the paw and begs the Indian to leave her a burning ember, but a toad spits on the remaining embers and puts them out (p. 71); and (3) an old woman is said to keep the fire in her vagina (p. 126, n. 9).

Acquainted now with several relevant aspects of the Amazonian myths about the origin of fire, let us turn to *The Flounder*, where, as we have seen, direct reference is made to myths that distinguish between "the raw and the cooked."

The narrator of *The Flounder* has his own version of the myth accounting for the origin of fire. He arrived at the myth, he says (parodying Lévi-Strauss's method), by examining "Ilsebill's tickler in the light of other myths" (F, 54). Introducing the myths, he describes conditions before the event:

In our early myths there was no fire. . . . And so we ate our badger, elk cow, and grouse raw or dried on stones. And we huddled shivering in the darkness.

> Then the rotten wood said to us, 'Someone whose flesh is also a pouch must climb up to the Sky Wolf. He is the keeper of the primal fire.... (F, 52).[2]

Grass's narrator continues his account by describing the woman's visit to the Sky Wolf. The Wolf says he must first test her "pouch," which he does "with his Wolf's member until he was all worn out and fell asleep on her flesh." She then tips the wolf off her and hides three glowing bits of charcoal in her "pouch" where they make the wolf's sperm hiss. The wolf wakes up and curses the woman, saying the fire will leave a scar which will itch. She laughs inordinately, and then pisses into the primal fire until it goes out. "And the old Sky Wolf wept, for that spelled the end of crispy brown roasts; he'd just have to gulp everything down raw. That, it seems, is what made earthly wolves murderous and misanthropic" (F, 53). The woman comes down from the sky and is indeed burned by the fire. When she screams with pain, she is given the name "Awa"—a deliberately intrusive element that gives the reader some distance from the myth ("Awa" or *Aua* is the German equivalent for "ouch"). And finally, by virtue of the fire she has brought back, the primordial woman establishes control over men.

This, then, is the myth of the origin of fire as told by the narrator of *The Flounder*. Comparison of his version with those of the Amazonian Indians shows extensive congruence as well as significant deviation. Setting the introductions side by side we find the following:

Lévi-Strauss	Grass
"formerly, men did not know how to make fire."	"In our early myths there was no fire."
"thin strips [of flesh]...laid out on stones to dry in the sun"	"We ate our [meat]...raw or dried on stones."
"They also ate rotten wood."	"Then the rotten wood said to us..."

After the "raw and the cooked" quotation, these explicit parallels are a clear indication that Grass intends for us to read his novel against the work of Lévi-Strauss.

Continuing the comparison:

Lévi-Strauss	Grass
Indian boy	woman
goes home with	visits
a jaguar	the Sky Wolf
who possesses fire	who is keeper of the primal fire

Besides the obvious parallel structure here, we notice the substitution of a woman for the male, allowing the narrator to depict a dominant matriarchy at the beginning of his "history." There is also a change from the South American jaguar to the European wolf, necessary for establishment of the myth as Pomorshian. Further:

boy mistreated by Jaguar's wife	woman tested by Sky Wolf

variation #1

boy refrains from laughing and consequently receives instruction from the jaguar (this actually happens at the beginning of the myth)	woman laughs inordinately and is cursed by the Sky Wolf

variation #2

toad spits on remaining embers and puts them out	woman extinguishes remaining coals by pissing on them

variation #3

old woman carries the fire in her vagina	woman carries the coals in her "pouch"

boy steals fire jaguar must eat raw meat and hates humans	woman steals fire Sky Wolf must eat meat raw and becomes murderous and misanthropic

We thus have ample evidence that the narrator's examination of "Ilsebill's tickler in the light of other myths" was done with *The Raw and the Cooked* in hand.

Although the comparisons we have just made show Lévi-Srauss's book to be a source for *The Flounder*, this information has implications beyond merely noting another source. Along with the blatant reference to "the raw and the cooked," the recognition of parallels consciously set up between myths of the origin of fire in Lévi-Strauss's work and Grass's novel lends credence to further use of *The Raw and the Cooked* in an attempt to interpret certain key metaphors in *The Flounder*. Three additional concepts developed in *The Raw and the Cooked* prove to be especially helpful.

First, writes the French anthropologist, "there seem to be two kinds of fire: one celestial and destructive, the other terrestrial and creative, that is, fire for cooking purposes" (p. 188).

Second, the opposition between the raw and the cooked has analogues in other opposing pairs: the "world of rottenness" and the "burned world," "nature" and "culture," "total disjunction" and "total conjunction," "woman" and "man," and "earth" and "sky." Using nearly two hundred myths related in some way to the cooking of foodstuffs, Lévi-Strauss points out that the cooking fire acts as a mediator between such oppositions. For example:

> the mediatory function of the cooking fire therefore operates between the sun and humanity in two ways. By its presence, cooking fire averts total disjunction, since it unites the sun and the earth and saves man from the world of *rottenness* in which he would find himself if the sun really disappeared; but its presence is also interposed; that is to say, it obviates the risk of a total conjunction, which would result in a *burned world*. (p. 293)

The following is a visual representation of this mediation according to Lévi-Strauss (p. 294):

mediation absent:	as excess: total conjunction "a burned world"	as lack: total disjunction "world of rottenness"
mediation present:	interposition of cooking fire: conjunction *plus* disjunction	

And third, the conjunction of a man and a woman is analogous in these myths to the feared union of the sky and the earth (resulting in a "a burned world"). "The birth of a child marks the emergence of a third term, which acts as a mediator between the two poles and establishes a certain *distance* between them" (p. 328). Further, "the child (especially the first-born) plays, between husband and wife, a part similar to that played by cooking fire between sky and earth" (p. 329).

The first of these concepts (that fire can be both destructive and creative) is amply reflected in *The Flounder*. Near the middle of the novel the myth of the origin of fire is continued:

> And once when Mestwina, while pounding acorns, told the story of the Flounder, she came close to the truth. "That," she said in Pomorshian, "was when Awa lived here and only her word counted. They Sky Wolf was angry, because Awa had stolen the first fire from him and made herself powerful. The men were all devoted to her. They all wanted to sacrifice to the Elk Cow, and not one of them to the Wolf. So the old Sky Wolf turned himself into a fish. He looked like a common flounder, but he could talk. One day when a young fisherman threw out his line, the Wolf in the Flounder bit. Lying in the sand, he made himself known as the old wolf god. The fisherman was afraid, so he promised to do whatever the Flounder commanded. Thereupon the Wolf said from inside the Flounder, 'Your Awa stole my fire, and the wolves have had to eat their meat raw ever since. Because Awa has won power over all men with fire, you must give a masculine nature to the fire that people use to cook and warm themselves and bake clay pots. The hard must be melted and grow hard again when it cools.' The fisherman relayed all this to the other men, and they

began to break rocks of a special kind. When they heated the lumps of ore in the fire, the iron in them melted and made the men into mighty smiths. Because the Wolf in the Flounder so commanded, they pierced their Awa with their spearheads. And I, too," said Mestwina whenever she pounded acorns to flour in her mortar, "will be killed by a sword forged in fire."

It seems, however, that when the Flounder of Mestwina's story heard of Awa's death, he turned himself back into a ferocious Wolf and brought war into the land with forged iron. For which reason Amanda Woyke always concluded her stories about Swedes Pandours Cossacks or Polacks with the words "They were like wolves. They wouldn't leave anything in one piece. They even ripped up the children." (F, 294)

The most important point made here is that the Sky Wolf/Flounder instigates the use of fire's destructive powers in war. In an earlier passage in the novel the Flounder likewise gives men instruction concerning the use of fire.

Just after catching the Flounder for the first time, the narrator tells him that Awa brought fire down from the sky with her. "She says fire is good for cooking meat, fish, roots, and mushrooms, or for keeping us warm when we sit around it chewing the fat. I ask you friend Flounder: what else can fire do?" (p. 25). The Flounder answers with information about other civilizations, with mythological gossip, and finally about metal that can be forged into spearheads and axes. This is the same fire/war constellation we have just seen, here in juxtaposition with fire/cooking—the creative half of the opposition. As the Flounder continues, he broadens the scope of the metaphor. Returning from a trip to Sweden with an ore specimen for the narrator, he counsels him:

"Take heart!" cried the Flounder. "Smelt down this and more like it and you will have not only acquired copper but also given fire a new, progressive, incisive, decisive, and masculine significance. Fire is something more than warmth and cookery. In fire there are visions. Fire cleanses. From fire the sparks fly upward. Fire is idea and future. On the banks of other rivers, the future is already under way. Resolute men are making themselves masters of it, without so much as asking their Awas and Ewas. It's only here that men are still letting themselves be suckled and lulled to sleep. Even your old men are babes in arms. Like Prometheus you must take possession of fire. Don't content yourself with being a fisherman, my son; become a blacksmith." (F, 26)

Not only can fire be used to smelt ore for weapons, the Flounder says, but in fire there are visions, ideas, the future. This is a key link, adding to fire's use in war the more subtly destructive dimension of the visions and ideas that fire here is made to represent.[3] These points are the Flounder's and lead us to an investigation of his role in the novel.

The narrator makes it clear that his account has two parts—the history of cooking and the story of the Flounder. He writes, "at first I was only going to write about my nine or eleven cooks, some kind of a history of human foodstuffs—from manna grass to millet to the potato. But then the Flounder provided a counterweight" (F, 147). Similarly, early in the novel, while describing "Nine and more cooks," the narrator says, "the talking flounder is a story by himself. Since he has been advising me the male cause has progressed." (F, 11). A counterweight to the history of human foodstuffs and a story separate from that of the cooks. Here we see the opposition set up between cooking and the Flounder that is basic to the novel. This opposition makes sense in light of the dual characteristics of fire as discussed by Lévi-Strauss. The cooking fire is creative, the fire used for war (and as we have seen, the visions and ideas represented by fire) is destructive, and identified with the Flounder.

In addition to his suggestion resulting in the use of fire for war, we can find numerous passages in which he teaches men potentially destructive ideas. The concepts of "ultimate goal," "ultimate victory," and "final solution"—they are to be found in the poem "At the end" (F, 95-96)—denote such destructive ideas. By introducing the "pure idea" (F, 96), "gods, from Zeus to Marx" (F, 150), myths (F, 97-98), and a Hegelian view of history, the Flounder hopes men will dominate women and create a world after his own image. But men have failed miserably in fulfilling their world-historical task, the Flounder says, and so he turns to women: "I'm coming more and more to like these ladies who are judging me. . . . All that untapped will to power—it gives me food for thought. . . . Slowly, a little late perhaps, I have discovered my daughters" (F, 150). As a result of the bankruptcy of male power, as an inevitable step forward in his dialectic process, as a manifestation of the predicted overcoming of the masters by the slaves, as a further step in the inexorable progress of the *Weltgeist* (read Flounder) toward actualization, the Flounder decides to offer his services to women.

Siggie, Maxie, and Frankie, progressive, liberated women, eager to continue their fight to overthrow their male oppressors, become the Flounder's targets. In the very moment they proclaim their need for a supernatural or ideological foundation for their actions the Flounder takes hold of their hook and lets himself be caught for the second time: " 'What we really need,' said Frankie while folding a boat, 'is an ideologically acceptable prop of our superegos.' And the Flounder bit" (F, 36).

If the women had simply made a deal with the Flounder and thrown him back into the sea (as did the narrator in the first place) the story of the Flounder's attempt to mold the history of the world would never have come to light (F, 39-40). But the women bring him to trial and he is forced to adopt another stance.

His plan is to attempt to discredit men and exculpate himself by playing on the culture/nature opposition we saw earlier in Lévi-Strauss. In an impassioned speech before the Tribunal, the Flounder says that women are, above all, mothers:

> "How poorly men are equipped by comparison. All they can conceive is absurd ideas.... The affairs and achievements of today: Calcutta. The Aswan Dam. The pill. Watergate. These are men's ersatz babies. Some principle has got them with child. They are impregnated with the categorical imperative.... Culture? Yes, if you will.... Canned music. Crumbling Gothic brickwork. In air-conditioned museums art has forgotten its origins.... Women, on the other hand.... will always—even with the fanciest hairdos—be nature. They menstruate. They give life even when they draw nameless seed from sperm banks. Milk wells promptly from them and them alone." (F, 396-97)[4]

Reading the Flounder's speech, however, we remember his role in introducing "culture" and remember as well another speech in which he berated men for their dependence on nature and the women who embodied it:

> "Breast-fed babies to the end of your days. But out in the world the future has started blazing trails. Nature is sick of being submitted to with womanish passivity; it wants to be mastered by men. Trace canals. Drain swamps. Fence in the land, plow it, take possession of it." (F, 32-33)

It was the Flounder who introduced history, who bullied men into leaving nature and women behind with their cultural achievements. Calcutta, the Aswan dam, the pill, and Watergate were in truth begotten by the Flounder. But before the Women's Tribunal he works to change the women's perception of his role in all of this.

Near the end of the novel the Flounder once again speaks out against the evils of male culture (even admitting his own role in its rise), all in a calculated attempt to bring women (whom he hopes we will see as a true antithesis to male/cultural hegemony) to power:

> "Yes. That's how it is. That's how it has been up to now. I declared war to be father of all things.... Time and time again I commanded death for one thing or another—the greatness of the nation, the purity of some idea, the glory of God, undying fame, an abstract principle such as the fatherland—my invention, incidentally—and exalted death as the essence of life.... And because history presents itself as an inevitable alternation of war and peace, peace and war, as though this were a law of nature, as though nothing else were possible, as though a supernatural force—take me as a captive example—had imposed all this as fate, as though there were no other way of discharging aggression, as though peace could never be more than a brief interval during which men prepared for the next day of wrath, this vicious circle must forever remain unbroken—unless it is broken by those who have hitherto made no history, who have not been privileged to resolve notorious historical

conflicts, whom I have subjected to male history, to whom history has never brought anything but suffering, who have been condemned to feed the war machine and replenish the human material it consumes—I am referring to women in their role as mothers." (F, 518, 521)

Thus far in his speech the Flounder has admitted his guilt, has pointed to abstract principles and supernatural forces as the causes of war and related conflicts, and has suggested mothers (nature) as the solution to history as it has been. Having been forced by the women of the Tribunal to admit this much (because they did not immediately make a pact with him) the Flounder/*Weltgeist* has gone through a process of de-actualization, represented by his increasing transparency. At this point we can see through him, recognizing his perfidy. But he is a crafty old fish and refuses to accept defeat. Playing on the women's feeling of historical importance, he says:

"No longer will women be compelled to stand silent and look on. The world is at a turning point. Today history demands a female imprint. Already the male is hanging his head, neglecting to play his role. Already he is unwilling to will. Already he is beginning to relish his guilt feelings. He's finished, and he knows it. The world awaits a sign from the Womenal, a sign that will put the future back in business. . . . The Womenal will have consequences. Our time-phase bears the imprint of the women's liberation movement. Women have been politicized. They have organized; they are fighting, refusing to be silenced. Already they have registered partial success." (F, 521-23)

Mixing his declarations against war and the male principle with rousing evocations of female will to power, the Flounder ends his speech with a telling suggestion:

"I am almost inclined to fear that womankind lacks counsel, sustained, reliable, or, to put it plainly, supernatural counsel. But as an embodiment of the guilty male and—as has been demonstrated—warlike principle, am I fit to advise the female cause, and henceforth the female cause alone?

"I want to. I could. I already know how. Let the Womenal judge." (F, 523)

He does, indeed, "already know how," and that is precisely the problem. His "supernatural counsel" has already led to male domination, to destructive technology, to war, and to ideological oppression. If the Flounder has his way, women will take up and advance these activities in which men excelled for so many centuries. Ironically, the Flounder has himself predicted that women, with such a takeover, "would develop an increasing disposition to male-type baldness" (F, 397-98). If women take over the direction of history with the Flounder's ideological base, following the *Weltgeist* as *he* strives for actualization, they will bring to the world the same consequences (war, destruction of nature, hunger, etc.) men have engendered over the ages.

Having turned for a moment from our discussion of the raw and the cooked to an investigation of the Flounder, and having recognized in him the destructive aspects represented by fire—the father of war, the embodiment of Hegel's *Weltgeist*, of ideologies, of goals that point beyond humanity—we can now return to cooking and its mediatory role. In *From the Diary of a Snail* Grass again and again calls on the snail with its slow, even, continuous progress (contrasting with the galloping, jumping *Weltgeist*) to mediate between melancholy and utopia.[5] Switching metaphors at one point, anticipating *The Flounder*, he writes of the mediatory power of cooking:

> In among the kitchen herbs, for instance. Believe me, children, if one of those quarrelsome ideologies that are always pulling out the carpet from under each other's feet, could manage, with their little articles of faith and ultimate goals, to raise so much as a sprig of fuzz-soft salvia, it might (possibly) lure me to the table. But my palate has been tickled by neither rosemary nor basil, thyme nor even parsley. What they've served me is tasteless. My spoon goes on strike. Marx boiled to a mash or—as more commonly—watered down, yields at best a foreboding of slobgullion, that dog vomit which promises equality and slobgullion freedom to all. (DS, 72)

If we look at the Flounder's attempt to overcome the contradictions of history, "patriarchy, the state, culture, civilization, dated history, and technological progress" (F, 452-53), we find that his list of achievements does not include cooking. In contrast, the persons who are most successful in ameliorating difficult conditions in the world of the novel are women like Amanda Woyke, with her potato soup, and the socialist Lena Stubbe, with her proletarian soups and cook book. When the narrator's wife tires of his tedious snail philosophy and tries to jump ahead (almost aborting their child), she laughs at the suggestion of historical progress through cooking: "Did the girls fall for that? Are aprons in demand again? Good God! Do they expect to emancipate themselves with cooking spoons?" (F, 332). One of the early women in the novel used a cast-iron spoon as a weapon (Mestwina killed Bishop Adalbert with such a spoon—again demonstrating the dual possibilities of fire); and the women of the "Womenal" also reject peaceful use of cooking as an historical force.

One of the versions of the fairy tale about the fisherman and his wife clearly sets forth cooking as the proper alternative to the Flounder and his historical manipulations:

> First the fisherman wanted to have him [the Flounder] cooked and eat him, but the fisherman's wife, Ilsebill, said, 'Let him talk.' Then Ilsebill wanted to put him in the pot, but the fisherman wanted to ask him a few questions. An-

other time, the Flounder wanted to be stewed—'liberated,' as he put it—but the fisherman and his wife kept having more wishes. (F, 293)

If the Flounder had been cooked when first caught, men would have been saved the crimes they committed while striving for spurious "ultimate goals." And if the women who caught him the second time had cooked him, either at once or at the end of the trial, instead of slowly accepting his "new" version of history and his offer of supernatural aid, the cycle could have been ended (however temporarily). But instead a ritual dinner is held and the Flounder is "set free to expiate his guilt" (F, 527). The expected expiation, ironically, will consist of counsel given by the "embodiment of the guilty male and—as has been demonstrated—warlike principle" (F, 523). Predictably enough, having convinced the women to accept his offer of aid, once more in a position of power, the Flounder loses his transparency. The *Weltgeist* is again moving toward total actualization.

As we have seen, then, cooking is given in the novel as a metaphor counterbalancing the Flounder. Like the snail in *From the Diary of a Snail*, cooking creatively mediates between historical contradictions (while the Flounder's ideological mediation is destructive). Nature and culture are both conjoined and disjoined by the cooking fire that prevents rottenness and a burned state. The mediation can fail, as when iron weapons are made with the cooking fire or when cooking is rejected as an historical alternative, but the possibility always exists. Cooking is not only a metaphor, however, but serves in actuality to combat the eternal problem of hunger. Soup kitchens do in fact aid the victims of atrocities committed in the names of ideologies. Cooking is a metaphor that deserves reification.

And finally, after pointing out the myths of the origin of fire in *The Raw and the Cooked* as sources for those in *The Flounder*, after discussing the creative and destructive aspects of fire as found in both works, and after demonstrating that the mediating cooking fire of Lévi-Strauss counterbalances the Flounder in a more than metaphorical manner, the mediatory function of a child remains to be discussed.

While the narrator writes of his past, reflecting on the respective historical roles of the Flounder and of his inner cooks, two ongoing events contemporary to the act of writing are also recorded. One of these events, the capture and subsequent trial of the Flounder, led, the narrator writes, to his narration,

because the Flounder, instead of being set free, had water poured on him, had his bleeding lip dabbed with Kleenex, and was finally brought ashore, everything came to light, the Vistula estuary became an exemplary place, and I an exemplary individual; because the Flounder was not set free, I must make a clean breast, confess to Ilsebill, and write it all down. (F, 40)

Of course, when the trial concludes and the Flounder is set free, the history quickly comes to an end. The second event contemporary to the narration is the conception, gestation, and birth of a child. Comparing the first and last scenes described in *The Flounder* in light of our previous discussion, we are able to add the child to the Flounder/cooking configuration already established.

In the very first paragraph of the novel we find reference to cooking, impregnation, and narration:

> Ilsebill put on more salt. Before the impregnation there was shoulder of mutton with string beans and pears, the season being early October. Still at table, still with her mouth full, she asked, "Should we go to bed right away, or do you first want to tell me how when where our story began?" (F, 3)

Still talking, Ilsebill tells the narrator that she has thrown her pills down the toilet and that there is no reason why they should not conceive a child. Here we remember the Flounder's comment that the pill is one of men's ersatz babies—along with other cultural monuments like Calcutta, the Aswan Dam, Watergate, and the categorical imperative (F, 397). Ilsebill has rid herself of the sterility foisted off on men by the Flounder and is ready to give birth. In addition, the meal consumed before going to bed is reported to be conducive to conception.

The important course of the meal, the narrator reports, is the fish soup:

> Eaten before the mutton with pears and beans, Ilsebill's soup, distilled from codfish heads that have had the hell boiled out of them, probably embodied the catalytic agent with which, down through the ages, the cooks inside me have invited pregnancy; for by chance, by destiny, and without further ingredients, it came off, it took. . . . In the fish soup, which Ilsebill had made green with dill and capers, codfish eyes floated white and signified happiness. (F, 4)

The intimation here that the fish soup is a catalytic agent inviting pregnancy supports statements quoted above as to the proper disposal of the Flounder. The society that cooks him and his ideologies instead of accepting his advice lives in peace and prosperity. Cooking the Flounder (fish soup) leads to conception of the child. And during gestation, the child mediates between the usually warring sexes. Codfish eyes floating in soup signify happiness.[6]

Three passages about children further identify them as metaphorical opponents of the Flounder. In the first instance Ilsebill, five months pregnant, becomes tired of the narrator's "obsessive insistence on slow, gradual, deliberately procrastinating change" (F, 330), and tries to leap over a ditch. Watching her fall, the narrator fears a miscarriage. Comparison is made to "The Great Leap Forward and the Chinese world food solution," an ideological attempt to solve the problem of hunger with a single leap forward. Such a solution (in either case) will prove abortive (as compared to careful gestation). The result is loss of the mediatory child.

A second reference to children and their natural function in society comes in the eighth chapter. Billy, who acts as cook for the three militant feminists, after being subjected to debilitating comments and unnatural acts during the course of the Father's Day excursion, decides to leave her companions and return to her child:

> What a new feeling: to be a woman. Even if she was hopelessly alone. But her mind was made up.... "I won't leave Heidi with her grandparents any longer—I'll go and get her and give her a real home. A child needs a mother's warmth and affection." (F, 491)

Even though Billy is brutally killed as a result of her decision, her motherly feelings contrast starkly with her companions' extraordinary attempts to conceive a savior son on the phallic pine tree. In the end, violence and perversion (both male and female) deprive a child of its mother.

The third example depicts a vicious opposition between the Flounder/Sky Wolf and children: "They were like wolves. They wouldn't leave anything in one piece. They even ripped up the children" (F, 294).

Turning now from the first scene where fish soup and throwing out the pill led to conception of a child, and from the near abortion because of a leap and Billy's decision to be a mother, we reach the final scene of the novel. The trial is over, the Flounder once again at large. As a result the narrator is no longer required to bare himself and the narration hurries to a close. The gestating child that formed a bond between man and woman has been born—a girl. The divisive war between the sexes has a new beginning. As the narrator visits his friend Maria in Gdańsk a scene is set that invites comparison with the novel's opening scene.

In the beginning a man and woman eat fish soup together, subsequently conceive a child, and embark on a lengthy reflection on history that reveals the Flounder as the instigator of war and ultimate cause of hunger. In the end a man and woman walk along the beach, saying not a word. Laying down in a hollow they have sex—impersonally, in direct contrast to the intercourse in the first scene and similar to the sex between Awa and the Sky Wolf. Only then do they eat—pork and cabbage, but no fish soup. Maria leaves the narrator and calls the Flounder out of the sea. She speaks with the fish until dark, laughing and listening to his "categorical finalities" (F, 547). Finally giving the Flounder back to the sea, Maria/Dorothea/Agnes/Sophie/Billy/Ilsebill walks past the narrator without seeing him. Once again the Flounder has caused a rift between the sexes. They should have cooked him.

Notes

1. Claude Lévi-Strauss, *The Raw and the Cooked: Introduction to a Science of Mythology I*, trans. John and Doreen Weightman (New York: Harper and Row, 1975). All quotations will be from this edition. The book was first published under the title *Le Cru et le Cuit* (Paris: Librairie Plon, 1964). Grass presumably used the German version: *Das Rohe und das Gekochte*, trans. Eva Moldenhauer (Frankfurt am Main: Suhrkamp, 1971).
2. B, 66: "das morsche Holz" can conceivably be translated as "the dry wood" (F, 52). But then the specific parallel to Lévi-Strauss is lost.
3. See Grass's statement on the destructive potential of ideas, in "Unser Grundübel ist der Idealismus," p. 94: "at any given time it is idealistic difficulties that make it impossible for the apostles of salvation to bear the contradictions of reality and to continually confront their own impotence."
4. For Lévi-Strauss the giving of milk is a primary indication of nature (see p. 270).
5. See DS, 91: "He apparently regarded them as sisters. How Melancholy and Utopia call each other cause. How the one shuns and disavows the other. How they accuse each other of evasion. How the snail meditates between them: punctilious, indifferent, and cynical as go-betweens can be."
6. An uneasy happiness, as signified by the overly obvious symbolism.

The Truth Told Differently: Myth and Irony

Winnifred R. Adolph

In the title character of his novel, *The Flounder*, Grass has created a figure that incorporates the most fundamental aspects of myth: a traditional or legendary story; an attempt to express or explain a basic truth; and a belief or subject of belief whose truth or reality is accepted uncritically.[1] Within the novel the one-dimensional, isolated world of the fairy tale is transformed into a myth.[2] The flounder of the fairy tale is a passive fulfiller of wishes, merely reacting to the requests of the fisherman's wife. Although the wishes violate the social order, the fish grants them until it becomes patently impossible to do so. This fish can turn a woman into a pope, but not God. In contrast, the Flounder of the novel implants wishes in men's minds. He guides them from primitive contentment into the worlds of commerce, politics and art. Cleverly, he imposes a social structure, which he maintains is world-wide. Thus a local fairy tale becomes a universal myth that explains a basic truth of existence: the division of society into male and female realms and the resulting social structures.

Myth, whether reflected in the uncritical tales of primitive tribes or in the sophisticated universal poetry of the Romantic era, has always played a major role in the life of human beings. Myths provide explanations of the universe and in so doing give cohesion and structure to society. Consequently, recent criticism has leaned toward the theory that for the modern era the function of myth is more important than its substance. As Ernst Cassirer writes:

> Thus while the study of the subject matter of myth may be highly interesting...it cannot yield a definite answer. For what we want to know is not the mere substance of myth; it is rather its function in man's social and cultural life.[3]

The myths that we have inherited give us an "eternal truth" against which to judge and understand our contemporary culture and values. As we approach the modern era, however, these truths often appear less eternal and less true. On the universal scales indifference appears to outweigh truth. As a result, man is not so much aware of a mythic truth as a "cosmic irony."[4] In relation to the powers of the universe man's existence is futile. Man often accomplishes the opposite of his intention as his every attempt to understand or progress is thwarted. Irony places the myth in doubt, for it reveals the futility of searching for meaning in an indifferent universe.

In Germany the preoccupation with both irony and myth received a renewed impulse during Romanticism. The desire for a unifying principle that would allow man to perceive himself and his surroundings as a totality led writers like Friedrich Schelling and Friedrich Schlegel to search for and pronounce a new, modern mythology.[5] Many believed that such a unity had existed in earlier times, in ancient Greece, for instance, and the new mythology expressed the hope that the lost mythic experiences could be regained through art.[6] The foundation of the new mythology was the belief that "the profoundest truths, whether of art or life . . . lie beyond the reach of any circumscribing analytical verbal formulation by scientist, philosopher or theologian."[7] An essential element of the new mythology was the longing to regain an organic, direct understanding of life's "profoundest truth." The facilitator and vehicle for this task was art. Running counter to these ideals of unity is the prominence of irony in Romanticism. Schlegel's famous aphorisms on irony: "Irony is a clear consciousness of an eternal agility, of the infinitely abundant chaos," and "Irony is the form of paradox," reflect his idea that irony exposes the conflict between the absolute and the relative.[8]

With these factors in mind the choice of the Flounder as the central conceit adds a mythological and ironic dimension to the novel. The discovery of the fairy tale takes place during Romanticism when the apparently conflicting concepts of irony and mythology were being used to investigate reality. There was the belief that art gives a premonition of truth in telling stories that both reflect and create reality. The appearance of reality is one of Grass's main concerns. In an interview with Dick Cavett Grass states that the committed writer is under the obligation to portray different realities.[9] By expanding the story of the Flounder from a fairy tale to a myth, Grass is able to exploit fully the potential of art to explore reality. He is able to jump from one time to another, from one reality to another. Through irony the author exposes the paradoxes and conflicts of these realities. In retelling the stories of days gone by the novel attempts to portray truth as it was understood at given stages of human history. The result, however, is not one final, absolute truth. The truth told differently reflects the infinite character of truth. That does not mean a relativistic escape, but the recognition that truth has a dimension beyond the limitations of one historical period or location. To interpret these historically limited manifestations as absolute truth is the unfortunate fate of people. Just as they see themselves defined by time and space, they believe that the truth must be just as definite. When the premise of a definite truth has been recognized as false, there arises the obligation to tell the truth again, differently and from new perspectives. Together with its permanent quality, myth possesses a dynamic property of constantly reshaping and retelling basic experiences. The reshaping quality of myth, the change of perspective, is basic to Grass's narrative technique and his treatment of myth. As a result, the novel derives its mythic dimension not only from the stories it tells, but from its narrative structure. Grass's principle of changing perspectives is seen in his use of familiar subject matters revealed in a new form. The bringing of fire, a myth known to most Westerners in the Prometheus story, becomes the accomplishment of prehistoric woman, and for this gift to human culture woman is punished with the eternal "itch," an insatiable desire for sex (F, 52-53). Similarly, the central story of the novel, the Flounder's, is told in an alternative version so that not the woman, but the man, is the greedy and destructive element of the tale (F, 345-53).

To understand the function of myth in *The Flounder* we must return to the beginning and commence our study where Grass begins his story: the conception of a child that coincides with the conception of myths. The gestation cycle is itself only a part of the larger life and death cycle. This again, although a limited period for one being, is of unlimited character as a part of the universal cycle. The conception of myths took place at a time of prehistory, as Grass writes, "a pleasantly historyless age" (F, 10). The myths were shadows waiting to be formed. Awa's benevolence provides a good life for the people: want is unknown; the men are suckled three times a day and live to a ripe old age. The state of bliss is, however, deceptive. The description is only from the standpoint of the narrator, who casually mentions that the women die younger than the men (F, 10). We do not know Awa's view of this time. Yet the utopia survives on her ability to maintain its tenuous balance.

When Awa brings fire to the world, she brings with it the destruction of her society. Although she hides the true story of the capture of fire, she cannot completely conceal the implications of fire. Fire provides the knowledge of opposites. Food is divided into the raw and the cooked.[10] Cooking is no longer an accident of nature through fire and lightning, but under control of human beings. This fact brings mankind the awareness that it can choose one form over the other. When the Flounder is caught, he exploits this limited knowledge and lures Edek into a world of opposites and ambiguity. He shows Edek the potential of fire as a tool; that is, the ability to create something outside of Awa's reality. Awa attempts to suppress new knowledge or retain it for her own use, as in the case of the knife that she secretly keeps (F, 27). She even forbids art, for it portrays things which she has not seen and, therefore, cannot exist. As the Flounder says of Awa: "Everything outside of her is ruled out" (F, 23). Despite her efforts, Awa's time is past. Edek has heard the Flounder's ambiguous voice that has awakened feelings of unrest in the male tribe. The Flounder leads man into a world where total male dominance will replace female dominance, and recorded history begins. It becomes the record of the male's attempt to restore and usurp the unity of the matriarchy. Yet the Flounder is never able to lead mankind to the same state of content that Edek perceived under Awa.

The era of Wigga is a time of transition. It is the era when reality as we know it emerges; that is, the time of two breasts, not three. Already male inroads have been made in the stories about the disappearance of the breast; it was lost when Wigga slept with the Flounder (F, 68); or perhaps it was the shock of seeing the Edek–idol with its monstrous genitals (F, 68); or maybe it was the withdrawal of the magical root that forced the men to see that there never had been a third breast (F, 69). According to the Flounder, it had all been a gigantic "hoax" (F, 69). At any rate, when the men no longer perceive the third breast, women's time is past. When Mestwina murders Bishop Adalbert in an attempt to preserve the old order, she accomplishes the opposite. With the martyrdom of Adalbert, the male principle suppresses the female, and the struggles of history become the struggles of man. History, however, as Grass stated himself, is not a chain of events, but a dynamic interplay of past and present experiences, attitudes and expectations.[11] Thus time in the narrative is not a linear progression, but a constant to and fro. The reader is not allowed to settle comfortably into one historical frame. Continuous and unexpected juxtaposing of historical and mythical time, of the imagined and the factual forces the audience to stay mentally alert.

The conception of the child is, of course, a metaphor for the birth of myths, and the history of the pregnancy is symbolic of the history of the world. In the context of the novel, the course of the pregnancy provides our primary sense of chronological development. As we go forward in time, it is usually in a spiral fashion. We go up and down in an increasingly complicated pattern that finally leads to the present. As the narrator writes: "On our paper most things take place simultaneously" (F, 123). This use of time complements and reflects the narrator's continuous encircling and probing of his subject matter in his search for the truth. The forms change, the names change, but the function remains the same: man's efforts to replace the matriarchy with new systems, and women's refusal to accept completely these systems. Men reconstruct their primal memory of Awa's time and attempt to impose unity through the Church, through art, through nationalism, supranationalism and socialism—all fail. Constantly in the background are the women and their insistence upon the value of food—of that which is.[12]

After the eras of Awa and Wigga women are relegated to a secondary role. Their lives are spent satisfying what Maslow calls "lower needs": the needs for food and procreation.[13] They are excluded from the higher needs of self-actualization: the making of history and the possession of an individual identity. Yet women assert themselves through their remaining duties. They both support and undermine the systems that men attempt to build. Through the eras food is manipulated and becomes both a weapon and a source of ridicule. The cooks of Grass's novel recognize the power of food and cooking. They cook not simply to eat, but with a purpose. Dorothea denies her husband tasty meals and devotes herself to mysticism; Fat Gret cooks her way through the reformation and laughs at the men and their new religious system; Amanda tries to save the world with her heavenly potato; and Lena cooks with a social purpose. Each of the cooks works her way through history, and each cook reveals the shortcomings of the male systems in politics and art.

Grass himself claims that *The Flounder* is a history of food and an attempt to show modern man the significance of food and the effect of lack of food on society.[14] "The book," writes the narrator, "deals with the history of human nutrition" (F, 183). Although both Grass and his narrator maintain that the book makes a political statement about the dangers of malnutrition, the images of starvation, as vivid as they are, are a minor part of the novel. The overwhelming impression is that of the "joy of cooking." The cooks prepare simple food so that it becomes an aesthetic experience; bad food becomes a punishment; good food provides comfort and reward; a heart is stuffed so that it illustrates theological truth. The narrator waxes eloquent over the virtues of millet boiled in milk and accords the potato its rightful place in history. This seemingly contradictory relationship to food is partially resolved in Grass's statement that all things come from food.[15] Food is not only necessary for physical survival but represents abstract and spiritual needs. In Christianity the fish symbolizes Christ, and Christ fed his people not only with his own body but with loaves and fishes. The combination of physical and spiritual guidance is echoed in the figure of the Flounder who shows little embarrassment at the preparation of his fellow fish for the sustenance of human beings. Food is the one element necessary in all societies, in all times, for all human activities. As Grass sees it, food is the basic element for all facets of life, cultural, erotic, and religious.[16]

The foods are combined in quixotic recipes that unite contrasting ingredients into ecstatic experiences. With the exception of the narrator in the present time, the preparation and manipulation of food represent woman's one remaining area of authority. The kitchen as a base of power (albeit unrecognized by men) is an ironic reversal of the Flounder's initial intent. During Awa's time the Flounder gave this advice: "It's time for you men to cut loose! How? With the kitchen knife. Kill her, my son. Kill her!" (F, 27). But the kitchen knife, intended to be used against women, is the only weapon left for women to wield against men. Paradoxically, the relationship of man towards food and cooks reflects both his ability to dominate women and his limitations. Similarly, woman, in accepting the domain of the kitchen, both limits her role in history and receives a powerful weapon. Neither man nor woman achieves the desired goal. Throughout the novel, we find this kind of ironic reversal that reveals fallacious attitudes that in due course become the reason for failure and self-destruction.

The myth of fire, for instance, was constructed to serve the matriarchy of Awa. It was to keep man subservient, for he did not possess the pouch to carry the fire. But the curse of the Sky Wolf realized itself not only in Awa's physical itch; more importantly, Edek is itching to know. And so one of his first questions to the Flounder is, "... do existing things also mean something else? Fire, for instance" (F, 25). With this question the world of Awa is shaken. The myth that she reluctantly constructed is not powerful enough to contain all the possibilities of fire. Her world, defined only by that which is and can be seen, does not admit the possibility that life may be different or more than Awa wants it to be. In the treatment of the two versions of the fairy tale we can see a similar reversal of the intended outcome. It is decided that only one version of the story will survive. The version in which the male's striving leads ultimately to disaster is fraught with doom, it is too "apocalyptic" (F, 353). It cannot be published, for to do so would be to challenge the very underpinnings of society; hence to insure the common good, that version of the tale is suppressed. But the destruction of the tale does not mean that the principle exposed in it does not exist. In fact, it is the unchecked spread of the male principle set forth in the suppressed version of the fairy tale that leads the Flounder to let himself be caught by women. Thus the benefactor and mentor of the principle must admit to its failure in order to prevent its further growth and its disastrous consequences.

Such ironic reversals are not isolated incidents within the novel, but rather fuse with the use of myth to provide the basic structure of the work. To a great extent, the irony complements the mythic structure. If we agree with Beda Allemann that ironic style alludes to a "hintergründig Mitgewusstes," further that it depends to a large degree on the relationship of the "Vordergründig-Gesagten" to the "Hintergründig-Gemeinten," and that it is the new and different artistic arrangement of these levels that allows ironic relationships[17]—then the complementary function of irony in the poetic treatment of myth and fairy tale, of history and fiction becomes evident. The ironic style together with the mythic structure of the novel is a tool that gives the author freedom to relate events and experiences as they would not normally appear in a historical (chronological) narrative by means of subtle transpositions and displacements of all relationships that emphasize their true character even more fully.[18] As myth enables Grass to encompass all times and places, the agility of irony enables him to explore these times and places from various standpoints.

The Flounder presents the reader with a *tour de force* in the use of irony. For the educated reader, the many historical characters are a constant source of amusement, and he feels that he is sharing an esoteric joke with the author. At the same time, the pseudo-factual style gives the impression that we are discovering the "real truth" about Opitz or Frederick the Great. Although such allusions contribute to the irony of the work, the novel in no way depends upon such shared knowledge for its ironic character. For the reader who comes to the work without such knowledge Grass has constructed a detailed world that contains its own irony. He clearly warns the reader not to take the printed word at face value. For those unfamiliar with the fairy tale of the flounder, its first mention places it in its proper context; it is a "phony fairy tale" (F, 20). The importance of myths is also ridiculed when the Flounder's lectures on the civilization of Greece and her gods are described as "mythological gossip" (F, 26) and "chit-chat" (F, 96).

The author commences his story in a time of which no one else has first-hand knowledge. Thus he provides himself with a *tabula rasa* on which to write the most outrageous stories, unafraid of anyone's contradictions except his own. We are totally dependent on the narrator for information, and his documentary style leads us to believe that we are now privy to life before history. The narrator can lead the novel in any direction, unencumbered by chronological time or historical fact. Allemann's statement that Thomas Mann's novel *Joseph and His Brothers* receives its poetic life from " the ironic interplay of two levels of consciousness: the dreamily mythic and the precisely scientific"[19] is just as valid for *The Flounder*. It is the constant interaction of these levels that gives the novel its tremendous flexibility. It was no doubt this same quality and the refusal of the work to be pigeonholed, which aroused the ire of those readers, among them many feminists, who demanded a consistent work with a clearly defined worldview. But the author uses irony to present many views and to investigate repeatedly the same idea or event from different angles.

Repetition as an element of ironic style is well known; for example, in Thomas Mann's works it is woven through the narrative—often as an ironic leitmotif. Through repetition otherwise neutral phrases or unimportant events gain increasingly ironic value as the novel progresses.[20] In *The Flounder* events and characters are rarely mentioned only once. On the contrary, the stories of the cooks and the Flounder are inserted time and time again, each time in a slightly different manner, or from a different perspective. An example of this technique is the letter at the end of the "Second Month" to Dr. Stachnik in reference to his efforts to have Dorothea canonized. The letter illustrates the variety of ironic modes and how these effect the narrative posture of the novel.[21]

The situation of the narrator (Dorothea's husband), who corresponds with Dorothea's biographer, provides an overall ironic setting. The narrator bows to Stachnik's erudition and admires his persistence with regard to proving to the world that Dorothea was "intellectually, morally, spiritually the most outstanding woman of Prussia during the period of the Teutonic Knights" (F, 165). But this deference is undercut by the explanations and asides of the person who endured married life with the real-life Dorothea. Within the novel the relationship of Stachnik to the narrator mirrors the relationship of the reader to the novel. From his position of first-hand authority, the narrator constantly challenges the body of knowledge that the reader has either brought with him or gained in the course of the novel. The narrator variously attempts to correct the reader's understanding of past times and figures or tells the reader that his historical conception is blatantly false because it is based on a hoax or incomplete information. Much of this irony is completely internal and requires no outside knowledge. The narrator, for instance, informs the reader that a seemingly innocent example of "a Pomeranian cooking utensil" (F, 87) was the spoon with which the Archbishop Adalbert was murdered. Later stories surrounding the event and its consequences are called "absurdities schoolbook history has handed down to us" (F, 88). In similar fashion, the narrator's neolithic version of a minotaur originally done at the insistence of the Flounder "to make figurines of comparable mythical import and to perpetrate a pious fraud" (F, 98) are later interpreted by archeologists as evidence for the "surprisingly early domestication of pigs in the marshes of the Vistula estuary" (F, 99).

In addition to the irony of the situation, Grass achieves irony through the use of unexpected, often inappropriate language. In regard to the period he is describing, he frequently chooses not the *mot juste*, but the *mot injuste*. When the narrator refers to the knights as "Schlägertypen" (B, 207) or "ruffians" (F, 165), he is using language familiar to the reader from twentieth-century gangster slang, and the Teutonic Knights become the hoodlums of the fourteenth century. The same juxtaposition of twentieth-century jargon and medieval life occurs when the narrator describes his forced sexual abstinence as a time of "langjähriger Lustverlust" (B, 208) or "years of sexual privation" (F, 166) and resents the fact that Dorothea "stopped doing it, she wouldn't let me in" (F, 166). In the original German, "sie ließ mich nicht mehr, ließ mich nicht ran" (B, 208). On a stylistic level, irony here brings the experience of modern man into contact with that of his predecessor. To appreciate fully the verbal irony of the work one has to refer to the German original of the novel, for in German the above phrases are undeniably twenti-eth-century in tone. Equally, many double entendres are lost in the English language; such as in the portrayal of Dorothea's relationship to the "Herrn Jesus (mit dem sie täglich verkehrte)" (B, 208), while she refuses to have in-tercourse (i.e., *verkehren)* with her husband. In addition, much of the emo-tionally charged language is toned down in the translation. In the description of Dorothea's first biographer, Johannes Marienwerder, the narrator shifts to a first-name basis and states that Johannes was determined, "come hell or high water" or "auf Teufel komm raus" (B, 207), to produce a saint for Prus-sia. The intrusion of such emotional language into the pseudo–academic style of the letter and the combination of different historical and verbal levels illus-trate the use of verbal irony and contribute to the basic narrative posture of the novel. In the example of (almost Saint) Dorothea of Montau, we can ob-serve how characters and events in the novel are described from many stand-points.

The letter summarizes the life of Dorothea and the various interpreta-tions placed on her deeds. As an advocate for her canonization, the Doctor has extolled Dorothea's piety and her role as the outstanding woman of the fourteenth century. The narrator responds with his personal knowledge of his wife: her refusal to have sex, her neglect of her children unto death for the sake of religion. The narrator also includes the judgement of the Tribunal that Dorothea was a precursor in the fight for women's liberation. The "Wo-menal" declares that Dorothea was one of the first women to win freedom from the demands of men and marriage. To this purpose she used the Church. Thus three attempts are made to interpret this woman's life, and all three are justified from the perspective of the interpreter: Dorothea the saint, the bitch, or the political activist. The letter reveals the clashing of various ab-solute principles, the Church, the family, and woman's need for identity. Each interpreter has chosen one aspect of Dorothea's life to elevate to the truth of her existence rather than come to terms with the many facets of her personal-ity. The narrator calls for a compromise proposal, "halfway between the Catholic and feminist positions" (F, 167).

The narrator's call for a compromise is telling of his persona in the novel. In a famous description of the Romantic, ironic writer, Ricarda Huch portrays a narrator who is spiritually free, as though suspended above the world.[22] The writer is not involved in the actions he describes nor is he subject to time. Although the critic may discern certain cultural biases in the narrative pose, the author writes as though his observations were timeless. In contrast, the narrator of *The Flounder* is very much a part of time. He has accumu-lated personal experiences throughout the eras and views his past actions with twentieth-century eyes. There is nothing to indicate that he is an especially distanced or astute observer of the era in which he is living. At the beginning of the letter, the narrator refers with some embarrassment to his time as "a dull-witted Hitler Youth" (F, 164). But the narrator is able to see his personal experiences in historical perspective and modify his initial reactions. Although still bitter about his treatment by Dorothea, the narrator acknowledges (reluctantly) that forces must be considered outside his personal happiness: "how insignificant was my squandered fortune weighed against what Dorothea gained each day pleasing God with her (bloody) flagellation" (F, 166). Even though he is willing to allow other considerations, he is not willing to abandon completely his personal experience. In his life as the swordmaker Albrecht Slichting the narrator had a miserable existence. He was, in fact, as much a victim of fourteenth-century systems as was Dorothea. Through its representative, the Church bribed and manipulated Slichting until he, not unwillingly, relinquished his claims on his wife. The narrator's call for a compromise is then also a plea for the recognition of the truth of personal experience, even when it contradicts historical truth or the claims of an institution on society. As the narrator of the epic he cannot permit the personal side to be completely disregarded in favor of the abstraction. The narrator closes his letter with the remark: "You and I, however, know that stories can't help being true. But never twice in the same way" (F, 168). There is little indication that after years of study Dr. Stachnik will revise his view of Dorothea and admit the possibility of a second truth. Therefore, we must view this remark as a plea, not only to the Doctor, but also as a personal call to the reader to be aware of the many possibilities of the truth.

Let us pause for a moment to consider the mythic and ironic elements in their relationship to truth. The mythic proportions of the novel attempt a unified understanding of human development. They illustrate the desire to look for one central truth to explain history and social behavior. The ironic elements counteract these tendencies by exposing facts and ideas not accounted for in myth. "It ain't neccessarily so," is the basic cord that is woven throughout the novel. Truth is to be found neither in the insistence upon universal principles nor in their negation. It is the tension between affirmation and negation, between different and competing world views that reveals the truth. As with electricity, it is neither the positive nor the negative pole by itself that causes the spark, but their proper alignment and the resulting tension. This spark can arc in any direction between two poles, or among many if they are situated correctly. Truth is like this electric arc that forms relationships between people and their world, and makes understanding possible. It would be dishonest for an author to present nowadays one truth from any one perspective, human or mythic. It would be equally dishonest for the author to deny the human desire for such a truth. The ironic stance of the novel captures the dynamic quality of this relationship and exploits the tension that arises from it.

In the figure of the Flounder, the tension between the mythic and the ironic is strongest. We are confronted with the image of a mythological demi-god attempting simultaneously to reverse and defend his myth. This is the final ironic reversal of the novel, and it negates the universality of the mythic proportions of the epic. We are left with a myth that offers no cohesion for the world. Indeed, a myth that admits its own failure and disclaims its responsibility with the words: "The present is not mine" (F, 453).

The Flounder's myth fails for the same reasons that Awa's failed. It did not encompass all the possibilities of the truth. The systems that men built at the advice of the Flounder were based on a narrow-minded view of unity. Men "in their use of power, in their delusion of power, and with their propensity to abstraction"[23] attempted to construct all-encompassing systems, but unable to do so they excluded one part of society. Each system is like an untried recipe in the hands of a bad cook who is afraid to add the one unusual spice or ingredient that would make the meal a new culinary experience. Because the systems depend on exclusion, they can never truly succeed. The world never really changes. Life in the Vistula estuary remains the same, whether the time is neolithic, medieval or contemporary. Danzig never attained freedom or stable food prices; nothing substantially different has been achieved; except "today the patricians have a different name" (F, 120).

In no part of the novel is the insistence upon exclusion clearer than in the discussion of the fairy tale. Each person wants to impose upon the tale his or her own vision of the truth. As Runge says: "It would seem . . . that we humans can tolerate the one truth and never the other" (F, 353). Yet the truth is many-sided and appears ambiguous, like the contents of an untried recipe. Without all it sides, the truth is less than a half-truth; it is a falsehood. Although the Flounder admits to the falsehood, his offer to go over to the women is not a solution. The Flounder cannot change the truth by exchanging one form of dominance for another. The trade-off does not make one version of the tale true and the other false. Both versions are true. If Grass portrays one myth, one truth in his novel, it is that there is no *one* truth. A myth that depends on separation for its meaning and demands that the world be divided into male and female, into raw and cooked, into hungry and sated, is not a valid myth. If humankind is to progress, we must abandon the principle of separation. We must see food with the awareness that it can be either raw or cooked. We must see not male and female, but be aware that human beings are both male and female. Only then can we break the pattern and accept that "the truth is told, a different way each time" (F, 545). The truth told differently is not simply a change in perspective and form, but a demand that the many sides of truth be recognized. Truth is ambiguous, and modern man—indeed, man or woman from any era—cannot impose clarity on the ambiguity of truth.

Notes

1. See *The Random House Dictionary of the English Language* (New York: Random House, 1968), p. 882.
2. "Eindimensionalität," "Fläche," and "Sublimierung" are criteria of the European fairy tale established by Max Lüthi, *Märchen* (Stuttgart: Metzler, 1968), pp. 8, 24-31.
3. *The Myth of the State* (New Haven: Yale University Press, 1946), p. 34.
4. For complete studies on irony, see Wayne C. Booth, *A Rhetoric of Irony* (Chicago and London: The University of Chicago Press, 1974); Charles I. Glicksberg, *The Ironic Vision in Modern Literature* (The Hague: Martinus Nijhoff, 1969); or D.C. Muecke, *The Compass of Irony* (London: Methuen, 1969). However, the term cosmic irony is not used here in Muecke's or Booth's technical sense; rather it corresponds more closely to Muecke's "General Irony": "It [General Irony] emerges . . . from an awareness of life as being fundamentally and inescapably at odds with itself and the world at large" (p. 123).
5. See Friedrich Schlegel, "Talk on Mythology," *Dialogue on Poetry and Literary Aphorisms*, trans., introd., Ernst Behler and Roman Struc (University Park: The Pennsylvania State University Press, 1968), pp. 81-93. See also the editors' Introd., pp. 25-29.
6. See Herbert Anton, "Romantische Deutung griechischer Mythologie," *Die deutsche Romantik*, ed. Hans Steffen (Göttingen: Vandenhoeck & Ruprecht, 1967), pp. 277-88. Anton states: "The lost natural state embracing life's totality was perceived in Greek mythology: it was to be regained by mythological-philosophical speculation and to be realized in a *new mythology* as art" (p. 281).
7. Ronald Taylor, ed., *The Intellectual Tradition of Modern Germany* (London: Bell, 1973), I, 148.
8. Friedrich Schlegel, *Dialogue*, pp. 155, 126, 131.
9. *The Dick Cavett Show*, PBS, 27 November 1978.
10. See also Scott H. Abbott, "The Raw and the Cooked: Claude Lévi-Strauss and Günter Grass," above, pp. 107-120.
11. See *Cavett*.
12. See Fritz J. Raddatz, "Heute lüge ich lieber gedruckt. *Zeit*-Gespräch über den *Butt* mit Günter Grass," p. 9.
13. Cited in Richard E. Simmons, *Managing Behavioral Processes* (Arlington Heights, Illinois: AHM Publishing Corp., 1978), pp. 64-70.
14. See *Cavett*.
15. See *Cavett*.
16. See *Cavett*.
17. Beda Allemann, *Ironie und Dichtung* (Stuttgart: Neske, 1969), pp. 12, 22, 23. "Hintergründig Mitgewusstes" refers to the knowledge the reader brings to a work, and that is constantly in the background while reading the work. "Vordergründig-Gesagtes," is that which is stated by the surface structure of language; "Hintergründig-Gemeintes," is that which is alluded to by the deep structure of the language. The latter can be a reference to something within the text, or it can be a reference to extra textual knowledge, i.e., knowledge the reader has to bring to the text in order to experience irony.
18. See Allemann, p. 20.
19. Allemann, p. 143.

20. Among those words and phrases that are introduced in the first pages of the novel and then gain ironic momentum are the references to the various foods, to cooking, to myth, and to Ilsebill's dishwasher.
21. Cf. Fritz J. Raddatz, "'Wirklicher bin ich in meinen Geschichten.' *Der Butt* des Günter Grass," pp. 892-901.
22. Ricarda Huch, *Die Romantik* (Tübingen: Wunderlich, 1951), p. 255.
23. Raddatz, "*Zeit*-Gespräch," p. 9.

On the Art of Garnishing a Flounder with "Chestnuts" and Serving It up as Myth

Otto F. Best

Translated by Albert E. Gurganus

"Literature is the orchestration of platitudes." Thornton Wilder
"All right, Mr. Flounder. There goes your other truth." Günter Grass

Press reviews and sales figures confirm it: Günter Grass is one of the most successful authors of contemporary German literature. His eminence is virtually undisputed. While some maintain that he has emerged as the representative of the German spirit and acknowledge him as a "champion of Democracy," others revere him as a *philosophe*, and "executor of the Enlightenment," and hail him as a "moral-political personality" and the conscience of the nation.[1] The fact that Grass, the renowned author and donor of the Döblin prize, takes every opportunity that presents itself in the Federal Republic and abroad to assume the role of *Praeceptor Germaniae redivivus*, that he enters into public discussions and voices forthright, unequivocal opinions, obviously renders examination of his literary works on the basis of their theoretical-philosophical substance a rather superfluous, futile endeavor. Is it really fitting to call Grass, enemy of theory, a *philosophe*, who by his activities, *per definitionem*, pursues the goal of leading mankind—read here: fellow Germans—out of "self-incurred immaturity?" Immaturity understood here, please note, in the sense of Kant's "inability to use one's own understanding without the guidance of another,"[2] that is, to critically analyze and order what historically has come to be.

In an equally comprehensive and penetrating analysis of Grass's *oeuvre*, published in 1975, the question is posed: How is it that in spite of the increasing topicality of his chosen subject matter and his innovations with form the author is no longer classed with "the representatives of topical literature?"[3] The author of the analysis, in which the German originals of the novel *The Flounder* (1977) and the narrative *The Meeting at Telgte* (1979) could, of course, not be treated, sets forth her answer in the form of theses. The first reads: "Grass and the heroes of his epics resemble each other in one critical point: their strong connection to the past through which they have lived renders them incapable of an adequate consciousness of the present." Grass's "ahistorical concept of history" is stressed in the third thesis.[4] The examination culminates in the "speculative assertion" that at a time when the author's interest became immersed in his political *Engagement* the significance of his work was reduced more and more to its purely "mechanical-literary" attributes.[5] Is the author of *From the Diary of a Snail* really lacking in social relevance, in "political substance"? And what about his belief in progress: does it ever become clear "where it all leads to"? Mere words? Or a philosophical-political concept?[6]

What one might be allowed to postulate in the meantime is this: the glimpses that Grass affords us into historical development tend to show history as an absurd process, as perpetual recurrence. "A keynote of resignation" is prevalent in them, a positive process of developement does not seem possible, "the impression of stagnation predominates."[7] If Grass sets up the evidently positive orientation of his political commitment primarily as a contrast to the "resigned" structure of his narrative works, he attempts to couple political and literary interest in *From the Diary of a Snail*. The history of the melancholiac and Schopenhauer disciple *Zweifel* (Doubt) find their correspondence and continuation in the commitment of the Social Democratic Party (SPD) campaigner. Whereas the tendency to show the fatality of history and to point to the basis of this fatality "in the structures of the individual consciousness and emotional ledger"[8] could, up until now, be discerned in the epics (the present—dominated as it is by the past—renders any hope for change futile) the alterability of the present now moves into the realm of possibility: it becomes a new goal—as the relativized utopia of the snail's pace.

Grass's new hope is embodied in the symbol of the snail[9]—"the snail is progress" (DS, 5)—and its party, the SPD.[10] With its slow but steady movement forward, the snail represents the desirable course of history. The image of the snail's pace replaces that of the leap forward that occurs mainly in *Local Anaesthetic* and in Grass's political remarks from the same period, describing the frustating element in the attempt at progress. Does this signal a disengagement from the retrospection that has predominated the literary work of the author up until now? Until the appearance of *The Flounder* one could have at least had that impression. In this novel, history is once again presented as an absurd process, as perpetual recurrence. Where, for example, in *Dog Years* the character of the German people crystallizes as an ahistorical constant, the nature of man as an ahistorical constant now determines the action.

Perpetual recurrence: Grass elucidated the notion in the clearest possible way in *The Flounder*. The duration of a pregnancy forms the frame of the novel. It establishes the basis for the narrative situation: story-telling as a remedy for depression. Yet the ironic element goes far beyond and is more profound than, Boccaccio's *Decameron*. "Entertainment" in a twofold sense: the appeasing and pacifying principle unites the narrtor and what he narrates. The narrator, temporarily the last link in a chain of men, the eternal Edek (Lud) appearing in numerous masks, relates to his pregnant wife, the eternal "Ilsebill. . . or whoever else may be listening to me" (F, 126), in the 1970s the story of nine cooks (in nine parts corresponding to the nine months of pregnancy) in whose shadow men make history, advised by the Flounder, whom they once caught. While the narrative "I" is telling his story, the Flounder is caught for a second time and indicted before the Women's Tribunal as an advocate of the male cause. A floating, romantic-ironic construction contained within a double frame. The entire construct resembles a "dream," an "idea," a "utopia"—a counterbalance to Ilsebill's melancholy and to the extant version of the *Märchen* "The Fisherman and His Wife." Conception, the months of gestation, during which the narrator nurtures his "cooks," are followed by the birth of a girl. The game can—as will be shown—begin all over again in accordance with the precepts of the Flounder Principle unless the "vicious circle" is broken, a "turning point" (F, 521) reached, a "new phase in human development" (F, 39) begun. Yet no change for the better comes about: the process of history is futile. The turning of Ilsebill (Maria) toward the Flounder at the end of the novel makes it clear: "And then the Flounder . . . leaped as though brand-new out of the sea and into her arms. . . . She overlooked me, overstepped me" (F, 547). Although the images associated with the Flounder serve as symbols for both phallus (fish) and vulva (mandorla), the feminine principle dominates the foreground—but in front of the masculine background and as yet another manifestation of perpetual recurrence.

Perpetual recurrence refers to the realm of myth. Mythology has one "great advantage," Friedrich Schlegel writes in his "Talk on Mythology": "What usually escapes our consciousness can here be perceived and held fast through the senses and spirit. . . ."[11] Myth is then the expression of primordial thought, primordial experience, formed by the imagination. Or, as Nietzsche writes, "symbols of the most universal facts." For the author of *The Birth of Tragedy*, myth is a "concentrated image of the world," a "condensation of phenomena," to which the miraculous is indispensable.[12] Mythology, Karl Kerényi writes, explains itself and everything else in the world. Whether one is seeking the cause of a natural phenomenon, the origin of a ritual or a custom, mythology consistently holds an answer for the perceptive person.[13] Since the myth represents an attempt at explaining the origin and relationships of the physical and metaphysical world as it was "originally," and thereby expresses how it actually "is," the myth becomes the agent of the paradox of the "simultaneous present and past."[14] The predominance of the static suggests inevitability.

The myth as an "essentially" explanatory narrative, as *Aition* with the question "Why?" at its core, may be considered the oldest form of narrative in human history. Yet A. E. Jensen points out that the descriptions in the aetiological myths, often very realistic and charming, cannot disguise the fact that the explanations they advance are "completely divorced from the senses."[15] The relationship between the "genuine" and the "aetiological" myth is similar to that between a cult ritual and a children's game. For Jensen, explanatory myths are therefore a "degenerate form" of the genuine myth.[16] They are related to those myths of political history, which "are presented as the truth, although they are only expedient, and as such correct only in a technical sense." As a product of the mythologizing of certain concepts, they present their own underlying phenomena as rationally incomprehensible and inexplicable. What they aspire to is the reverential acceptance of what they present. The authoritarian state (Hegel) and the insatiable will (Schopenhauer) may both be considered myths of this type. Thus the creation of myth serves as a means of creating an ideology. It is not without reason that Friedrich Nietzsche calls the myth a "repose of thinking" ("Faulbett des Denkens") that offers itself as an alternative to "cold abstraction" and "strict science."[17] Myth provides floating fantasy instead of the procrustean bed of thought. Recognition and perception as "penetration into the world in order to gain insight into its nature" are then enemies of the myth.[18] The inductive principle is pitted against the deductive, the dynamic versus the static—enlightenment serves as the explorer of myth. To be sure, C. G. Jung is convinced that even "if it were to happen that all tradition in the world was to be eliminated all at once, . . . the entire system of mythology and religion [would] begin all over again."[19] All enlightenment would be of no use, for it would only destroy the temporary manifestation of the creative impetus, not the impetus itself. One is reminded of Schopenhauer, who posited the irrational of the will as opposed to the optimism of humanism and the enlightenment, and who was convinced that perception can be altered but the will cannot.

Grass's explanatory myth revolves around the fish: the Flounder. Together with the snake, the fish tallies as one of the oldest symbols of mankind. Among those who have investigated that fish is C. G. Jung.[20] The significance he ascribes to it can be measured in the breadth of his analysis. Particularly in the Near and Middle East the fish symbol has a long and colorful history. Its incidence ranges from the Egyptian symbol for the soul, to the Babylonian god Oannes, to the sacred fish feasts in the cult of the Phoenician goddess Derceto-Atargatis (Astarte), whose son was named Ichthys. The role of the fish in Jewish and Christian tradition is also a part of this historical antecedent. The fish has a messianic significance in Jewish belief. Leviathan, the messianic fish signified eucharistic nourishment. In the symbology of Christianity the fish appears as Christ. He too is eaten "eucharistically"; in paradise he is the sustenance of the blessed. An object of veneration, on the one hand, the fish also bears the connotation of uncleanliness and is used to represent hate and *sensuality*. Thus, in the hermeneutical writings of the church fathers Christ shares a number of symbols with the devil, among them the fish shape. Were these darker associations known to Grass? Many things may attest to it.

In the immediate context it is immaterial where the boundary between myth and literature is drawn. Poetic invention begins with the "active involvement" of the individual imagination in the mythological, with the conferral of a subjective significance.[21] Grass's explanatory myth is poetic invention; as a blending of the literary form of both myth and *Märchen* it confirms the interest in the mythological occuring in modern literature.[22] It is well known that the heroes of *Märchen*—a form that is related to the myth in many respects and that cannot be separated from it in principle—undertake wonderful adventures and arrive at their intended goal aided by magical helpers or by unusual means. Animals interact with people as equals and assist in their affairs to the end that wishes are realized in an unexpected fashion. Alfred Döblin,[23] Grass's "teacher" (AL, 60-91) wrote in 1936 that the "present-day form of the *Märchen*" is the novel. In it the author may jockey with his material, for the reality he creates is an "as if." In the "present-day novel" Döblin recognized two interweaving tendencies: one toward the *Märchen* and another toward reportage. Two currents that did not flow from the "ether of the aesthetic," but rather sprung from the "reality of life." For Döblin, "the active, progressive levels" tend toward reportage; the inactive, tranquil, and satiated tend toward the *Märchen*. Just as the dreamer is constantly grappling with the dream material, so the author orders the novel around characters and a course of action. Literature as the "super dream," as a *Märchen* embodying simple, elementary, fundamental situations such as the relationship of the sexes, that is, their conflict.

There is little purpose to searching for a specific "Flounder myth" in antiquity. As a synthesis of universal images and structures fundamental to several myths, "archetypal patterns,"[24] Grass's explanatory myth of the Flounder is his own creation: "That . . . was when Awa lived here and only her word counted. The Sky Wolf was angry, because Awa had stolen the fire from him and made herself powerful. The men were all devoted to her. They all wanted to sacrifice to the Elk Cow, and not one of them to the Wolf. So the old Sky Wolf turned himself into a fish. He looked like a common flounder, but he could talk" (F, 294). The (sky) wolf as fish, as a divine principle influencing human lives. Poseidon, the sea-god capable of transforming himself, whose union with Medusa produced the winged horse Pegasus,[25] is certainly a relation of the Flounder: "My role was comparable to that of Poseidon in relation to the Pelasgian Athene—I was expected to assert myself alongside the Awa cult" (F, 70). It was Poseidon, to whom the Flounder appealed after being caught, who enlisted him "as a propagandist" in the fight against "Hera, the Pelasgian Athene, and related exponents of matriarchy" (F, 31). As a "swimming newspaper" (F, 35), he tells of Poseidon and Hera, enlightens the advice-seeker about "mythological gossip" (F, 25-26). Later he "goes on" about "the refinements of Minoan culture," "deplores" that "a seaquake (or the wrath of Poseidon) had recently destroyed the capital city of Knossos," and exclaims, however, that "King Minos was miraculously saved!" (F, 98) and that "the Zeus principle, the male seed, the pure idea triumphed" (F, 96). And thus it is high time that the men of the Baltic create their own myth: the "masculine myth" as "Jovian head-birth" in the "Minoan manner" (F, 98-99). The masculine cult of the "flounder-headed god" arose, substitute for matriarchy, the third breast: "Dissatisfaction set in" (F, 69). The "legend" spreads "that the Flounder—one had only to call him—would grant wishes and give advice. . . ." (F, 85). Just as Beelzebub became the Devil, and daimon became demon, the flounder-headed god, by Christian interpretation, became Satan: the principle of sensuality (F, 86).

As has already been mentioned, the fish as a symbol alludes to the religious (Christ) as well as to the sexual (phallus, mandorla) realm. It represents vitality, rejuvenation, and wisdom.[26] The punishment the Tribunal metes out to the defendant consists of a "memorable," "ritual," "solemn," "grandiose flounder dinner" to be held "at a long table" before the eyes of the prisoner (F, 524). The allusion cannot be ignored: once the emancipation from "ever-loving womanly care" had been achieved, he and his ilk would be "simmered in white wine seasoned with capers . . . and served on Dresden china" (F, 31). The Flounder feast, conceived as punishment, is a symbolic act: a "communion" of sorts. Is this parody on Christ's sacrificial death or on Christ's Last Supper with the believers? It comes through more clearly elsewhere: "Verily I say unto you . . ." (F, 296). The Flounder is then "eucharistic" food as indicated in fish mythology.

The narrator calls the Flounder, who has pledged himself to the male cause and who is as old as the eel (F, 226), an "omniscient Flounder, who advised, taught, and indoctrinated me . . . and told me in no uncertain terms

how to . . . teach the womenfolk to suffer in cheerful silence" (F, 30). It was
under his influence that "we became men. . . . men with principles who invented their own enemies, loved honor for honor's sake, and yet saw themselves in the mirror of irony" (F, 33). Embodying the "male principle" (F,
322), or more precisely, "the principle of male domination" (F, 177), the
Flounder is presented as "the male *Zeitgeist*" (F, 408), inventor of "the Prometheus story" (F, 50), for whom "fire is masculine thought and action in
one" (F, 51). As (twisted) "reason" (F, 54) he deprived woman of "a logic of
her own" (F, 133). As the narrator's "foster father" (F, 133) and advocate
of the male cause, he effects the end of "matriarchal absolutism" (F, 132).
From the third mammary, the "fatherless matriarchate" (F, 39), when "only
matriarchy held sway" (F, 10), to the "patriarchal self-justification" (F, 23)
of "male divinity" (F, 68). In place of the third breast the "eel," who, tired
of the male cause, voluntarily forces his way into the (female) fishtrap. An allusion, of course, to the dropping off of the corresponding organ as the expression of male realization of the individuation principle, of the appearance
of the "recent male deity who went by the name of Ryb" (F, 86)—a punning
allusion to the phallic quality of the "floundergod" (F, 87). With the Flounder as god of males, "dull reality" (F, 69) has made its entrance, to be escaped (return to the mother myth)[27] by means of fly agaric mushrooms, collected and dried by a female hand.[28]

With the help of Christianity, hostile to women and favorable to men,
the Flounder had achieved the complete elimination of female domination.
Since Christianity, however, relies on "alternate fasting and feasting" (F,
132), a remnant of female domination would nevertheless have to be tolerated
in the future in the form of jurisdiction over hearth (kitchen) and home.
Woman's sphere of activity is reduced to kitchen and bedroom, to recipes and
dream-inducing mushrooms—last island in a sea of male conquistadorism,
brimming with the "spirit of violence" (F, 518). The "life-negating" principle (F, 518) is victorious over the life-affirming one, that is, woman. The
Flounder seeks to join their side: "Never again . . . In the future I will . . ."
(F, 517). In order to attain this goal he outlines once again the stark contrast
between man and woman: "Women have no need to worry about immortality, because they embody life; men, on the other hand, can only survive outside themselves, by building a house, planting a tree, doing a deed, falling
gloriously in battle, but after first begetting babies. Persons who can't give
birth to children are at best presumptive fathers; nature has not done well by
them" (F, 397). They set their "ersatz babies" (F, 396-97), their milestones
"on the treadmill known as history" (F, 396) up against the eternal cycle of
conception birth, and death, against nature, against life. Which has led to the
present state of affairs of "everywhere . . . madness impersonating reason"
(F, 453). Male pregnancy gives birth to the "categorical imperative" (F, 397);

only men can "antedate death as birth into the unknown" (F, 397). In brief, the Flounder is "the destructive, life-negating, murderous, male, warlike principle," as one of the female prosecutors says (F, 518).

The age of the Flounder is the brazen age; it dispels the timelessness of the Golden Age of the matriarchate, of paradise. The Flounder teaches counting, algebra (F, 28); the theoretical reason of the male world supplants the practical reason of the matriarchy (F, 46). "I admit," the narrator has the Flounder recapitulate, "that on my advice the oppressed male terminated many thousands of years of historyless female domination by resisting the servitude of nature, by establishing principles of order, replacing incestuous and therefore chaotic matriarchy with the discipline of patriarchy, by introducing Apollonian reason, by beginning to think up utopias, to take action, and to make history" (F, 46). There is the innuendo of the evil one: history versus "historylessness," order versus chaos, Apollo versus Dionysus, utopia verses melancholy—Hegel versus Schopenhauer. A dualism emerges that warrants inquiry. Hence: Why is it thus? On "principle" (F, 397) men discover and destroy; on principle women are "mothers," life-dispensing child-bearers and life-sustaining cooks: melancholic collectresses. "Death wish" (F, 519) versus life wish; the male, destructive principle versus the female, protective principle. It was determined such at the ultimate source, in the "primordial darkness" (F, 41), from which the Flounder emerges. The "will" wills it that way.[29]

The narrator confirms my previous hypotheses by having the Flounder emerge from the "shadowy, in-between realm of the subconscious" (B, 50; missing in F). As the embodiment of the urge that bade Adam to eat of the Tree of Knowledge, he led mankind out of paradise, where the question of meaning did not yet exist—and consequently no melancholy either—where things were still identical with one another. With its just under six hundred pages *The Flounder* is a most voluble, indeed garrulous, book. In any case, anyone who would exclusively fault the author for this loquaciousness, would be guilty of a *faux pas* of poetic logic. It has a function in the mythologizing process. Thus, it is not merely that the Flounder is omniscient; another characteristic gives rise to his volubility. He likes to tell "amusing little anecdotes" (F, 48), to engage in "gossip" (F, 26). His mirthful banter runs the gamut from the aetiological explanation of Earthmother Awa's name (F, 53), to the phallic mangel-root business (F, 72), the frequently heralded breaking winds (F, 135, 205, 210, 478), the biting-off of the testicle (F, 195), the vaginal transubstantiation (F, 209), gossip on impotence (F, 375), the snapped noose (F, 421-22), all the way to the notion of frying eggs in Ilsebill's "belly fat" (F, 536), which is exposed during her Caesarean—a notion that may, however, be reckoned to the account of the narrator. It might be apt to term these facetious anecdotes obscene or racy jokes. For the most part they are, quite obviously, the silliest, dullest, or corniest of jokes—"chestnuts." Their function may be to emphasize the situation; the amusing effect they aim at is merely comic affirmation. Nonetheless, some bounds—if at most only those of so-called "propriety"—are overstepped. Is this the joy of story-telling gone overboard or Rabelaisian provocation? There has to be another explanation.

If one proceeds from the premise that the Flounder is, all told, the embodiment of the instinctual drive, of the will, then he represents sensuality. It has already been demonstrated that this interpretation accords with the traditional use of the fish symbol. The Flounder's mania for story-telling is more than a part of his defense strategy: it is his essence. Sensuality and loquaciousness (garrulity as leaving nothing unverbalized) belong traditionally together. The history of this association goes far back; it always became manifest when the official Christian order was questioned. Christian moral precepts proscribe the immediate gratification of the instinctual drive—carnal pleasure. As the expression of sensuality, which *per definitionem* stems from the Devil, it represents a deviation from the norm, from the established order. It is the sinful transgression of proper bounds—proper because the Church has established them as such—and its consequence is spiritual as well as physical. Hence the censure of deviant life-styles *and* deviant spirituality that was passed from time to time on the sectarians, libertines, and others.[30] Such deviation was denounced as a manifestation of sexual desire, of a proud life given both to fantasizing and to giving voice to that which was fantasized. These accusations elicited considerable comment in the discussion of the novel. Hence it comes as no surprise that Rabelais also appears in the handbook of the "libertine." The censure passed on others applied to him too: that he reeled "unsteadily between his idle and frivolous fantasies."[31] It may also be said then of the Flounder that "frivolous anecdotes" alternate with "grotesque episodes" in his flow of words (F, 217). But in the seventeenth century the reproach against disobedience, curiosity, and sensuality was really meant in earnest, whereas the transgressions against which the reproach was once directed have become for Grass mere collapsible scenery that may be best justified as a narrative stratagem. The ornament of sensuality—in spite of the efforts to endow it with a "deeper meaning"—comes across much more as a rather presumptuous end in itself like an oversized clove of garlic used in a dish concocted to regale the gourmet's palate.

The apostrophization of the Flounder as "super-Hegel," "*Weltgeist*," and the allusion to the principle of Apollo and Zeus brings the name Hegel into play. It is already well known how aggressively the antitheoretical, anti-ideological creator of *The Flounder* rejects Hegel and his consequences. The basis for this hostile image certainly seems to be an imperfect understanding of Hegel, predicated only on the precepts of the objective spirit and the "consequent absolution of the individual from personal responsibility in favor of a state responsible unto itself, and of historical progress as something unaffected by the conscious efforts of the individual to influence it."[32] Grass's criticism of ideology in general focuses merely (and inadequately) on Hegel. History is interpreted as the history of the *Weltgeist* that negates individual significance. The myth of the *Weltgeist* and the belief in it—which eradicates reason and delivers history over to the knifepoint of the tragic—are indicted. From what position does Grass criticize and by what means does he propose to combat the effect of the *Weltgeist* (a concept I do not advocate)?

It has already been mentioned: the principle of the snail,[33] the very picture of tedious as well as individual progress and locomotion. The aptness of the image must be considered.[34]

Probationary schoolmaster Hermann Ott, central character of the novel *From the Diary of a Snail*, who searches for years for proof that depression is curable (DS, 274), is depicted as a disciple of Schopenhauer. He writes philosophical treatises, "which for the most part picked bones with Hegel and drew inspiration from Schopenhauer" (DS, 38). As a guide in Schopenhauer's birthplace Ott explains "Schopenhauer's melancholy as the heritage of a family of Hanseatic merchants" (DS, 24). Ott wants to go beyond Hegel with Schopenhauer (DS, 46). "It appears that even before his university days snail collector Ott had learned from Schopenhauer to put observation first and knowledge second and to avoid the Hegelian method of proving preconceived knowledge by the results of observation" (DS, 45). Such a reference to Schopenhauer, when it has to do with (inductive) reasoning, has to be surprising, not to say shocking. Doubt, the melancholiac, sides with Schopenhauer and his "skeptical view" (DS, 26) as opposed to the "ignoramuses who with Hegel hurry past Schopenhauer" (DS, 301); like Schopenhauer he sees himself as a victim of Hegelian philosophy. For Schopenhauer the inventor of the *"Weltgeist"* was a "dull, spiritless, nauseatingly repulsive, ignorant charlatan." What he "scribbled with unprecedented impudence, conceit, and absurdity" has had as its consequence the "intellectual ruin" of an entire generation.[35] The future, the proponent of the "will" predicts, will bring the truth to light about the "mind-perverter" Hegel. But time was on Hegel's side, whose thought, among other things, exerted a molding influence on the character of the Prussian state. The powerless, melancholic bourgeoisie, of course, felt themselves more or less at one in suffering with Schopenhauer[36]—even if the prime premise of reality for Hegel is love, which in the form of the dialectic rules the world. Nascent self-consciousness—which Hermann Ott (and Günter Grass) quite clearly understands as little as Hegel's contemporary and rival Schopenhauer—follows the laws of the dialectic. On the other hand it is a fact that Hegel, who through his philosophizing became the personification of the *Weltgeist*, failed to recognize the "chaotic element" of sensuality in mankind. A failing that Schopenhauer corrects when he counters Hegel's optimism, his "genuinely profligate way of thinking" (that Schopenhauer considers a "bitter mockery of the nameless suffering of mankind") with his own philosophy of the "melancholic and inconsolable."[37] The will appears as the innermost essence of mankind: a blind, irresistible impulse, the objective manifestation of which is "nature." From the insight into suffering and misery that characterize human life arises compassion, the feeling of responsibility, the prerequisite for human love. The last of which may be the reason for Ott's attraction to Schopenhauer. Like the novelist Grass later, the author of *The World as Will and Illusion* sees the agent of history in man's "humanness." It is this trait that gives rise to melancholy—a melancholy born of recognition of the denial of (male) order and its conventions. If the basic tone of resignation that characterizes the epic works of Grass can also be discerned, in spite of itself, in the reconciliation of the principles of melancholy and utopia in *From the Diary of a Snail*, then *The Flounder*, in a *tour de force*, presents melancholy and depression as a "female ailment." Men—active, ambitious, exercising power, and pursuing utopias—are immune to it. Thanks to the advice and assistance accorded them by the Flounder. Female melancholy is the price for insatiable male domination.[38]

Behind the Hegel-Schopenhauer dualism is yet another dichotomy. Among the topics on which the omniscient Flounder lectures is that of "culture and civilization" (F, 238). He does so from an "enlightened bourgeois approach . . . relatively progressive," as even the (female) prosecutor must acknowledge (F, 333). Even if the narrated material is presented from various, jumbled perspectives, it is obvious that the male cause and that of civilization are one and the same (F, 517). Grass draws a distinction between culture and civilization: "culture" as a potential male achievement is surmised with a question mark and disparaged with a "Yes, if you will" (F, 397). Civilization appears as the destructive application of the "unto death" principle of reason (B, 659; the rendering in F, 519 is unsatisfactory).[39] Only in German has "civilization" taken on a counter-meaning to "culture." Kant was the first to make use of the antithesis.[40] He reckons the "idea of mortality"—which according to Schopenhauer is the only possible help for mankind—as "still belonging to culture." Wilhelm von Humboldt employs the contrast in the sense of "internal" and "external." And for Oswald Spengler, civilization is culture's phase of perversion and disintegration: civilization as a "termination"; it follows "the process of development like the end-product, life like death." In fact it is Spengler who utters this and not the Flounder while defending himself before the Tribunal.[41] Both civilization and culture are classed under the rubric of "betterment" in German, yet above and beyond that they are related to different concepts: culture is ascribed to "taste"; civilization to "custom," "convention."[42] Regulation, expediency on the one hand; tact, sensibility on the other: that which has organically grown is opposed to that which has been artificially created. The analogies to the poles of Grass's system of reference are conspicuous.

Is a new, revisionist rendition of Thomas Mann's concept of the aforementioned dichotomy being served up here?[43] The central theme of the cultural-political polemic, in which Thomas Mann developed his thoughts on the democratic form of government in the modern era (1918), is the antithesis between culture and civilization,[44] the individual and society. The (male) corporate state instead of (female) democracy, the (western) peoples of disintegration and "destruction," of reason and "rhetoric," instead of the (German) "people of life." Doesn't the contrast recur in Grass as the antithesis between the (female) principle of affirmation of existence, of life, and (male) destructive civilization, populated "with rhetorical figures" (F, 517)? Patience versus force (F, 53), Dionysian versus Apollonian (F, 46), practical reason versus theoretical (F, 29), sensibility (taste) versus (rationalizing) intellect, historylessness versus history (F, 46), nature versus "principles of order" (F, 46)? The melancholy of woman versus the utopia of man (F, 46).

Among the topics for discussion, by one of the women's groups is that of the "Great Leap, which was said to have already begun" (F, 334-35), "not a precipitate action," but rather "a continuous process, unfolding in several phases" (F, 335). In the next paragraph, as a contrasting illustration, the author has Ilsebill leap over a ditch: corresponding to that "unfathomable law," which he does not understand, "that governs her actions" (F, 335). She falls. The narrator would have liked to engrave her in copper as a "leaping *Melencolia*": her "defiant goat face, as if the whole world had offended her" (F, 335). Melancholy appears as the expression of powerlessness, sadness, pessimism. Depression, "well-deep," prevails when, for the women celebrating Father's Day in the Grunewald Forest, the preliminary euphoria has passed (F, 481). First the "male competition" (of women) takes place (F, 471), then the leap onto the "phallic pine tree" (F, 472), then the question as to "the meaning of it all" (F, 481), then the " aftertaste of absurdity" (F, 480). And finally Billy's Father's Day realization: "I am a woman, a woman, a woman!" (F, 492)—the jubilation of "normality." In the end, the devastating rape as the extreme form of the perversion of the aggressive male will: "lust" (F, 520). The circle closes brutally.

On the advice, and under the influence, of the Flounder the male had learned to "think up utopias" (F, 46). The side-effect of male domination is female melancholy. What could possibly reconcile them? Hardly the intrusion of woman into the male utopia, as it is portrayed in an absurd fashion in the description of the Father's Day celebration and the business with the artificial penis (F, 464-65).[45] Something new would have to take shape that cannot be found in *The Flounder*. The women succumb to the same mistakes as the men; they turn to the Flounder, who, tired of the male cause, had rammed his upper lip through a blade of "a pair of sexless nail scissors" (F, 36). The new possibility was alluded to in *From the Diary of a Snail*: the reconciliation between circle and straight line, fire and water, the active and passive principles as a spiral, snaillike transformation that evolved from reason and will.[46] However: in the realm of an axiomatically fixed will the vicious circle cannot be broken, the horizon remains obscured. As Schopenhauer says: "the individual is nothing more than his [or her] will." It determines "perception" and "intellect," which is merely an "organ" of the will; its "sense antennae to external stimuli." The will is and remains paramount, the "snail" to which the "antennae" belong.[47] The evolution principle finally reveals itself as utopia. Perpetual recurrence as the final word: melancholy, which creates utopias, creates that which "did away with the sexes and the battle of the sexes: equalized and harmonized, free from hatred of father's suspenders, free from hatred of mother's apron" (DS, 232). For the story of the Flounder or of the perversion of the male principle and the vitality of the female principle ends at the threshold of renewed perversion: the fishtrap instead of the eel.

Notes

1. See Manfred Jurgensen, *Über Günter Grass*, pp. 6, 179; Gertrude Cepl-Kaufmann, *Günter Grass*, p. 215.
2. Hans Reiss, ed., *Kant's Political Writings*, trans. H. B. Nisbett (Cambridge: Cambridge Unversity Press, 1977) p. 54.
3. Cepl-Kaufmann, *Günter Grass*, p. 12.
4. Cepl-Kaufmann, p. 4.
5. Cepl-Kaufmann, p. 204.
6. Helmut Koopmann, "Günter Grass: Der Faschismus als Kleinbürgertum und was daraus wurde," p. 180.
7. According to Jurgensen, *Über Günter Grass*, p. 182, for Grass the "historical reality" of progress could "never be rendered comprehensible by any philosophical system."
8. Cepl-Kaufmann, pp. 181, 165: "The general tone of resignation in the author's prose works is readily discernible in the immediately conspicuous basic premises, which simultaneously determine the structure of the work."
9. Cepl-Kaufmann, p. 78.
10. Concerning the snail as a symbol, see Max Horkheimer and Theodor W. Adorno, *Dialektik der Aufklärung* (Frankfurt am Main: S. Fischer, 1969), p. 274, who compare the "spiritual life" with the "antennae of the snail," its "feeling face." See also *Dialectic of Enlightenment*, trans. John Cumming (New York: Herder and Herder, 1972).
11. Friedrich Schlegel, *Dialogue on Poetry and Literary Aphorisms*, trans., introd., Ernst Behler and Roman Struc (University Park: The Pennsylvania State University Press, 1968), p. 85.

12. Friedrich Nietzsche, *The Birth of Tragedy and the Case of Wagner*, trans. Walter Kaufmann (New York: Vintage Books, 1967), pp. 127, 135.
13. Karl Kerényi, "Was ist Mythologie," *Europäische Revue*, 15 (June 1939), 17.
14. Karl Kerényi, *Wesen und Gegenwärtigkeit des Mythos* (Munich and Zurich: Droemer and Knaur, 1965), p. 129.
15. Adolf Ellegard Jensen, "Echte und ätiologische (explanatorische) Mythen," *Die Eröffnung des Zugangs zum Mythos. Ein Lesebuch*, ed. Karl Kerényi (Darmstadt: Wissenschaftliche Buchgesellschaft, 1967), p. 268.
16. Jensen, p. 270.
17. Friedrich Nietzsche, "Wissenschaft und Weisheit im Kampfe," *Sämtliche Werke*, ed. Karl Schlechta, Vol. III (Munich: Hanser, 1956), p. 335.
18. André Jolles, "Mythe," *Die Eröffnung des Zugangs zum Mythos*, pp. 199, 203.
19. C. G. Jung, "Über die zwei Arten des Denkens," *Wandlungen und Symbole der Libido* (Leipzig and Vienna: Deuticke, 1912), p. 27.
20. See Carl Gustav Jung, *Aion: Untersuchungen zur Symbolgeschichte* (Zurich: Rascher, 1951).
21. Wilhelm Wundt, "Unterschied zwischen Mythos und Dichtung," *Die Eröffnung des Zugangs zum Mythos*, p. 138.
22. Rainer Stillers, "Erzählen als Mythologie. Zur Rolle mythologischer Motive im Werk Maurice Blanchots," *Elemente der Literatur: Beiträge zur Stoff-, Motiv- und Themenforschung. Elisabeth Frenzel zum 65. Gebutstag*, ed. Adam J. Bisanz and Raymond Trousson, Vol. II (Stuttgart: Kröner, 1980), p. 159.
23. Alfred Döblin, "Der historische Roman und wir," *Aufsätze zur Literatur* (Olten: Walter, 1963), pp. 166, 183.
24. John J. White, *Mythology in the Modern Novel: A Study of Prefigurative Techniques* (Princeton: Princeton Unversity Press, 1971), p. 38.
25. Edward Tripp, *Reclams Lexikon der antiken Mythologie* (Stuttgart: Reclam, 1974), p. 446.
26. See also Carl Gustav Jung, *Symbols of Transformation*, Vol. V of *Collected Works*, 2nd ed. (Princeton: Princeton University Press, 1956), p. 198; Juan E. Cirlot, *A Dictionary of Symbols*, trans. Jack Sage, 2nd ed. (New York: Philosophical Library, 1971), pp. 106-107.
27. See Carl Gustav Jung, "Mythendeutung," *Die Eröffnung des Zugangs zum Mythos*, p. 169: "dreams, dream visions, fantasies, and delusions" are the ultimate origin of all mythology; the archetype of the "Earthmother," which appears in *The Flounder* as "Awa," is one of the constants common to all of them.
28. Kerényi, "Das Wesen des Mythos," *Die Eröffnung des Zugangs zum Mythos*, p. 245. According to Kerényi, the use of mushrooms (*Psilocybe Mexicana*) is one way of opening up the dimension of the myth. See also F, 69, 77, 102, 352, and elsewhere.
29. See also DS, 155: "In his cellar Doubt . . . pursued his will. He wanted something, didn't want something. He wanted to want something, wanted not to want something. And his will to want something was preceded by another will that wanted or didn't want to want something."
30. See Gerhard Schneider, *Der Libertin. Zur Geistes- und Sozialgeschichte des Bürgertums im 16. und 17. Jahrhundert* (Stuttgart: Metzler, 1970), p. 57.
31. Schneider, p. 191.
32. See Cepl-Kaufmann, *Günter Grass*, p. 118.
33. Concerning the image of the snail in the works of Günter Grass, see Cepl-Kaufmann, p. 247, nn. 69-70.

34. See my forthcoming article "Doppelleben zwischen Evolution und ewiger Wiederkehr: Zum postgastropodischen Werk von Günter Grass," *Colloquia Germanica*.

35. See Wilhelm Weischedel, *Die philosophische Hintertreppe: 34 grosse Philosophen in Alltag und Denken*. 6th ed. (Munich: dtv, 1980), p. 251.

36. Concerning the ongoing reception of Schopenhauer, see my afterword to Thomas Bernhard, *Der Wetterfleck* (Stuttgart: Reclam, 1976), pp. 63-65.

37. Weischedel, *Die philosophische Hintertreppe*, p. 267.

38. Concerning melancholy as the result of exclusion from real power, see Wolfgang Lepenies, *Melancholie und Gesellschaft* (Frankfurt am Main: Suhrkamp, 1969), p. 118; concerning work and activities as a remedy for depression, see Arnold Gehlen, *Der Mensch: Seine Natur und seine Stellung in der Welt* (Berlin: Junker und Dünnhaupt, 1940); see further Lepenies's discussion of Gehlen, p. 232.

39. Concerning the "self-destruction of the Enlightenment," see Horkheimer and Adorno, *Dialektik der Aufklärung*, p. 15.

40. W. Perpeet, "Kultur, Kulturphilosophie," *Historisches Wörterbuch der Philosophie*, Vol. IV, ed. Joachim Ritter and Karlfried Gründer (Basel and Stuttgart: Schwabe, 1976), col. 1309-1324.

41. Oswald Spengler, *Der Untergang des Abendlandes*, 32nd ed. (Munich: Beck, 1932), pp. 42-43. See also *The Decline of the West*, trans. Charles Francis Atkinson (New York: Knopf, 1932).

42. Wehrle-Eggers, *Deutscher Wortschatz* (Frankfurt am Main and Hamburg: Fischer Bücherei, 1968), pp. 658, 850.

43. Thomas Mann, *Betrachtungen eines Unpolitischen* (Frankfurt am Main: S. Fischer, 1956). See also Otto F. Best, *Das verbotene Glück: Kitsch und Freiheit in der deutschen Literatur* (Munich: Piper, 1978), pp. 171-79.

44. See Jürgen Rothenberg, "Grosses 'Nein' und kleines 'Ja': *Aus dem Tagebuch einer Schnecke*," p. 147: Grass's address on the occasion of the five hundredth anniversary of Albrecht Dürer's birth "may, in many respects, be appropriate, but at the same time, . . . it places too much emphasis on the negative results of our civilization."

45. See Grass's reference to the melancholy of the "suburban widow" and her intimacy with the "object made of India rubber, supplied by certain mail-order houses" (DS, 296).

46 Concerning the snail as the embodiment of the active and passive principles, as the symbol of the spiral reconciling circle and straight line, see my article mentioned above, n. 34.

47. Arthur Schopenhauer, "Über die Freiheit des Willens," in *Kleinere Schriften*, Vol. III of *Sämtliche Werke* (Stuttgart and Frankfurt am Main: Insel, 1962), p. 625.

The Swan Song of a Male Chauvinist

Erhard Friedrichsmeyer

Initially, the narrator of *The Flounder* tells us, he meant to write a history of foodstuffs and nourishment (F, 147). Befitting the original idea, the novel opens with a meal, shared by the narrator and his wife. But here as everywhere in Grass's monumental tale, food and its history, cooking and recipes, though a formidable stratum in the narrative, are overshadowed by much more private concerns. The narrator has problems with women. The history of food and feeding is the antidote the speaker as artist applies to his problems as a man. In the artist's vision, women stand central in a counter-proposal to history as we generally understand it.[1] As the narrator invents the lives and deeds of a number of women cooks, not violence but care is the essence of this alternate perception of history. Never having been told before in this fashion, it is an imaginative chronicle the narrator is fully qualified to tell. He is a cook as well as a writer.

The civilizing value of the food story is prefigured in the opening scene in which the meal is a calming prelude to the main event, a skirmish in the battle of the sexes. After eating shoulder of mutton with beans and pears, the narrator and his wife procreate. Though it is an act "in love," its choreography points more to the harshness of combat than to the tenderness of harmony: "And so we lay down, arming and legging each other around, as we have done since time immemorial. Sometimes I, sometimes she on top. Equal, though Ilsebill contends that the male's privilege of penetrating is hardly compensated by the female's paltry prerogative of refusing admittance" (F, 4). If the combatants appear to be equal in this duel, it becomes more and more certain as their story unfolds that the narrator is losing in the "Armageddon of the sexes," as the male-female relationships in *The Flounder* have been described.[2] His marriage is under terminal strain; he is, all in all, an attested to, and even self-admitted failure (F, 39, 149).[3] In the closing scene of the book there is also an act of procreation; but now the speaker is hardly more than a device for artificial insemination. To his partner, Maria Kuczorra, he is "nobody" (F, 104).

The narrator's apology for what he as a man has bungled, his proposal of history as cooking, marks an historical turning point. It is a leitmotif of *The Flounder* that the era of male domination is at an end. The future belongs to women. The narrator's stories about foodstuffs and his women cooks may constitute an acquittal on the grounds of good intentions to some of the novel's readers, but to the women in the speaker's life they are more like an ineffectual rear guard action. In the last analysis, the women find them inconsequential, entertaining at best, boring at worst. Maria Kuczorra, his indifferent sex partner in the book's closing episode, seems equally indifferent to his stories. She rather listens to the words of the Flounder who in Grass's adaptation of the Grimm Brothers' tale, "The Fisherman and His Wife," now no longer functions as adviser and confidant to men, but of women. The words of the Flounder can make this somber woman laugh again. But rather than cheering the narrator, this laughter seems to imply a threat. We do not know what the fish says, but the male reader is likely to feel worried. Maria, emerging from her consultation with the Flounder, becomes a woman *per se*, a forboding figure in her total obliviousness to the man with whom she has just mated. In the context of Grass's *oeuvre*, Maria merges with that sinister *Urbild* of woman who dominates the end of *The Tin Drum*, the black cook. From the male point of view, *The Flounder* ends on a threatening, even a somewhat apocalyptic note.

The fiction of history as cooking can be read without misgivings only if we believe it to undermine the cliché that places women in the kitchen, thus "in their place." The negative stereotype disappears indeed if we focus on the cooks' role as contributors to a counterhistory. But in another perspective, the women do not escape the confines of cliché, notwithstanding their unquestionable dominance over the men in their lives. They are creatures shaped by an unmistakably male imagination. Small wonder, for the cooks are conceived in the narrator's own image; they are his *Kopfgeburten*, or "headbirths," incubated parallel and in response to his wife's pregnancy. His paternity is indelibly stamped upon them in the mark of male stereotyping. He does his wife one, or in fact, nine—or eleven—better when he gives birth to his nine—or eleven—cooks. So potent is he that they remain his creatures for life. He is not only their progenitor, but their mate as well, for he projects himself into their lives as lover or husband. As author or mate, he reduces them to some of the oldest patterns of masculine typecasting: There are the primeval mothers, Awa and Wigga, suckling their men as babes. There is the opposite cliché, the avenging furies Mestwina and Sophie Rotzoll.

Because of her disinterest in marriage and family, Dorothea of Montau is disfigured to the contours of a fanatic. Agnes Kurbiella is the woman as clay, given identity by the male of her first sexual encounter, here grotesquely so by a man initiating a gang-rape. Amanda Woyke, an independent-minded woman with little respect for her bungling husband, nonetheless submits to one pregnancy after another whenever her man, insignificant though he is, returns home the hero from some battle. Lena Stubbe is a socially conscious, indeed class-conscious, person who authors a proletarian cookbook, yet submits to weekly beatings by her husband as if succumbing to a fate natural to her sex. Worse, she is loyal to him even when he becomes the cheapest of thieves.

Among the nine "invented" cooks—Sibylle Miehlau and Maria Kuczorra are contemporaneous figures in the life of the narrator— seemingly the exception to male chauvinist framing is Fat Gret. She is a comic heroine and since literature lacks comic protagonists—as the Flounder states[4]—we are to think that Fat Gret is unprecedented, thus not stereotyped. The opposite is true. She is the mirror image of the boisterous, lustful, crafty, obscene, and gluttonous male comic figure of literature, a cross between Falstaff and Gargantua. In short, she is unmistakably a male derivative, not a "female companion piece," as the Flounder has us believe (F, 218).

Despite their reduction to stereotype, it must be emphasized, these cooks are presented as heroines one and all; they tower above the men around them. Men in *The Flounder* do hold power collectively, but individually they are a sorry lot. Since above all the speaker is no exception, male inadequacy becomes transparent as the personal cause for his condescension toward women, be they real or imagined. The most obvious example of this reductive attitude is the name he confers upon his wife. He calls her Ilsebill, because of its negative associations with the fairy tale mentioned above, a virtual impossibility as a given name.[5] Rather it is an insult by which the narrator labels his wife the eternal nag, lusting for riches, social status and dominance. Actually, her cravings are hardly excessive; she insists on an automatic dishwasher, some vacation travel, and on her husband's presence at the birth of their child. In essence, she runs afoul of her husband because she has a will of her own. Thus she rejects the identification with Awa (F, 4), the primeval mother, sensing, it must be assumed, that she is being typecast. When the narrator, on the other hand, reincarnates himself time and again, it is an attempt at self-elevation, a fictive triumph of male permanency as lover and husband. His historical omnipresence is to overshadow the sum of inadequacies he reaps in each of his life spans. Since the speaker heavily stresses his role as sexual partner in all his reincarnations, his projections into historical permanence are, moreover, much in line with the male fantasy of the omnipotent lover. So dear is this fantasy to him that he resorts to it also in order to offset his insignificant role during the trial of the Flounder. He insists that he has bedded the entire Women's Tribunal (F, 380).

If so far the case for the narrator's chauvinism toward women has been made in terms of examples rather than extended argument, it is because the obvious needs only be glossed, not proved. The narrator himself is quite open about his attitudes. When he has some of the female characters merge with Ilsebill, he underlines her role as synecdoche: women, one and all, are shrews, forever pestering men with their quirks and demands. When the narrator—and also Grass, for the two are never very far apart if the narrator is willing to tell us he is at work on a book entitled *The Flounder* (F, 453)—makes no attempt to disguise his negative feelings about women, offensive though they must be to many of his readers, there must be good reason for doing so. We can rule out the possibility that he is an unabashed male supremacist, for time and again he counteracts his antifeminine stereotypes by equivocation. Nonetheless one can speak only rarely of true objectivity in his posture or of an effective dialectic in his presentation of the male and female views. The portrayal of Dorothea of Montau is a case in point. The zealot is painted in lively if not garish colors, at length and with passion, while the apology of her as a woman in search of liberation is a rather perfunctory and paltry exercise in evenhandedness (F, 167). To the reader, the fanatic is the person, the quester for self-liberation the shadow.

Granting that it is not the perverse pride of a male supremacist that accounts for the openness of the narrator's bias, I suggest that it is a proclivity for the truth, however troublesome. Without doubt his frankness tarnishes him, yet to the writer that honesty is essential if he intends to make his world transparent. The speaker's truthfulness has two aspects here: one is its implication that no man or woman can escape living his or her life without being trapped by the patterns a world of male dominance has wrought over the ages; the other is that a serious novel whose central theme is the relationship of the sexes cannot have a narrator feigning neutrality if he takes part in the plot. The alternative, a narrative voice equivocating from a neutral, androgynous zone, would be a presumptuous form of charlatanism.

Irritating or even offensive though Grass's novel must be to any reader who has any sympathy at all for the aims of feminism, so far very few serious critics seem to have condemned it wholesale on these or any other grounds. One simply cannot deny that it contains superb episodes and characterizations, given with a degree of stylistic vitality rarely equalled in contemporary fiction. I submit one must grant this even to the novel's most offensive segment, the " Father's Day" chapter. Its effectiveness is rooted in Grass's virtuoso exploitation of the grotesque. The formula here is total subjugation of the women figures to masculine perspectives of dominance. It is quite obvious to the reader that Grass's use of the strategies of the grotesque springs from the fear that feminism is about to pervert its aims. He seems to believe that women wish to achieve dominance on male terms, emulating the worst masculine traits, and thereby inviting a backlash of horror. Although the women in this scene are largely the agents of their own demeaning, it is the narrator (as author, since he is not a witness to the scene) who prescribes their activities, if not their fate. It is difficult to imagine at this stage of women's liberation that a female author would envision the movement in terms of *mundus perversus*. Grass's judgment rests not so much on a presence of fact, but on a future imagined. Therefore his vision of horror seems not so much a warning against potentially dangerous trends, as it seems a punishment for crimes not yet committed. When one of the women, for example, climbs a pine tree, laboring at its top to achieve orgasm, the incident as metaphor is impaling by phallus. The metaphor contains its own brutal justification: Women ask for it. Here the woman has gone to the tree, not the tree to her.

The strain of male chauvinism in *The Flounder* is much too pronounced to have gone unnoticed. Yet only a few critics have taken Grass to task on the issue. Gunzelin Schmid Noerr, one of the few, is certain that readers sympathetic to feminism will see Grass as a male chauvinist. His women are either "strapping" and "lascivious," in charge of bed and kitchen, or else they are reduced to "anemia" and "quarrelsomeness." Noerr judges *The Flounder* primarily in psycho-political terms, as the "patriarchy's attempt to last a little longer by means of self-criticism," and as the "deliriousness of a man who, no longer taken seriously by women, pours forth a flood of words . . . in order to prevail against woman's ever potent . . . nature." Noerr grants value to Grass's "episodes and little tales," but denies that the novel is a successful construct of art because its author failed to make full use of his own principle of structure, to Noerr the interplay of three dimensions of experience: history, the contemporary context, and the confrontation with the feminists.[6] G. P. Butler is willing to give *The Flounder* more credit as a novel, but also registers a strong protest against Grass's attitude toward feminism: "Irritation at the antics and the stridency of certain feminists . . . is a poor excuse, in a writer who expects to be heeded, for trivializing the problems or lampooning the protagonists and supporters of a movement which has rightly changed the world most of us grew up in. . . . the women . . . 'Manzis' (sc. 'emanzipiert') Grass calls them — are presented in far more injurious fashion [than the men], with at best a mixture of affection and condescension . . . . " Convinced that Grass has always been "something of a male chauvinist, even a misogynist," Butler nevertheless thinks that much of what Grass says about the "libbers" is "good rollicking fun," and further, that Grass, although falling short of dealing with feminism in a nonchauvinist fashion, reveals his humanity in the autobiographical accounts of his travels to Gdańsk and India.[7]

It needs to be observed that the travel episodes are not often singled out by critics for praise. It is not the melancholy, subdued, and wistful Grass of the autobiographical accounts that rivets our attention, but the reemerging Grass of old, that is, the writer of *The Tin Drum* — ebullient, aggressive, vital and burlesque. To Marcel Reich-Ranicki the strength of *The Flounder* is its episodic denseness. Grass, he holds, is a highly inventive storyteller, a pastichemaker, not a novelist. He falls off when he does not so much invent as report, for example, in the accounts of his travel to India and Gdańsk, which Reich-Ranicki finds superfluous.[8]

If not dispensable, the travel segments do pale when measured against the purely invented scenes and images. The best passages of *The Flounder* are those in which Grass's imagination is the freest; and when at his most imaginative, he is by no means the least chauvinistic in his treatment of women. In consequence, we must ask if *The Flounder* has literary merit in spite of, or because of, its strain of male chauvinism. Butler seems to think the former; I contend the latter. The narrator's male chauvinist imagination energizes some of the best scenes and episodes. To deny its artistic function and value would be, in a doubly figurative sense, to emasculate Grass's novel.

To make a case for the narrator's male chauvinist imagination as a *sine qua non* in the narrative texture of *The Flounder,* we return to one of its most powerful segments, the "Father's Day" chapter. In spite of the narrator's claims to having been present (F, 96), he does not appear as an eyewitness to, or within earshot of, the events narrated. They are fictive and understood as such by the reader since the intensity of the grotesque achieved gives the chapter much more the mark of fantasy than fact. Central to the "Father's Day" chapter is Sibylle's dildo-rape by her women friends. Walking into the woods after her ordeal, she has an awakening. Some of her thoughts are put in quotation marks. Technically, they are audible; but unless one is the total literary purist, Sibylle's quoted words must be attributed to the narrator's imagination. He is inventing, not reporting. Her ruminations begin as follows: "She felt (so she mumbled to herself) as if the scales had fallen from her eyes. 'It took those bastards to buck some sense into me'" (F, 491). They end in the triumphant and jubilant outcry: "'I'm a woman, a woman, a woman!'" (F, 492).[9]

Noteworthy is that Sibylle credits her friends as males with her new awareness of what is "natural." Though her deliberations are termed "forward-pointing" by the narrator, they indicate anything but a new departure in female consciousness. Her pride in being a woman is a revisionist somersault back into the most ubiquitous cliché of all, the traditional glories of motherhood and domesticity. Keeping in mind that only her shouted words, "I'm a woman," can be assumed to have been heard—by the motorcyclists who are about to kill her—the remainder of her words are the narrator's interpretation of what being a woman means to Sibylle. Quite naturally, we look for irony to offset the odiousness of this portrayal. Is the narrator saying that in our world there is no alternative for Sibylle but to either emulate men or be the "total woman?" If there is this irony, it does not absolve the narrator. He, not Sibylle, is speaking, and it is he who reduces her awakening to cliché. To give him as much license as possible, let us assume he is the satirist who, as Reich-Ranicki observes in his review of *The Flounder,* is allowed anything at all, if the results justify the means.[10] Against this esthetic criterion stands a moral one that imposes limits on the satirist's instincts for punishment: He is not to punish the defenseless. This tabu seems to hold even in our day. Heinrich Böll, for example, subscribes to it in his search for the confines of satire in *Frankfurter Vorlesungen.* The satirist of *The Flounder,* who claims to be "all in favor of the libbers" (F, 6), disregards these boundaries. Although in her rape Sibylle has been made to pay horribly for whatever her aberrations might have been, the satirist dismisses her awakening as cliché. Thus the "moral" satirist who supports feminism is likewise a male chauvinist. By extension the moralist who envisions disaster for the cause of feminism in the "Father's Day" chapter is the male chauvinist who seems to want no liberation for woman at all when he advances the "total woman" as the alternative to surrogate masculinity. The line between him and the horrifying world of the males who people the chapter becomes blurred. In sum, the chapter seems more a vision of woman tried by ordeal than a testimonial to the victims of male supremacy.[11]

For all the misgivings the reader may have about the "Father's Day" chapter, some of its scenes, especially the one discussed here, have stunning power. It is a power that is fueled, above all, by the narrator's male chauvinist imagination, as indicated by the crescendo of the scene discussed above. There is intense emotionality, a mega-punch of violence, pathos and catharsis. The instances of male chauvinism cited above are clearly more intrinsic to the dynamics of an episode than, for example, the narrator's insistence on calling his wife Ilsebill. But because in the Sibylle incident a male chauvinist imagination is at work under the surface, it would be wrong to assume that it is unintentional. If there is near consensus on one trait of Grass's work, it is the critics' conviction that he is a highly conscious artist. Thus it is fitting that in regard to the question of women the narrator confesses to a sense of guilt as *man* and as *author* (F, 147). He signals a self-indictment that encompasses not only social, but artistic attitudes as well. He does not, to put it bluntly, suppress elements of fiction springing from a male chauvinist imagination if he deems the dynamics of the scene demand their inclusion.

For one other example, I would like to turn to the biography of Lena Stubbe, on the whole one of the most sympathetically drawn characters in the novel. Author of a proletarian cookbook, her form of emancipation is class consciousness. Yet the narrator maneuvers her into a position that violates the dictates of that consciousness. Though this formulation seems harsh, I believe it is supported by a critic whom no one would accuse of being reticent in his praise of Grass. In an open letter, Wolfgang Hildesheimer pays tribute to *The Flounder* on the occasion of Grass's fiftieth birthday. Reminiscing that Grass years ago said that the personal judgment of a few friends meant more to him than all printed criticism put together, Hildesheimer declares *The Flounder* a *Jahrhundertbuch* or "novel of the century." Since this monumental tribute is not private communication but public fanfare, it would be an embarrassment of excess were it not laced with irony. Hildesheimer's kudos contains, I believe, a disguised exposé that indicts the narrator *and* Grass, without distinguishing between them, for male chauvinism: "You rarely have been a hero, my friend. You fall off, sometimes miserably, against all too many of your . . . great women." To Hildesheimer, the narrator does not deserve Lena, as she does not deserve the "hypocritically kind rebuff" by her hero August Bebel. Lena's reaction to his refusal to support publication of her cookbook, a resigned "It don't matter," contains for Hildesheimer an "acceptance of a death sentence to her life's work"; it is one of the "hidden deemphasized high points" ("versteckten weggewischten Höhepunkte") of the book.[12] The phrase with which Lena accepts her "death sentence" is a high point played down for these reasons: It minimizes Bebel's insensitivity to Lena's wishes; it minimizes Lena as a person. It is this latter aspect, I believe, that Hildesheimer's irony exposes. Lena's "It don't matter" (F, 438) must be understood as the author's language; it rings of heroic suffering, but is nonetheless painfully implausible. True, Lena submits to the beatings by her husband, knowing that he, dwarfed as he is by her strength of character, needs to elevate himself at her expense. But it is precisely the strength of her character that has enabled this woman to undertake the task of the proletarian cookbook. It is, given her time and place, a feat of formidable tenacity. It does not follow that she would submit so abjectly to what Hildesheimer aptly calls a "death sentence to her life's work." To be sure, she is a modest woman, but she does speak her mind, even to the educated. If she can speak out on her way to Bebel's funeral in the encounter with Rosa Luxemburg and Robert Michels, she can speak out to Bebel. From the perspective of psychological stringency, her response to Bebel seems unlikely indeed. Lena's "It don't matter" does give luminance to the episode, but it moreover shows an author who, in Hildesheimer's words, "falls off miserably" against Lena. If he does not deserve her, the opposite is true as well. Lena does not deserve being forced into the demeaning frame of the woman who is ennobled by sacrificing her

wishes to those of the great man. In Grass's defense one might argue here that
psychological plausibility is secondary to the law of character he has designed
for Lena: She never falters in her care of others. Bebel comes to her worn and
tired, and she cannot help being an aid and comfort to him. Admirable
though this at first seems, this caring, if so relentlessly and self-effacingly
practiced, reveals a conception of character by the author that is dogmatic
and slighting. Is Lena not, ultimately, a derivative of the suckling mother,
which seems to be, after all, Grass's most positive image of woman in this novel?

If Hildesheimer recognizes a male chauvinist at work in *The Flounder,*
how can he call the novel a *Jahrhundertbuch?* Perhaps here the term means
not so much "book of the century," but "book of, or about, a century." Understood as the latter, *The Flounder* might be regarded as an exemplary
chronicle of an age in which male dominance issues into woman's liberation.
Hildesheimer's kudos is best explained as an evaluation of *The Flounder* as a
supremely honest book. Grass not only deals harshly with the narrator, but
also, most importantly, with himself. That Grass is, above all, honest with
himself becomes especially clear if we see him as a satirist, a perspective that
has been alluded to by several critics.[13] Seen as a satirist, Grass undertakes in
The Flounder what satirists worth their salt have done throughout the history
of their craft. At one point or another in their careers they go through the
painful process of revealing themselves in all their misery as being both criminal and judge in the world they attack. Grass's self-indictment is not limited
to labeling himself a failure as a man and author, but it includes self-exposure
of what, in the perspective of the relationship of the sexes, might be termed
the essential Grass: In the very fiber of his craft, Grass has been a male chauvinist writer.

Nevertheless, only the sternest ideologue and moralist would deny that in
The Flounder Grass demonstrates a high degree of artistry. Even when we see
through Lena's "It don't matter" and Sibylle's "I'm a woman" as being authorial straight jackets foisted upon them, there is indeed an element of
pathos in their words. It is the pathos of the victims of the male world, a
world that above all includes the artist as victimizer. Therefore these women
of Grass's imagination reveal a reality more true to the essentials of our world
than a lesser writer's adherence to psychological plausibility in character
development might have shown.

In order for a self-indictment to ring true, it cannot be an exercise in
self-justification. The self-pity of the narrator, surfacing time and again, is to
be dismissed with laughter. If justification is not possible, there can only be
an invocation of justice. The satirist as judge pronounces it by declaring the
dominion of men to be morally bankrupt. Consequently the male chauvinist,
who derives his posture of superiority from the collective social power of the
males, will vanish with that power. *The Flounder* is a swan song. This chroni-

cle of the battle of the sexes does not, as Noerr asserts, attempt to make the patriarchy last a little longer by dint of self-criticism, but graces and hastens its demise by virtue of truthfulness. Grass heeds the Flounder, who advises the narrator on how to make his exit: "'The male cause is bankrupt. Time to knock off, my son. To abdicate. Do it with dignity'" (F, 453).

Grass's penchant for the truth, his labor to make our world transparent, has in at least two instances, I believe, cathartic power over his male chauvinist imagination. In Ms. Schönherr and Ulla Witzlaff he concedes that in our day there are women who have escaped the world of male will and representation. It is worth noting, however, that in their names even these figures come with strings attached, be they ever so weak. Ms. Schönherr, although exercising power, is no man in woman's dress, lording over the trial. Her ample humor, her dignity, her intelligence and competence seem impervious to undercutting. Ulla Witzlaff is great fun to be with, but she is not reduced to "being one of the boys." She is not the prisoner of kitchen, dress code or shrewishness. These two figures lend support to the "third possibility" in the struggle of the sexes alluded to in the book (F, 5). Their suggestion for punishing the Flounder for having supported the excesses of male dominance throughout history is not the justice of that history, the way of the "killer males," nor is it that utopian justice that some feel will come in a peaceable world to be ushered in by women. The Flounder is neither killed nor forgiven. The verdict is instead a pragmatic one, applicable to our time: the Flounder is symbolically killed while actually remaining on trial as adviser to women. He does have, after all, a proven record of working against inequality.[14]

In the hope, however slight, that the Flounder can profit from experience, we might speculate that some day he will be an adviser to both sexes in the struggle against excesses. This novel, as all of Grass's work, rules out a utopian balance; the tension between the sexes will continue. But a Flounder tied neither to male nor female chauvinism may help greatly in the quest for the "third possibility," a workable approximation of balance. A cool head and ironic wit such as his then may even be a model for the male artist's re-emergence without his chauvinist coat of arms. To this end, Grass's novel, understood as the swan song of a male chauvinist, is a persuasive prerequisite.

Notes

1. In an interview with Richard Plant, "Answers by Günter Grass," p. 14, Grass says: "My first notes . . . had to do with food. To me food plays a decisive part in world history. Most historians, however, are more concerned with wars, congresses and ideological hair-splitting. . . . I also discovered that they tended to

slight the contributions of average, anonymous women to history. History is made by men, written by men. . . . From these two sins of omission, I developed the conflict of the sexes."

2. Paul Zweig, "Too Many Cooks," p. 80.
3. "I made messes" (F, 91); in the original: "Ich habe versagt" (B, 115).
4. The translation is slightly amiss here because Manheim mistakes "fehlen" (to lack completely) for "fehlen an" (to be in short supply): "For literature is short on comic female protagonists" (F, 218), does not entirely correspond to: "Denn uns fehlen weibliche Literaturpersonen in komischer Hauptrolle" (B, 275–76).
5. When the narrator's wife signs a telegram to her husband as "Ilsebill" (F, 533), asking him to be present at the birth of their child, she ironically refers to her nature, alleged by her husband, of always making "excessive" and "unreasonable" demands.
6. Gunzelin Schmid Noerr, "Über den Butt," pp. 92–93.
7. G[eoffrey] P. Butler, "Grass Skirts the Issue: A Reaction to *Der Butt*," pp. 26–27.
8. Marcel Reich-Ranicki, "Von dem Grass un synen Fruen," pp. 183, 189.
9. For a more complete quote of the passage in question, albeit in a different context, see Scott H. Abbott, "The Raw and the Cooked: Claude Lévi-Strauss and Günter Grass," above, p. 119.
10. Reich-Ranicki, p. 190.
11. Fritz J. Raddatz, "Wirklicher bin ich in meinen Geschichten. *Der Butt* von Günter Grass," p. 900, devalues this episode as follows: ". . . the only text whose trenchancy one could call merciless, indeed, malicious."
12. Wolfgang Hildesheimer, "Butt und die Welt. Geburtstagsbrief an Günter Grass," pp. 965, 970.
13. See Reich-Ranicki, p. 190, and Morris Dickstein, "An Epic, Ribald Miscellany," p. 12.
14. For a different view of the outcome of the trial, see (this book) Otto F. Best, "On the Art of Garnishing a Flounder with 'Chestnuts'," pp. 140–47, and Helmut Koopmann, "Between Stone Age and Present or The Simultaneity of the Nonsimultaneous," pp. 79–88.

The "Professorial" Flounder: Reflections on Grass's Use of Literary History*

Siegfried Mews

The Flounder has been justifiably called an "historical, encyclopedic, picaresque, satirical . . . novel" that not only offers "a cultural history of cooking . . . [and] a fresco of the political history of a landscape between East and West," but, in addition, a sketchy literary history.[1] Indeed, it is truly amazing how Grass incorporates a wealth of encyclopedic material into his novel—material that was culled from the most diverse branches of extant knowledge, including literature. Even the casual reader—if the complex novel can be read in casual fashion at all—cannot fail to notice the frequent references to writers, works, and characters that pertain to world literature. Thus, for example, Homer and Shakespeare, the *Nibelungenlied (Song of the Nibelungs)* and Boccaccio's *Decameron*, Cervantes' Don Quixote and Grass's own Oskar Matzerath from *The Tin Drum,* are mentioned. Further, a number of poets from two different periods of German literary history make their appearance in the novel as fictionalized characters or are specifically referred to.

It is clear, then, that literature and literary history form an important stratum of the novel and require analysis to elucidate their function and meaning—particularly, since critics have so far mainly contented themselves with registering that "Grass's historical sweep through the ages also involves literature."[2]

To begin with, we may dismiss the notion that Grass amassed his encyclopedic material solely to display his erudition or to engage in an intellectual game for the benefit of those *literati* who will be able "to twig the more exotic references and allusions."³ Although a self-taught person by his own admission, Grass must be considered a *poeta doctus*⁴—though certainly not in the somewhat stodgily respectable mold of a T. S. Eliot or Thomas Mann—a *poeta doctus,* moreover, who constantly acquires new knowledge not for the sake of enshrining it but to use it imaginatively for his artistic purposes.⁵

In fact, Grass's own creature, the Flounder of fairy-tale renown, exhibits a combination of omniscience and self-indulgent garrulousness that lends itself readily to satire. Thus the Flounder displays "his wide reading," which includes "all the intellectual giants from Erasmus to Marxengels" (F, 517), with occasional "scintillating arrogance" (F, 516). From his very first appearance in the novel he maintains his "know-it-all superiority" that makes him "garrulous, . . . nasally professorial, . . . infuriatingly paternal" (F, 44); further, anxious to have his ideas and pithy sayings attributed to the proper source, the Flounder wishes "to be quoted" (F, 103). In the same vein, he lets "his philological fancy run away with him" (F, 44): in short, for the radical feminists, who reject all forms of traditional learning that smack of academia, the Flounder is "nothing but a shitty Germanist!" (F, 253).

Although there is some justification for this hardly flattering appellation, the Flounder does not employ his omniscience for rhetorical effect only; when he is first caught by the fisherman Edek "toward the end of the third millennium before the incarnation of our Lord," he uses his access to "certain information pointing beyond the neolithic horizon" (F, 23) as an enticement for the fisherman to shake off the yoke of Awa's and her successors' benevolent matriarchy and to establish the patriarchal order. Actually, in recalling the beginning of his advisory role to men, the Flounder reduces the problem of female rule versus male rule to the question of "informational superiority" (F, 45). Men finally began to dominate when "those impulses that . . . led to all the manifestations we casually refer to as culture" (F, 45) were set free by abolishing Awa's taboos. Culture does, of course, include literature; hence it is not surprising that the cultured Flounder gives the present-day narrator "literary advice" (F, 413) with regard to the composition of his novel. Since the Flounder is not self-effacing, however, he insists that the book be named after him (F, 413).

To be sure, there is ample justification for entitling the novel *The Flounder.* The present-day narrator, who bears a strong resemblance to the author Grass himself,⁶ informs us that his original concept, "to write about my nine or eleven cooks, some kind of a history of human foodstuffs" had been changed through the Flounder, who provided a "counterweight" (F, 147).⁷ The Flounder who, as a sort of Hegelian *Weltgeist* (F, 150), has promoted the male cause from the Neolithic Age to the beginning of the twentieth century, stands accused as "the destructive, life-negating, murderous, male, warlike principle" (F, 518). By introducing him, Grass could turn the novel into the "great historical accounting . . . the balance sheet" (F, 413) of the relationship of the sexes—the novel's overriding theme that evolves in a complex structure.

Suffice it to sketch the salient structural features that are relevant for our discussion. The external frame of the nine "months" or chapters encompasses three intermingling strata: first, the conception, gestation, and birth of the child of the narrator and his wife Ilsebill—a period of frequent domestic quarrels; second, an analogous conception and birth on the part of the narrator who intellectually delivers himself of his nine or eleven cooks; third, the Flounder's trial before the Women's Tribunal.

Embedded in all three strata of the nine-months time frame is the story and history of the cooks with its vastly expanded time span of approximately 4,000 years. Although ostensibly told by the narrator to his wife Ilsebill in the privacy of their home (F, 3), this history assumes exemplary significance that far surpasses the domestic sphere. It is primarily the trial that offers the author opportunity to examine each of the nine historical cooks in particular and the role of women in its political, socioeconomic, and cultural-literary context in general by contrasting the often diametrically opposed views of the radical feminists on the one hand to those of the Flounder on the other.

To be sure, a semblance of chronological sequence has been preserved by devoting one chapter each (with the exception of the first one) to one specific cook, beginning with neolithic Awa. Nevertheless, the traditional sequence of past, present, and future has been suspended and simultaneity has been elevated to a principle governing the narrative.[8] The constant intermingling of various time levels is reinforced by the present-day narrator's ability to be present simultaneously in various "time-phases," to see Ilsebill in each of the cooks, and, finally, to recognize the women of the Tribunal as embodiments of the cooks.[9]

The highly original structural device and narrative stance are, without doubt, attributable to Grass's conviction that the specific aspect of "reality" he is concerned with, that is, the role and contribution of women, cannot be adequately grasped by relying on conventional, purportedly objective historiography. Hence a more imaginative approach is needed.[10] There is, actually, one telling incident in *The Flounder* that amounts to a tongue-in-cheek poetological statement. In one of the affidavits by literary critics that were read at the trial to assess both the character and literary achievement of the eminent Baroque poet Martin Opitz, the priority of literature over life is unequivocally postulated. According to this affidavit the young Grimmelshausen, who in 1669 was to publish his picaresque novel *Simplicissimus*, possibly compared the battle scenes at the Battle of Wittstock (1636) with "the printed metaphors" in Opitz's translation of Sir Philip Sidney's *Arcadia* and "recognized their authenticity . . . so demonstrating once again that nothing happens but what has first been prefigured by the written word" (F, 255).[11]

Although this bold statement, which reverses the ordinarily assumed cause-and-effect relationship between life and literature, rests on shaky foundations,[12] the passage offers an instructive example of Grass's imaginative adaptation of the results of literary scholarship—explicit mention is made of "a deserving Germanic scholar" (F, 254) or, rather, "Germanistenfleiss" (B, 322). The statement gains added weight if we recall that Grass conceives of *The Tin Drum* as a continuation of the picaresque novel, a subgenre of which Grimmelshausen's *Simplicissimus* is such an outstanding example.[13] Further evidence for Grass's artistic affinity to Grimmelshausen can be seen in the close, though not exclusive identification of the narrator with the character of Gelnhausen/Grimmelshausen in *The Meeting at Telgte,* whom he causes to pronounce a poetic program (MT, 112–13) that can be easily applied to Grass himself.[14]

At any rate, not everything has been "prefigured by the written word," but the narrator, who is hardly less well read than the Flounder, makes also ample use of literary references. The narrator's interest in literature should not surprise us; for example, he introduces himself as a contemporary "writer" (F, 22) and, from the very beginning, he has pronounced artistic inclinations. Thus, in his first "time-phase" as the neolithic fisherman Edek, the narrator experiences his "obsessive drive to leave . . . marks" (F, 22), that is, to create images. In all of his "time phases" the narrator is either a writer, artist, or artisan, but in the "Fourth Month" he appears as "poet and painter at once" (F, 227)—the combination of Baroque poet Opitz and Danzig painter Möller corresponds most closely to Grass's own artistic bent as both writer and graphic artist.

Owing to his artistic-literary propensity, the narrator uses "prefigurations" in the form of quotations to comment upon events, to concisely provide the gist of specific situations, to allude to states of mind, or moments of emotional stress. Thus he quotes, in fearful anticipation of an argument with his wife Ilsebill and one of the women from the Tribunal, from Luther's hymn: "'Out of the depths to Thee I cry . . . '" (F, 382). Further, he appropriately comments on the Flounder's refusal to continue serving as advisor of the male cause with the last words of master carpenter Anton, the staunch upholder of the old order in Friedrich Hebbel's middle-class tragedy *Maria Magdalena.* For the Flounder's proclamation that "the world is at a turning point" (F, 521) and that the age of women is beginning, leaves the narrator utterly disoriented. His confusion is only inadequately expressed by the colloquial phrase, "I'm completely at a loss!" (F, 530), because his entire world has become incomprehensible to him—a condition comparable to that of master Anton: "Ich versteh die Welt nicht mehr" (B, 673). At first glance, the function of other quotations, for example, the oblique reference to Brecht's famous phrase "talk about trees" from his poem written in exile, "To Those Born Later," is less evident.[15] To be sure, the reference characterizes Jan Ludkowski, one of the narrator's friends, who accompany him through the ages and whose names invariably contain the syllable "Lud-", as a highly imaginative person with a keen interest in literature. Like the narrator, Jan has the ability "to see historical episodes in detail, as if he had been there" (F, 541). On the basis of Jan's ability we may see in the following passage one of the instances in which parallels between different ages, here by using analogies of a literary nature, are being drawn: "With Jan you could sit and talk. About mouth-blown glasses. About poems. Even about trees. We talked about Gryphius and Opitz, just as they may have talked about heaven knows what. About the burden of an evil day" (F, 542-43). The allusion to Brecht is too strong not to be deliberate; the "evil times" evoke both Opitz and Brecht (and the contemporary narrator/author).[16] Hence history appears to follow a repetitive pattern, the idea of progress proves to be a delusion. To underscore this point the Flounder mentions the similar views on hope held by both St. Augustine and the twentieth-century philosopher Ernst Bloch in the same breath (F, 145); he further assigns the same function to the "gods" Zeus and Karl Marx, that is, to prop up the ideological "superstructure" of the male-dominated world (F,150).[17]

Literature is clearly part of this superstructure. For example, when the Flounder is accused of having urged the husbands of Lena Stubbe, the seventh cook, to beat her, it is alleged that this advice was based on the nine-teenth-century male *Zeitgeist* as expressed in "pertinent quotations from Nietzsche" (F, 408). Conversely, when the Flounder, who had initially pro-moted the cause of men with yet another quotation,[18] decides to support women, he cites their Nietzschean "will to power" (F, 150) as an appealing quality. Needless to say, the adoption of male attitudes and forms of repres-sion on the part of the females bodes ill for the resolution of the conflict be-tween the sexes. This point is driven home forcefully in the grim "Father's Day" chapter that ends with the failure of the new woman and the "brave new world" they seek to establish.[19] Again, literature— from Homer to the nineteenth-century writer of historical novels, Felix Dahn—provides the models for the exhibition of sheer bravado on the part of the four emanci-pated women with which they want to outperform their male competitors: "and then . . . the great, the unprecedented male competition began . . . . That's how it's always been, as you can see recorded in Old Man Homer and Old Man Moses, in the *Nibelungenlied* or *The Struggle for Rome*" (F, 471).

It is understandable that the feminists of the Tribunal bridle at the idea of male role models supplied by literature. But when the Flounder recom-mends elevating the "cooking nun" Fat Gret and her exploits to world-liter-ary status by considering her "a female companion piece" (F, 218) to François

Rabelais' Gargantua—Rabelais, incidentally, is also one of Grass's favorite authors—the Flounder is reprimanded for cracking "literary jokes at the expense of the world's oppressed women" (F, 219). The humorless rebuttal of the Flounder by the prosecutor of the Tribunal serves to remind us of the feminists' dogmatic ideological fixation that does not permit them to use the escape valve of humor and, hence, a means of questioning their own position. The feminists, it seems, are headed for perishing in the "unrelieved tragedy" of their literary forebears—Schiller's Mary Stuart, Euripides', Sophocles', and their subsequent adaptors' Electra, Hebbel's Agnes Bernauer, and Ibsen's Nora—whom the Flounder, ever "hooked on culture" (F, 22), lists in catalog fashion (F, 218).

True, although the narrator realizes that the "male cause and with it civilization" has been a "failure," at the same time, he implies that this failure possesses "tragic grandeur" (F, 517). Ultimately, however, the "tragic grandeur" of men is only one step removed from the "unrelieved tragedy" of the heroines. But male protagonists such as Cervantes' Don Quixote, Sterne's Tristram Shandy, Shakespeare's Falstaff, and Grass's own Oskar Matzerath are able to overcome tragedy by making "comic capital" of their "despair" (F, 218).

Yet there is another type of heroine who has succeeded in subverting the Flounder's scheme. The Flounder had originally intended love as "an ideational superstructure" (F, 262) that would establish female emotional dependency and thereby assure male domination. But through their selfless love such literary figures as Shakespeare's Juliet, Hölderlin's Diotima, Kleist's Käthchen von Heilbronn, and Goethe's Ottilie in *Elective Affinities*, managed to turn the Flounder's "so craftily devised instrument of oppression into a symbol of eternal womanly greatness" (F, 267). In the Flounder's view the hitherto unsung Agnes Kurbiella, the cook of the "Fourth Month" and unconventional "muse," who serves both the poet Opitz and the painter Möller, is clearly of the same caliber as Juliet and her ilk. Conversely, the Women's Tribunal considers Agnes a victim of "male pimping" (F, 257) and adamantly rejects the notion "that the role of women in art can only be one of passive, servile, manuring mediation" (F, 255), and that "such summits of art" as "Handel's *Messiah*, the categorical imperative, the Strassburg Cathedral, Goethe's *Faust*, Rodin's *Thinker*, and Picasso's *Guernica* . . . are beyond [their] reach" (F, 256).

Although the narrator largely confines himself to reporting the contrasting views, the passages relating to women's role in art and literature reflect Grass's underlying assumption that women pertain to the realm of nature, whereas men pertain to the realm of culture.[20] At any rate, the crafty Flounder's wholesale disparagement of men's cultural achievements (F, 396-97), which is dictated by his desire to serve the cause of women, cannot hide the fact that the contributions of women in the novel remain largely outside the cultural-literary sphere. In contrast to the narrator in his various "time-phases," his companions, the cooks, display litle artistic talent; after Awa's matriarchal rule, which was inimical to artistic endeavor, had been abolished, the fourteenth-century Dorothea of Montau with her "slight lyrical gift" (F, 167) emerges as the sole exception.[21] If the cooks engage in writing at all, this activity is directed towards practical, humanitarian ends, as the notable examples of the seventh and ninth cooks demonstrate. The correspondence of the eighteenth-century Prussian serf Amanda Woyke with the colorful, adventurous, American-born Benjamin Thompson (later Count Rumford) is interpreted by the Flounder as "a harbinger of the future, already burgeoning Chinese World Food Solution" (F, 313). Likewise, the socialist Lena Stubbe aims to improve the lot of the working classes by means of her *Proletarian Cookbook* that, alas, remained unpublished.

As we may gather from the Flounder's previously mentioned, ferocious denouncement of men's cultural achievements, in the Grassian scheme of things women's lack of artistic talent does not amount to a flaw—quite the contrary. Just as the act of procreation at the beginning of the novel takes precedence over over the telling of the story, so the intellectual endeavor of writing is clearly subordinated to the biological act of creating new life. Implicitly the superiority of women is postulated precisely because of women's ability to give birth. All that men are capable of creating are "ersatz babies" (F, 396–97) or "headbirths" (*Kopfgeburten*), as Grass entitled his latest narrative. "'Men survive only in the written word'" (F, 103), the Flounder pontificates. The superiority of women is also attested to by the fact that the comparatively few well-known historical male figures who appear in person in the novel are depicted as devoid of greatness; rather, they tend to seek warmth, understanding, and comfort in their encounter with women whom the history books do not list. Frederick II of Prussia and Amanda Woyke, the socialist August Bebel and Lena Stubbe, Martin Opitz and Agnes Kurbiella, are cases in point. The novel as a whole, then, seeks to redress the injustice of neglecting and suppressing women's contributions in both historical accounts and literary histories—a point that will be discussed in greater detail later on.

To return to literary history proper, we have seen that the Flounder's praise of the "muse" Agnes Kurbiella inverts, for all practical purposes, the conventional relationship between the famous and the unknown; in these endeavors the Flounder is supported by the narrator who, in his "time-phase" as Opitz, was too occupied with producing "courtly flattery and lamentations of various kinds,"[22] so that he never succeeded in turning out "a poem to her kindness" (F, 15). Therefore, it is not primarily Grass's intent to provide an assessment of Opitz's significance for literary history—although this aspect certainly is not neglected. In his account in the "Fourth Month," which is presented from both an omniscient narrative perspective ("The burden of an evil day"; F, 240-48) and as the narrator's report from the trial ("Why the Flounder tried to rekindle two cold stoves"; F, 249-58), Grass presumably excerpted and paraphrased those unnamed "prominent literary critics," notably one Opitz biographer, whose affidavits are cited at the trial (F, 254).[23] Like Opitz, Grass himself makes exceedingly "skillful use of quotations from other authors" (F, 254). But, apart from the "invented" muse Agnes Kurbiella, who attempts in vain to inspire the prematurely aged Opitz, Grass reserves his most imaginative touch in the "Fourth Month" for the hypothetical encounter between the young Gryphius (1616-1664), who was later to be considered one of the strongest lyrical talents among the Baroque poets, and the older Opitz (1597-1639) in 1636.[24] Gryphius' accusation that Opitz had "squandered his [poetic] strength in politicking" (F, 243) echoes the charge that critics had leveled at Grass himself;[25] conversely, Opitz's remarks concerning Gryphius' "immoderation" in his sonnets that exhibit "the condemnation of all earthly pleasure . . . as vanity and vexation of the spirit" (F, 242) implicitly endorse the poet's active participation in worldly affairs, including the realm of politics, so that such lofty goals as "peace" and "universal tolerance" (F, 245) might be achieved. Not only does Gryphius stuff himself "ravenously" at the meeting with Opitz (F, 246)—thus savoring to the fullest the goods this vale of tears has to offer—in *The Meeting at Telgte*, in many respects a continuation of the "Fourth Month" of *The Flounder*, he publicly recants his previous condemnation of the deceased "Opitz's only too adroit diplomacy" and opts for public service in Silesia (MT, 32). Of course, Grass wants us to view the mature Gryphius' complete change of heart with suspicion—owing to the fact that he "continued in ever-new images to proclaim the death of literature" (MT, 33). "The death of literature" is precisely the slogan the radical students of the 1960s adopted to express their contempt for literary pursuits that were supposedly totally irrelevant from a socioeconomic point of view.

There is yet another episode in the novel that has been adapted from literary history. The "Sixth Month" not only offers another loving female cook but also includes a subchapter that is of utmost significance for the entire novel. The title of the subchapter in question, "The other truth" (F, 345-54), is of programmatic importance, for here the author creates a both plausible and effective setting for his endeavor to offer an explanation for the "other truth" that had been lost since 1807. The surmised "other truth" rests on the assumption that there had been two totally divergent versions of the fairy tale "The Fisherman and His Wife." Both versions had been told to the painter Philipp Otto Runge by an old woman on the isle of Rügen in the Baltic. Runge is supposed to have traveled to the Oliva forest, in the vicinity of Danzig, to meet some well-known literary figures, that is, the brothers

Grimm and the editors of the first volume of *The Boy's Magic Horn* (1805), Clemens Brentano and Achim von Arnim. The purpose of this meeting was "to discuss a publishing venture [i.e., the fairy tale in Low German dialect] and exchange ideas" (F, 345). But after heated debates the lovers and collectors of fairy tales—Bettina Brentano, who later married Achim von Arnim, was among them—decided to suppress the version that presented woman in a positive fashion and to publish the version that depicted man in a favorable light. Eventually, the latter version appeared in the first volume of the Grimms' well-known collection of fairy tales, the *Kinder- und Hausmärchen* (1812), and has dominated the "fairy-tale market" ever since "in defense of the patriarchal order" (F, 20), as the narrator remarks.

Grass follows literary history to a considerable extent. During the last months of 1807 Arnim and Brentano, with the aid of the brothers Grimm, did, indeed, work on the continuation of *The Boy's Magic Horn*, the second and third volumes of which were published in 1808. They did so, however, in the city of Kassel, since August 1807 capital of Napoleon's creation, the kingdom of Westphalia. Kassel was, at the same time, the residence of Jakob and Wilhelm Grimm as well as that of Brentano, who had married for the second time. Thus the meeting has some basis in fact. Grass further adheres to literary history when he has Arnim travel west from Königsberg after the peace treaty of Tilsit in October 1807. To be sure, Arnim did not end his journey in Danzig or the Oliva forest, as Grass has it. Bettina Brentano, who returned from Berlin to Frankfurt on the Main, met Goethe in Weimar on 23 April 1807; on no account did she travel to the Oliva forest after her meeting with Goethe.

There is an obvious explanation for Grass's choice of the Oliva forest instead of Kassel that is so geographically remote from Danzig: just as Danzig and environs play a significant role in Grass's previous work, notably in the so-called "Danzig Trilogy," so the Vistula estuary and Danzig/Gdańsk provide not only the setting of *The Flounder* (with the exception of the "Father's Day" chapter) but also an exemplary locale in which the stages of world history, as reflected in the fates of the cooks, unfold. Choosing Danzig as the meeting place between Opitz and Gryphius was quite justified; Grass attempts to lend a higher degree of probability to the meeting of the fairy-tale collectors by having it take place in utter secrecy, "in the heart of nature" (F, 346). The Romantics' propensity for such settings is well known; one is inclined to cite Ludwig Tieck's apt term *Waldeinsamkeit* in this connection. Needless to say, Grass is not primarily interested in creating a "romantic" mood; rather, the secret meeting place is an important ingredient in the story about the lost "other truth." Thus the peaceful tranquillity of a moonlit night—another favorite romantic motif—is disturbed by Runge's burning of the one version of the fairy tale. Runge's ominous deed with its far-reaching implications is reminiscent of other, more recent book burnings that were designed to serve as a means of suppressing oppositional or undesirable literature.

It has been suggested that Grass's attention was drawn to the fairy tale about the fisherman and his wife by an article published in 1973.[26] Should this be the case, then we are faced with yet another facet of Grass's creative adaptation of the results of literary scholarship. Apart from the meeting in Kassel, which Grass transferred to Danzig, an actual, scholarly debate took place that resulted from Runge's authenticated writing down two divergent versions of the fairy tale.[27] But Runge sent the two versions—both of which showed an antifemale tendency—to different potential publishers; they both appeared independently from each other in print in 1812. As a consequence, philologists began to assume that there must be one original version or *Urtext* of the fairy tale[28]—perhaps Grass derived the idea for the discussion about the "true" version in *The Flounder* from this scholarly debate about the correct version.

At any rate, the narrator had not participated in the burning of that version that showed "a modest Ilsebill and a fisherman with immoderate wishes" (F, 349). In contrast to the chapter devoted to Opitz, Grass here foregoes the opportunity of having his narrator appear as one or several of the writers gathered in the Oliva forest. But the narrator's general, pervasive guilt feeling as a man (F, 147) induces him to proclaim near the beginning of the novel: "Of course, I'm going to write the other truth that Philipp Otto Runge took down, even if I have to pick it word for word out of the ashes" (F, 20). And after the burning the narrator exclaims: "And now I must write and write" (F, 354)—a clear indication that the novel as a whole is designed to counteract that "phony fairy tale" (F, 20), or, as the Flounder says, "the misogynistic propaganda tale" (F, 20), the "Grimms' distortion of his legend" (F, 34). Although the narrator's efforts result in a novel, this novel originates from the initial narrative situation in which the narrator tells a story to his wife Ilsebill. Hence the narrator is able to claim that his narrative deviates from the unequivocal ("eindeutig"; B, 374), published narratives: "But the text of the story . . . had already been established and made ready for the printer, whereas the unpublished storyteller always has the next, entirely different, very latest version [actually: story and history; B, 374] in mind" (F, 294). This kind of narration is akin to that of the storytellers among the cooks whose literary talents, as we noted previously, tend to be slight or nonexistent. Mestwina, Fat Gret, and Amanda Woyke in particular are formidable storytellers; their style is determined by the rhythm of the work they perform. Despite their "reprehensible attachment to the past" (F, 299), their storytelling is not, by any means, mere "escapism, flight from reality" (F, 298). On the contrary, by remembering past events they help perpetuate a kind of reality that is ordinarily not to be found in print.

The fairy tale "The Fisherman and His Wife," which received possibly more attention than any other fairy tale,[29] offered Grass the opportunity of replacing woman possessed by hubris with man filled with boundless ambition. The possibility of applying the fairy tale with its theme of rise and sudden fall to overweening men was, in fact, recognized by the Grimms' contemporaries. In 1814 the fairy tale was widely interpreted as a comment on Napoleon's fate.[30] In the novel, however, Napoleon, like other great historical individuals, is primarily viewed from the kitchen perspective—somewhat in the manner of Brecht.[31] During his brief appearance Napoleon engages in political decision-making while he is eating "smoked Vistula salmon" (F, 363) that is being served to him by Sophie Rotzoll, the eighth cook and main character in the "Sixth Month."

For, despite the central thematic significance of the events in "The other truth," and despite the numerous allusions to these events throughout the novel, the subchapter is a comparatively self-contained episode in the "Sixth Month" with, perhaps, only a tenuous link to the main plot, that is, the story of the cooks. The link is provided by Sophie who visits her relative, the wife of the woodsman in whose cabin the collectors of fairy tales have gathered. (An additional link is established by Sophie's former employment in the household of Pastor Blech, the Danzig historian whom Grass quotes (F, 362, 365-66) and who, as one of the narrator's incarnations during his Napoleonic "time-phase," had recommended the Oliva forest as a meeting place.) As the historical cook who most clearly anticipates the modern feminists, she is convinced that only the "truth" depicting men as acquisitive and ambitious is right. Sophie is wont to express her revolutionary convictions in "rousing kitchen songs" and "rhymed barricade songs" (F, 360, 361) in which the spheres of the kitchen and politics are fused by means of rhyme—a poetic device also used by Heinrich Heine.[32]

Sophie had initially adored Napoleon as "the savior of the Revolution" (F, 360) and the representative of the idea of freedom. Her admiration turned to hatred, however, when, after the French occupation of Danzig in 1807, her beloved Friedrich Bartholdy was not released by General Rapp, Napoleon's governor in the city and Sophie's second employer. As a youth Bartholdy had been incarcerated by the Prussians because of his sympathies for the French revolution and his founding of a Jacobin club. Sophie then begins to act in accordance with her revolutionary kitchen songs; she uses the kitchen as a political weapon by endeavoring to poison Governor Rapp with mushrooms "by way of avenging the betrayed revolution" (F, 355), as the Women's Tribunal sees it. One of the Tribunal's member's states categorically that Sophie acted "not out of childish love but for the sake of freedom. For reasons of principle" (F, 376). The narrator, although he "was" Friedrich Bartholdy, Pastor Blech, and Governor Rapp during his Napoleonic "time-phase," remains purposefully vague as to Sophie's true motives and refrains from committing himself. But it seems obvious that the narrator, who shares with the author Grass his pronounced "dislike of ideology" (F, 388),[33] wishes to warn of that "diffuse freedom that lasts only as long as a song in several stanzas supplies a cramped soul with air" (F, 376). How easily abstract ideals can become perverted and how easily their adherents can shift allegiances is demonstrated by Sophie. At first her songs are "sans-culottish," but after her "brief period of Napoleonic enthusiasm" has waned, they take on a distinct "fatherlandish tone" (F, 376). The narrator's (and author's) criticism of the kind of activist political lyrics that appeal directly to the masses and seek to produce an intoxicating effect is reinforced when we learn that the aged Sophie and her Friedrich Bartholdy, who has finally been released from prison, can only experience the idea of freedom as an escape from the present by partaking of fly agaric.

It has been shown that Grass makes extensive use of literature in his novel. Grass's creative adaptations extend from the folk tale to "high-brow" poetry, from the employment of single-line or cryptic quotations to creating plausible literary discussions among writers, from exploring the relationship of writing and politics in particular to that of writing and reality in general. Grass derives his learning, which in the novel is displayed by the omniscient and loquacious Flounder as well as the narrator, from many sources. Yet there is no gratuitous exhibition of insignificant facts; rather, literature and literary history are fully integrated and subordinated to the novel's central theme. Of particular importance, of course, is the fairy tale "The Fisherman and His Wife" that, in the version handed down to us by the brothers Grimm, "couched a centuries-long and hence complex historical development . . . in simple words appropriate to the popular tradition" (F, 43-44), as the Flounder remarks. Since the entire novel is, in a sense, a vastly expanded refutation of the Grimms' fairy tale by providing an elaboration of the "other truth," it has a "compensatory function" like the fairy tale.[34] However, the complex structure and innovative narrative stance of *The Flounder* have no equivalent in the traditional fairy tale with its naiveté, uncomplicated, linear plot, and easy-to-grasp moral. On the contrary, there is no clearcut and, necessarily, simplistic message in *The Flounder*.[35] For example, the novel's "open ending"[36] has been a contributing factor to the critics' lack of unanimity with regard to Grass's stand on feminist issues.[37] Despite man's abdication at the end of the "Seventh Month," despite the dismal failure of the new woman in the "Eighth Month," the "Ninth Month" offers a semblance of hope. The new-born human being, a girl, will, perhaps, shun the imitation of male patterns of exploitation and power-wielding—a course the radical feminists seem bent on pursuing with the help of the Flounder. There is, after all, an indication of a third possibility that would overcome the domination of one sex by another. Near the beginning of the novel the narrator muses: "Maybe we've simply forgotten that there is still more. A third something. In other respects as well, politically for instance, as possibility" (F, 7). And, lest we forget, in the fanciful conceit of the two versions of the fairy tale there is inherent a third way that would overcome the dualism, the antagonism of the sexes. For when the painter Runge had asked the old woman on the isle of Rügen which version of the fairy tale was the correct one, she had replied: "The one and the other" (F, 349), or, to translate more literally: "Both of them together" (B, 443).

Notes

*An abridged version of this article will appear under the title, "Der Butt als Germanist: Zur Rolle der Literatur in Günter Grass' Roman," AoF, pp. 24-31.

1. Anton Krättli, "Danziger Butt mit Zutaten. Zum neuen Roman von Günter Grass," p. 486.
2. Leonard Forster, "An Unsystematic Approach to Der Butt," p. 75.
3. Geoffrey P. Butler, "Grass Skirts the Issue: A Reaction to Der Butt," p. 24.
4. See Forster, "An Unsystematic Approach," p. 75.
5. "Am liebsten lüge ich gedruckt. Interviews mit Günter Grass," pp. 219-20.
6. See Grass's statement concerning the correspondence of the authorial "I" and narrative "I" in Heinz Ludwig Arnold, "Gespräche mit Günter Grass," TuK, p. 28. As to the function of the narrator, see especially Gertrud Bauer Pickar, "The Prismatic Narrator: Postulate and Practice," above, pp. 55-74.
7. Grass confirmed this history of the origin of the novel: "My first notes and etchings...had to do with food...I can't remember when I first encountered the flounder legend, which seemed to serve as just the right metaphor [for the conflict of the sexes]." See Richard Plant, "Answers by Günter Grass," p. 14. In other interviews Grass stated the matter similarly. See Arnold, "Gespräche mit Günter Grass," p. 31.
8. See Helmut Koopmann, "Between Stone Age and Present or The Simultaneity of the Nonsimultaneous," above, pp. 75-89.
9. For a listing of the various correspondences, see the Structural Diagram, below, pp. 198-199.
10. See Arnold, Gespräche mit Günter Grass," p. 31.
11. For a somewhat different interpretation of this passage, see Judith Ryan, "Beyond The Flounder: Narrative Dialectic in The Meeting at Telgte," above, p. 42.
12. According to Ulrich Stadler, Der einsame Ort. Studien zur Weltabkehr im heroischen Roman (Berne: Francke, 1971), p. 104, the lack of realism ("Wirklichkeitsgehalt") in chapter 27, book II of Simplicissimus, for which the text of Arcadia provided the model, is particularly pronounced. Further, Grimmelshausen could not have read "Opitz's translation," i.e., Opitz's adaptation of Theodor von Hirschfeld's translation (1629) at the Battle of Wittstock (1636) because the adaptation was not published until 1638. Hence one should not overlook the element of irony in Grass's acount—despite his obvious exploitation of the products of "Germanistenfleiss," among which we may, perhaps, also count Hans Geulen,"'Arcadische' Simpliciana. Zu einer Quelle Grim-

melshausens und ihrer strukturellen Bedeutung für seinen Roman," *Euphorion,* 63 (1969), 426-37, and Walter Holzinger, "Der Abentheurliche Simplicissimus and Sir Philip Sidney's Arcadia," *Colloquia Germanica* (1969), 184-98. For the references to Stadler, Geulen, and Holzinger, I am indebted to my colleague, Christoph E. Schweitzer. At any rate, Grass strives for consistency within his fictional universe. In *The Meeting at Telgte,* for example, Gelnhausen/Grimmelshausen is reported to have "quoted a passage from Opitz's translation of the *Arcadia*"(MT, 7).

13. See Arnold, "Gespräche mit Günter Grass," p. 6. As to the picaresque features of *The Tin Drum,* see the bibliographical references in Volker Neuhaus, *Günter Grass,* p. 35.

14. See Ruprecht Wimmer, "'I, Down Through the Ages': Reflections on the Poetics of Günter Grass, above, pp. 25-38.

15. See Hiltrud Gnüg, "Gespräch über Bäume. Zur Brecht-Rezeption in der modernen Lyrik," *Basis,* 7 (1977), 89-117, 235-37. It should be added that one cannot, with absolute certainty, state in each case whether Grass is quoting intentionally or merely using phrases that do not, at first glance, betray their literary origin. For example, the context would suggest that the Flounder quotes the "voice of God" from the epilog of Karl Kraus's drama *The Last Days of Mankind* when he proclaims the bankruptcy of the male cause: "That's not what I wanted" (F, 453), or, "Das habe ich nicht gewollt" (B, 572). Kraus, in turn, uses, in slightly altered form, the Kaiser's statement with which he commented on his declaration of war in 1914.

16. Opitz's line, "Die Last der bösen Zeit" (B, 306), which is also used in altered form as the heading of a subchapter (B, 305-15; F, 240-48), does evoke Brecht's first line in "An die Nachgeborenen" ("To Those Born Later"): "Wirklich, ich lebe in finsteren Zeiten" ("Truly, I live in dark times"), especially since the "talk about trees" is mentioned in the same passage.

17. See also Osman Durrani, "'Here Comes Everybody': An Appraisal of Narrative Technique in Günter Grass's *Der Butt*," p. 120.

18. Presumably, ". . . Zukunft. Schon hat sie . . . begonnen" (B, 36), is a reference to Robert Jungk, *Die Zukunft hat schon begonnen. Amerikas Allmacht und Ohnmacht* (Stuttgart: Scherz & Govert, 1952), an erstwhile bestseller. ". . . the future is already under way" (F, 26) bears only a faint resemblance to the English translation of Jungk's book by Marguerite Waldmann, *Tomorrow Is Already Here* (New York: Simon and Schuster, 1954).

19. Grass quotes George Orwell's "utopian novel" *1984* (F, 189) but does not mention Aldous Huxley's *Brave New World.* The reference to Orwell follows the subchapter on Calcutta, "Vasco returns" (F, 173-88)—an indication that, in Grass's view, Calcutta with its horrid slums and permanent food shortages offers a preview of that "dark side of utopia" (DS, 310) Grass spoke of in a different context. See also Grass's essay, "Im Wettlauf mit den Utopien" (AL, 129-49).

20. For a fuller discussion of the nature/culture dichotomy, see Scott H. Abbott, "The Raw and the Cooked: Claude Lévi-Strauss and Günter Grass," above, pp. 107-120.

21. Forster, "An Unsystematic Approach to *Der Butt*," p. 75, calls Dorothea's verses in "mixed High Alemannic and Low Prussian . . . perhaps not entirely successful." At any rate, the "Fourth Month" in general and the subchapter "My

dear Dr. Stachnik" (F, 164-68) in particular offer another example of Grass's imaginative appropriation of sources. Dr. Stachnik, Dorothea's biographer and Grass's Latin teacher in Danzig, also appears in *Dog Years*. See "Am liebsten lüge ich gedruckt," pp. 219-20. The criticism by Anneliese Triller, "Grobe Verzeichnung. Die Darstellung der Dorothea von Montau durch Günter Grass," p. 20, that Grass "distorts" Dorothea, misses the point.

22. "Jammertalallegorien" (B, 23) with its "vale of tears" overtones is both far more expressive and indicative of the Baroque period than the English rendering. See also Arnold, "Gespräche mit Günter Grass," p. 29.

23. Theodor Verweyen and Gunther Witting, "Polyhistors neues Glück. Zu Günter Grass' Erzählung *Das Treffen in Telgte* und ihrer Kritik," p. 462, n. 13, draw attention to the brief passage about Opitz, the "irenist" (B, 322; F, 254), which has most likely been derived from Marian Szyrocki, *Martin Opitz* (Berlin: Rütten & Loening, 1956), p. 95. There is additional evidence for Grass's use of Szyrocki's biography. Thus the quotations from Opitz's poems in B, 396 (F, 241): "Mein Geist . . ."; B, 309 (F, 244): "Du hebst . . ."; B, 321-22 (F, 254): ". . . die Freyheit . . ."; B, 322 (F, 254): "Gewalt macht . . ."; are all quoted, often with the corresponding context, by Szyyrocki, pp. 111, 83, 47, 46. It is not quite clear, however, why Grass changed the spelling of Opitz's Danzig publisher Andreas Hünefeld to "Hühnerfeld" (B, 306; F, 241).

24. The meeting could not have taken place on 2 September 1636 (F, 241) because, by that time, Gryphius had left Danzig. Opitz, in fact, did not settle in Danzig until after Gryphius' departure, although he had visited the city while Gryphius still resided there. See Marian Szyrocki, *Andreas Gryphius. Sein Leben und Werk* (Tübingen: Niemeyer, 1964), pp. 20-24, 121, n. 38. Szyrocki is more explicit in his *Der junge Gryphius* (Berlin: Rütten & Loening, 1959), pp. 75,79, where he states that, in all probability, Gryphius never met Opitz face to face.

25. See Arnold, "Gespräche mit Günter Grass," pp. 23, 34.

26. Hanspeter Brode, *Günter Grass*, p. 182, infers that Grass came across the fairy tale in 1973, as a result of the publication of the article by Heinz Rölleke, "Von dem Fischer un syner Fru. Die älteste schriftliche Überlieferung," *Fabula*, 14 (1973), 112-23. Brode bases his inference on the introduction to Rölleke, *Der wahre Butt. Die wundersamen Wandlungen des Märchens vom Fischer und seiner Frau*, although Rölleke does not explicitly state that Grass was introduced to the fairy tale by his article. Grass, incidentally, claimed that he did not remember when he first "encountered the flounder legend." See n. 7, above.

27. Rölleke, *Der wahre Butt*, p. 8.

28. See Rölleke, "Von dem Fischer un syner Fru," pp. 112-23.

29. Reinhold Steig, "Literarische Umbildung des Märchens vom Fischer und siner Fru," *Archiv für das Studium der neueren Sprachen und Litteraturen*, 57 (1903), 8. The popularity of the fairy tale is also attested to by the retelling of Uwe Johnson, *Von dem Fischer un syner Fru. Ein Märchen nach Philipp Otto Runge* (Frankfurt am Main: Insel, 1976).

30. See the letter by Friedrich Karl von Savigny to Wilhelm Grimm (Berlin, 29 April 1814) in Adolf Stoll, *Friedrich Karl v. Savigny. Professorenjahre in Berlin 1810–1841* (Berlin: Heymann, 1929), p. 104. Grass's mention of the 1814 publication of an "attack on the tyrant . . . in High German" (F, 353) probably derives from Savigny's letter, which is frequently cited in secondary literature. However, Kayser's *Vollständiges Bücher-Lexikon. Ersther Teil A-C* (Leipzig:

Schumann, 1834), p. 216, lists only a Low German version of the fairy tale: *Von dem Fischer un syne Fru. Eine plattdeutsche Erzählung* (Hamburg: A. Campe, 1814).

31. See, e.g., Brecht's poem, "Fragen eines lesenden Arbeiters" ("Questions from a Worker Who Reads").

32. See, e.g., Heine's ironically titled poem, "Zur Beruhigung" ("Consoling Thoughts") from *Neue Gedichte* (*New Poems*) of 1844.

33. Grass's "dislike of ideology" is already evident in *Local Anaesthetic*, but even more so in *From the Diary of a Snail*, in many respects a forerunner of *The Flounder*. In *The Flounder* the narrator appears as the representative of the "snail philosophy," i.e., slow progress, whereas his wife Ilsebill wants to take Mao's "Great Leap Forward" (F, 330)—both literally and figuratively.

34. Lutz Röhrich, "Argumente für und gegen das Märchen," *Sage und Märchen. Erzählforschung heute* (Freiburg: Herder, 1976), p. 25. See also Johnson, *Von dem Fischer un syner Fru*, p. 47.

35. Grass had considered subtitling *The Flounder* fairy tale (*Märchen*), but refrained from doing so as a "concession" to prevailing literary norms. See Fritz J. Raddatz, "Heute lüge ich lieber gedruckt. *Zeit*-Gespräch über den *Butt* mit Günter Grass," p. 9.

36. Arnold, "Gespräche mit Günter Grass," p. 30.

37. See, e.g., the reviews by Jessica Benjamin, "The Fish That Got Away," pp. 41, 44, 78, and John Simon, "What's Cooking?," p. 59.

The Critical Reception of *The Flounder* in the United States: Epic and Graphic Aspects

Sigrid Mayer

When *The Flounder* first appeared in English and American bookstores in November 1978, Günter Grass's latest major novel had been a bestseller in Germany for eight months. The popularity of the book came as a surprise to literary critics who had received the novel rather cautiously until its overwhelming success confirmed the author's position—not only as writer on a grand scale (*Grosschriftsteller*) but also as writer for the people (*Volksschriftsteller*).[1] But whatever happened in Germany, where Grass is not necessarily seen as "the prophet in his fatherland," did not remarkably affect American reactions to the book. Here *The Flounder* had not been introduced to the general public by years of public readings by the author or by excerpts published in major newspapers prior to its publication. The one reading that took place at the New School in New York in April 1977, had been noticed by the press mostly in connection with an exhibit of the author's graphic work. But the public's awareness that the author was once more working on a lengthy novel, which had been skillfully aroused in Germany for five years, was certainly missing in this country—although a national advertising campaign was launched and the author undertook a promotional tour in the fall of 1978, such publicity did not reach readers much in advance of the reviews in popular magazines.

After a record translation time of only one year *The Flounder* was published in November 1978 and greeted in some review sections as Grass's first major novel since *The Tin Drum* (1962), the novel that had been on American bestseller lists for several months in 1963.[2] In the same year *Dog Years* had been published in Germany and was followed by its American edition in 1965. It seems noteworthy, moreover, that *Local Anaesthetic*, for which the author was praised in a cover story by *Time* magazine (13 April 1970), is not considered, in retrospect, one of Grass's major novels. Nor is there any mention in any of the reviews of the author's plans to write a "cookbook" that were first announced in *From the Diary of a Snail*, published in English in 1973.

The first fact, then, about the general reception of *The Flounder* is that it is primarily identified as a work by the author of *The Tin Drum*. This applies especially to readers and reviewers who are old enough to have some literary memories of the early 1960's. Dick Cavett, for example, on whose show the author appeared in the fall of 1978, spent the entire thirty minutes of the interview, not in discussing any aspect of *The Flounder*, but in exploring once more the author's personal memories of his country's Nazi past and the beliefs he held as a Hitler youth and as a seventeen-year old at the end of World War II. To be sure, the fifty-one year old author did not mind these questions, nor did he lose his cool when it was pointed out to him, as he took out tobacco and cigarette paper, that a person by the name of "Grass" rolling a cigarette might look suspicious.

As early as December 1978, Richard Howard (then president of the PEN American Center) observed "a good deal of . . . critical resistance to this insistently ambitious work." (30)[3] He mentions a "Keep Off The Grass" attitude inspired by the author's previous international successes and seeks to elucidate this phenomenon with the "old pervasions of genre." He writes:

> It is difficult to be comfortable with a novel that has no mortal characters, no plot and no modesty. (But being uncomfortable is just what we should expect: It is the one posture any 20th-century novel with claim to salience has imposed upon the public of what was once a popular form.) Indeed, most of the dissent I have read about this whopper . . . has been a kind of scepticism—is the thing a novel at all? As if we knew, any more, what a novel was!

These observations are borne out in part by Nigel Dennis's evaluation of the book in the *New York Review of Books* as "a very bad novel" (18). But instead of backing up this judgment with some good reasons, this reviewer attributed the book's success in Germany to some 4,000 complimentary copies that supposedly induced their recipients to squander lavish praise on the work. When Dennis professes to "a personal approach" to the novel "because it is a work about which one is certain to be wrong" he is absolutely right. His "personal approach" has little to do with valid literary criticism and a lot with criteria that are quite extraneous to the work itself. However, Dennis's reaction to the book was exceptional, if challenging. The overall response by critics turned out to be refreshingly unbiased, spontaneous, often casual. It also revealed a broader spectrum of critical reactions than that evidenced by the reception in England, for example. Very clearly, the book will never attain the bestseller status of *The Tin Drum* in this country, although *Time* magazine declared it (with four other titles) as belonging to the "Best Fiction of 1978"[4] and listed it under "Editor's Choice" during the first five months of 1979.

As one reviewer correctly observed: "The book invites its own cliches" (23), as a feast, a stew, a fishpot, and the like. In order to analyze some of the major points addressed by the critics it will be useful to separate a few of the stew's diverse ingredients.

I. Genre

A major objection to the novel, voiced by several reviewers, is its length, its "tediousness" and lack of clear focus. The richness of the "stew," so many critics felt, demanded too much digestion. John Updike, who reviewed the book for the *New Yorker* (61), confessed: "My consumption, at least, of large portions of 'The Flounder' was spurred on by no other hunger than the Puritan craving to leave a clean plate." And Paul Zweig reported in *Harpers* (65): "I found myself wading forward in places as if through glue." The reviewer of *Newsweek* (16) felt "relieved to have finished it," while William McPherson in the *Washington Post Book World* (41) concluded: "After finishing it, I felt stuffed, rather like the man in the old Alka-Selzer commercial who exclaims, 'I can't believe I ate the whole thing.'" Maureen Howard in the *Yale Review* (29) sounds more resentful: "I pushed through all 547 pages with the dogged persistence of a hack reviewer." Obviously, what these critics were looking for was a clear, if involved, development of plot, a linear kind of novel that required a straightforward reading from beginning to end. Yet none of these start-to-finish readers would be likely to advocate such an approach in the case of a history book (where you would probably select the historical periods of your choice), *The Arabian Nights*, a book of poetry, or a cookbook. "Puritan" or not, "the old pervasions of genre," or what befits a novel, turned out to be the reviewers' criteria for the enjoyment of this work or lack thereof. The reader's independent value judgment—like the reviewer of *Punch*, he might have concluded, "no need to read from start to finish, it can be started at any point" (60)—fell prey to his preconceived concept of the "novel." As Richard Howard pointed out, in the case of *The Flounder* the exigencies of genre are conflicting. To the extent that this book is an epic, "it offers a totality of life received complete, whereas insofar as it is a novel it seeks to discover and to construct a secret totality" (30).

Those who could not come to terms with the book as a "novel" also found that its characters leave a lot to be desired, that is, they don't appear to be "real." While not many reviewers went so far as to ask: "But what if none of the nine [cooks] is interesting to read about?" (18)—some maintained that, "In the long annals of his [the author's] historical 'cooks', the vivacity belongs nine-tenths to him and only one-tenth to his characters" (6); or, "Only at times do Grass's 'Cooks' and their men come alive as more than counters in a vast thematic chessgame" (65); or, "It is a novel of ideas (as such it could have used a name and subject index) not of character" (41). We also find the following astute observation: "But the women are all fictional, inventions to play against the facts which the men act out" (43). A more comprehensive view (and review) of the novel, on the other hand, reached this conclusion: "Mr. Grass's cooks save him for they give body to his politics and unite them with his gustatory temperament. Though comic creations, Mr. Grass's cooks, like Oskar, are all unyielding obsessional types, hedonists, ascetics, patriots, all mute but enduring witnesses to the special horrors of their age" (19). When the same reviewer explained, "The cooks bring together Grass the novelist and Grass the socialist," he might as well have added, "Grass the portraitist." For as such, as "Gunter Grass, Portraitist," the author was introduced by the *New York Times* when he brought an exhibit of his recent etchings to New York in April 1977 (36). The art critic observed: "In the present show there are portraits and self-portraits—but there may be an insect oddly placed on the face of a portrait, as in 'Ute und ich'—and in the rendering of virtually every observed object, there is an element of fantasy and paradox." Here it seems that the characteristics derived so readily from a look at Grass's artwork go a long way in answering the criticism levelled at the cooks. As is the case with the author's protrait-etchings, their "characterization" is not so much achieved through the description of inner psychological complexities as through a combination and confrontation with phenomena from another realm that serve as characterizing attributes. In the poem "All" (F, 415) it can be seen, for example, how Sophie's mushrooms, Awa's third breast, Amanda's potato-peelings, Sibylle's Father's Day celebration, and so on, have become inseparable attributes reflecting the unique make-up of each individual character. As a matter of fact, several of these cooks, notably the more "fictitious" ones, such as Awa, Dorothea, Sophie, are concretely visualized in the author's graphic experiments.[5]

II. Woman as Cook and the Feminist Point of View

In stating that "Grass's novel . . . is a celebration of cooks" one reviewer raised the question whether "woman as cook" was likely to win feminist endorsement (47). This, to be sure, means opening a can of worms since the feminist issue is so aggressively dealt with in the novel that John Simon in the

Saturday Review proclaimed it "the first major satirical anti-feminist novel" (54). The same thesis is advanced elsewhere: "The book is a feminist tract," and, "the book is an antifeminist tract" (30). Other male reviewers were less willing to take a stand on this issue. The reporter for *Newsweek* concluded, "A feminist argument is advanced, relentlessly," but he wonders "how feminists are going to react to a boar in their ranks" (16). And a reviewer in *Prairie Schooner* sounded a rather defensive note: "(But, as the Flounder once said, 'All men are interchangeable.' Women, I guess, are different)" (2). Nor can further enlightenment with regard to the feminist aspect of the novel be gained from the following: "Clearly Grass is highly critical of women, but no more so than he is of males . . . One might guess that much of the thrust of Grass's account—women through the millennia—is aimed at *épater les femmes*" (27). Luckily, there were also women reviewers. While some seemed to sense that this aspect of the novel is hardly its most important criterion, a reviewer for *Ms.* provided an analysis. She found the book disappointing on account of its troubling cynicism:"Despite Grass's attempt to ironize the narrator's pride in his exploits and his selfpitying passivity, he indulges them in a way that suggests an innocence that history hardly confirms. The narrator never tires of repeating that he only followed the flounder's orders." Conversely, she noted that "not one female character ever speaks for herself in the novel, including his present-day puppet Ilsebill. The novel's mythical zigzag through history relieves Grass of the narrative problem of giving his female characters a life of their own." She accused the author of "the lack of an alternate vision" and maintained that "all the possibilities—for love, autonomy, change—that feminism celebrates are omitted" (13). Another reviewer concluded: "Hope, perhaps, lies in the fact that in the narrator's equivocation between sexist and liberal, infant and artist, consumer and about-to-be consumed, there is abundant wit and deep irony" (29).

In this context it may be noteworthy that the most frequently quoted line from *The Flounder*, especially in short accounts of its dialectic development, is the statement from the Flounder's final speech at the Women's Tribunal: "Today history demands a female imprint" (F, 529).

If the premise holds that women's liberation is the "the main theme" of the book, the conclusion reached by a reviewer for the *New Boston Review* is inescapable: "Despite Grass's efforts to avoid sounding fashionably chic on the subject of women's liberation, this is exactly what he does . . . Günter Grass wants to instruct the children of the modern world. This time, on this subject, they know as much and perhaps more than he does" (17). Many readers might also agree with Morris Dickstein's reservations in the *New York Times*: "By temperament Mr. Grass seems attached to his masculine prerogatives though depressed at the havoc they have wrought in the world. But the challenge of feminism does not possess his imagination the way the spectacle of the Nazis once did. The sardonic ferocity of *The Tin Drum* turns more pensive and playful here" (19).

In some regards it seems unfortunate that a comparison with the author's first novel—to which renewed attention has been called by the internationally successful film directed by Volker Schlöndorff—is time and again used as criterion to evaluate *The Flounder*. Few reviewers seem to have read any other of the many texts by Grass available in English; even those who did cannot resist some lopsided analogies: "With the Flounder, Günter Grass creates a character whose combinaton of intelligence, amorality, self-irony, and curiosity makes him almost the equal of Oskar . . . The Flounder . . . is obviously an image of the typical, essentially amoral contemporary artist" (17). Typical of the critics' preoccupation with the stereotype created by *The Tin Drum* is the last line of an account in *Village Voice*: "But privately: You want Grass, read *The Tin Drum*" (23). Yet noone seems to have noticed that already in that first novel a fantastic or "mythical" cook—who, in the English version, is called the "Black Witch"—makes numerous appearances. The novel even concludes with a play on the nursery rhyme of *die schwarze Köchin* or the "Black Witch." In fact, the motif of the cook, male or female, "wicked" or not, can be traced throughout the author's work, his poetry, drawings, etchings, and early plays.

III. Food

Few readers recognize that, "throughout the book, sounding a steady note in the midst of the encyclopaedic obsession with provender and nourishment, there runs a utopian dream . . . of a universal kitchen steaming with magical soups . . . that will feed the world forever" (39). In other words, in this book the author is not so much intent on analyzing past history as he is on conjuring up a vision of the future. When, in a penetrating account of the novel, Saul Maloff also points out that, "for all the exuberance and comic inventiveness, despair lies palpably close to the roiling surface" (39), he has in essence identified the inseparable sisters pictured by the author in one of his graphic self-portraits and described in his *From the Diary of a Snail*: "How Melancholy and Utopia call each other cause. How the one shuns and disavows the other. How they accuse each other of evasion. How the snail mediates between them" (DS, 91).

A genuine misunderstanding has apparently occurred with respect to the function of the food in the novel. Some critics generally refer to it in terms of food for food's sake; others infer that the author had some gluttonous hang-up about food, that he recorded recipes for the purpose of creating a gourmet cookbook, that food and sex were the only things the author considered of cultural significance. Here are some examples: "Could Grass have been on a diet when writing *The Flounder*? Many novelists have lovingly described enormous meals as if their famished faces were pressed against the windows of the rich" (45); "But mostly he talks about sex and food. Especially food" (23); "The two binding and almost endlessly suggestive themes are food and male/female relations" (3); "The flounder [is] hoping to end a matriachal age in which eating is the sole event" (2); "Mr. Grass has undertaken . . . to recount the history of Europe in terms of an eternal triangle consisting of man, woman, and food" (1); "Cooking and sexuality, from which derive all family, cultural, and ultimately even political relationships" (54); "The book, for example, is a history of German and Polish peasant cooking. And the narrator/fisherman eats . . . throughout our history" (22); "Günter Grass's . . . novel, which simplifies human history to the primal activities of eating and sex, opens with a heavy dinner" (16); "But history cannot be only recipes, and even the most iron-stomached reader must sometimes feel . . . stuffed" (61); "The passages on cooking and the history of nutrition in particular are unique" (65); "Sex and food are as far from the dry rumblings of *Weltgeist* and *Historismus* as one can get" (53); "Better still, . . . leaf through *Julia Child and Company*, a new cookbook that is attractive, unpretentious, and instructive" (29). "What I liked best, though, was the food" (51); "(It is, among other things, a cookbook with recipes for mushrooms, millet, lots of fish, various stuffed organ meats, even roasted goddess)" (41); "When women leave cooking pots and beds and reject their traditional roles, they become unlikable" (55). Perhaps these reactions reflect a cultural difference between the American people who take enough or plenty of food for granted and the citizens of the Federal Republic who, surrounded by a worrisome surplus food production in Europe, can never quite rid themselves of a sense of moral guilt. Issues concerning the Third World are topical in Germany; anxiety about the future of mankind in terms of nourishment appears to be more prevalent than most other concerns. In the view of many the question of war and peace, for example, hinges directly on securing an adequate food supply for the countries of the Third World. Seen in this light, Grass's preoccupation with food throughout history takes on a future dimension; it reveals itself as a kind of utopia. If his American readers would take the trouble of looking for a common denominator in most of those recipes that have come across as so much gourmet cooking, they might discover that they are frequently inspired by "what is left over," or "bones, husks, innards, and sausage" ("What I write about," F, 8-9). The abstract lesson of filled calf-heads, stuffed hearts, lambs' lungs, pork kidneys, stirred blood, wild mushrooms, millet, potato soup, and soup of fish heads is not so much a gourmet cookbook as a reminder that these items, unavailable in modern supermarkets because nobody wants them, could be turned into a tasty nourish-

ment by the inventiveness of cooks. In other words, the answer to mass starvation lies not solely in more and more ample supplies but also in making the
most of the resources nature will provide in a given environment. In this context it is noteworthy that the fourteenth-century Dorothea of Montau is often
perceived by critics as "a bad cook" (48, 51) because she insists on lenten fare
the year round. Yet it is precisely her invention of lenten dishes, such as
"Scania herring," that makes her contribution to cooking invaluable.

The misconceptions about the function of food are paralleled by the notion that the author chose the region of his hometown of Danzig as locale for
his historical cooks for no other but sentimental reasons. Although the stages
of cultural and historical growth of civilizations are regularly observed near
river deltas, reviewers tend to refer to the mouth of the Vistula as a strange
and exotic strip of Baltic coastline. The question has been raised whether "in
the brooding insistence upon the regional... there may be a difficulty for
American readers" (30). The failure of some reviewers to correctly locate the
Women's Tribunal (it is taking place in Berlin) indicates some confusion.
Paul Zweig has this trial take place in the 1960s (65) in a moviehouse in Danzig, while Nigel Dennis has the Flounder "stand trial at the hand of the libbers of Bonn" (18). The latter also maintains that "Grass says, when God
made Frankfurt-am-Main he shat a lump of concrete." Dennis draws somewhat farreaching conclusions from this statement when he assumes that the
work's "soft and flaccid element... has pleased the Germans," because, he
argues, "much as his [Grass's] countrymen have the right to admire the
strength they have shown since 1945 in emulating the deity, the need
for... tears in the *Biergarten* and sentimental laughter—is as strong today as
it was in the Prussian Reich" (18). However, Grass (or the narrator) expresses himself in hypothetical terms: "If God had shat a pile of concrete, the result would have been Frankfurt" (F, 186).

Related, perhaps, to the conceptions or misconceptions about the role of
food in this book is the role of excrement, or, as reviewers would have it, the
role of scatology. There is no question that many American readers are turned
off by those passages or even subheadings that refer in some way to the end
results of digestion, such as "Inspection of feces" (F, 235), "Excrement
rhymed" (F, 280), and others. An editorial writer for *The Christian Science
Monitor* clearly states as his major objection to the book "a lack of discern-
ment" on the part of the author: "These [excesses] go well beyond any hearty
vulgarian's glorification of bodily functions to the rankest sort of blasphemy.
It may be 'the puritanical mind' which finds this obscene, as the narrator suggests. But an author so undiscriminating as to include it makes his own judgment look suspect" (45). At the other end of the spectrum *Playboy* magazine
presented several pages of extracts from *The Flounder* as a "first look at a
new novel" in the December 1978 issue (25). In addition to having discovered

these "spice-filled morsels" in Grass's prose, the magazine also discovered the author as a graphic artist. The extracts from *The Flounder* were accompanied by a small reproduction of the 1973 self-portrait "Sated" (*Gestillt*) and a full-page reproduction of "Kiss II" (*Kuss II*, 1975)—an etching that shows the head of a woman in close contact with that of a fish. The footnote to these etchings is slightly misleading, however, in claiming that they were made "to illustrate the book." At any rate, the idea of presenting some excerpts from Grass's novel and illustrating it with his art work proved so appealing that the editors of *Esquire* decided to do something similar. But apparently they encountered problems when they assumed that the purchase of an author's prints automatically provides the copyright for their reproduction.

IV. The Poems

Only *Time* and *New Yorker* quoted an example of the forty-six poems that are interspersed throughout the novel. Several reviewers did not mention the poems at all. For instance, *New York Review*, in a report of three thousand words ignored this aspect of the novel entirely. The comments of those who do mention the poems are mixed and quite general: "The whole [is] seasoned with a liberal sprinkling of poems about which the best I can say is that they don't survive translation" (65); "There are, to be sure, interpolated poems that do not seem to live up, and thus advance the cause of, the prose" (54); "Prose chapters alternate with free-verse poems whose verbal energy, if it exists in the original, didn't travel" (16); "In tone it ranges . . . from mock-lyrical scatology to a grim description of a visit in Calcutta" (43); "He also lards his narrative with mock-epic poetry" (53); "There are also poems" (23); "I, for one, find the poems preferable to the whole, long—if masterfully structured and expertly translated—novel" (33); "The novel is a dramatized vision of history, with horror, humor, lyricism, pathos and scatology . . ." (3); ". . . prose episodes are balanced by about forty passages of poetry, all in Grass's free verse, low keyed and often witty manner. Not a few of the latter are extremely successful" (27); "Grass's . . . historical consciousness pulses heavily but not so much as to drown the comedy and lyricism" (8); "The clangorous prose debauchery . . . is set off by less successful but welcome poems, a recurrent punctuation" (30); "Nor is it to mention the wonderfully suggestive, witty, elusive poems strewn about with a prodigal hand, enough of them to compose a volume in themselves" (39); "These poetic summaries of comments . . . are pointed and witty and provide relief for the reader in breaking the voluminous flow of the sixty-some episodes of the book" (55).

There may be a certain justification in the implied criticisms of the translation of the poems in the novel. A comparison of the English and German

versions reveals that Ralph Manheim may have been overly careful in repro-
ducing every word and nuance of the original—thereby losing some of the
terseness, conciseness, and elliptical quality of Grass's poetry. In England,
the publication of *The Flounder* by Secker and Warburg coincided with that
of a volume of Grass's poems in a bilingual edition. These poems under the
title *In the Egg*, translated by Michael Hamburger and Christopher Middleton, were selected from Grass's earlier poetry and had been published previously in the United States.[6] As in British publications *The Flounder* and *In
the Egg* were usually reviewed together, in several instances these early Grass
poems received a more favorable evaluation than his new novel (14, 7). This
may be more attributable to the critics' implicit view that poetry has no apparent function in a major prose work than to the fact that Grass's independently published poetry and the poems included in *The Flounder* were rendered
into English by different translators.

V. The Translation

The English translation of the book drew a surprising number of comments—surprising, because Ralph Manheim has been Grass's unusually successful and loyal prose translator ever since *The Tin Drum*, for whose English
version he won the PEN translation prize in 1964. Those referring to the
translation in passing as "excellent" or "valiant," "astonishingly lyric and
precise," or "capturing the gusto of Grass's pungent and punful prose" are
judging presumably by the richness of the English prose, its inventiveness and
resourcefulness in reflecting a variety of lingos and jargons, and its overall air
of "authentic Grass." They are right, especially with regard to the narrative
parts of the work. However, at least one reviewer, John Simon of the *Saturday Review*, went to the trouble of carefully checking out details; he indig-
nantly reported on a number of inaccuracies he found. Yet, a more comprehensive study of Manheim's English version would indicate that it is a rather
nitpicking exercise to argue whether, for example, *bei Gelegenheit* should, in
a given context, be translated as "when the occasion presented itself" or
"circumstances permitting." Such minor inaccuracies as Simon detected are
usually outweighed by considerations of overall stylistic unity, variety, or
complexity. Measured by such standards it is not really critical whether *spitzfindig* is rendered as "meticulously" or "cunningly, resourcefully." Indeed,
these questions seem in themselves *spitzfindig* in view of the fact that Manheim had to find convincing English equivalents for such alliterative terms as
wortgewaltige Wortspalter (B, 44). Moreover, he was confronted with the
staggering task of researching colorful names for an endless variety of
mushrooms, roots, herbs, grain, deer, fish, and dishes ordinarily not to be
found in English dictionaries, in addition to finding tribal and personal

names that corresponded as closely as possible to the many historical and geographic terms. The difficulties arising from the translation of the title are revealing in this respect (cf. the "Translator's Note," F, xii). This is not to mention Manheim's ingenious recreations of Grass's pseudo-Middle High German rhymes for the High Gothic Dorothea, or the verses and little songs that characterize the Baroque poets Opitz and Gryphius. In fact, one gets the impression that Manheim must have met the challenge of recreating this whopping volume in English not merely with unsparing dedication but also with a good deal of personal enjoyment and enthusiasm.

When asked in an interview what he thought of Manheim's translation, the author, who must be considered a competent judge of literary translation (11, 64), replied: "Manheim has done a first-rate job. He has adapted the book for the American reader—you can't ask for anything better" (48). One reviewer goes even further. In comparing the two versions of the notorious Father's Day chapter he finds "that although Mr. Manheim is faithful to his author, his American-English version is the more impressive. Here, as elsewhere in the novel, Mr. Manheim uses a cooler hand and chooses his words from a harder vocabulary" (18). Here could be an explanation, why this chapter has not elicited the shocked reaction among American readers that it provoked initially in some German reviews (31).[7]

There is, however, one problem related to Manheim's American adaptation—owing to the fact that the work was published in the same translation by Secker and Warburg in London. Not a few of the British reviewers of *The Flounder* emphasized that they consider the translation to be "American." The reviewer of the *Spectator*, for one, conceived this to be a shortcoming: "I trust that Secker and Warburg, if they use Mannheim's [sic] otherwise excellent translation, will retouch it in British English: obscene idiom in particular jars for the English reader when it is translated into American slang" (49).

VI. Readers' Expectations

If, in the English-speaking countries, *The Flounder* has so far not yet met with the same popular acclaim that it was accorded in Germany, it is not on account of an inadequate translation. For example, Michael Hollington writes: "It is possible to claim that critical reaction to the book in English-speaking countries was short-sighted." He believes "that as the novel is digested [at an appropriately slow rate] its distinction will gradually be recognized."[8] Obviously, if a book is to become a popular success, it has to speak to some other need besides private enthusiasm (or lack of it) on the part of reviewers and critics. While it is easy to see what needs this book could be addressing in today's German society, it is also evident that such factors as historical consciousness on the one hand and concern with utopian solutions to world crises on the other are not what the American reader is primarily looking for. As Roger Sale wrote in the *Chicago Tribune*: "Since it is a book very much rooted in German experience, it won't do anything like that well here . . . It is not the sort of book we make into a best seller" (51).

In his review for the *New York Times* M. Dickstein points out that, "It is a truism to say that, except for Southerners like Faulkner who inherited the consequences of the Civil War, American writers have a relatively undeveloped sense of history" (19). Such sense of history may simply reflect Americans' greater degree of security and autonomy with regard to history's past and future burdens; conversely, writers and readers in Germany (that is, in the Federal Republic) apparently feel the need to rediscover history without the severe ideological restraints of the Third Reich.

"A run to the encyclopedia reveals that many of the characters are historical figures," one reviewer informs us (16). Indeed, many names will have a greater resonance for German readers. Actually much of the "fun," that is, the irony and parody that the book provides, arises because traditionally exalted figures from every branch of the humanities are removed from their pedestals and shown—still within their historic roles—as human beings. For instance, to see such revered but rarely read Romantics as Achim von Arnim and Bettina Brentano get high together on fly agaric (a colorful but poisonous good luck symbol), or to have the highly respected Grimm Brothers indicted for taking editorial liberties with the sacred "truth" of fairy tales, or to look at the time of the Reformation from the viewpoint of a "liberated" abbess, must be "fun" for young readers—provided these perspectives are part of their lessons in history and literature. Similarly, some encrusted notions about the past held by many adults since their school days are shaken loose and seen in new contexts. Removed from this kind of social or cultural environment, the book, as one reviewer predicted, "may delight a few and will bore many" (33).

Recently, American moviegoers rejected a lengthy movie about the Old West because it seemed like "a four hour guided tour through your own living room."[9] In a sense, *The Flounder* is a guided tour of another living room, with some of its more permanent fixtures irreverently covered by graffiti.

A sampling of the critical reaction to the publication of Manheim's translation of *The Meeting at Telgte* in May 1981 does not yield any conclusive answer to the question whether the epic dimensions of *The Flounder* have been its major drawback or whether it is Grass's play with European political and cultural history that caused its lacking impact. On the one hand, *Telgte* is called "an imaginative leap . . . easily accessible . . . even to those unfamiliar with the details of German life in this or the 17th century" (67). On the other hand, one reviewer opines that, "in English," there is an overabundance of "encyclopediana" (69); in a similar vein another reviewer concludes that the book "is likely to be a mystifying disappointment for American readers" (71).

Like its predecessor *The Flounder*, the German original of *Telgte*, which was published in April 1979, met with great success and immediately climbed to the top of the bestseller lists. As he had done in the case of *The Flounder*, the author met with the translators of *Telgte* for a question-and-answer session in January 1980 to fulfill his obligations to his foreign readers (62). The difficulties of translating are illustrated by the fact that, at the time of the translators' meeting in Frankfurt, no decision had been made concerning the title of the English version (62)—presumably because of the English-speaking reading public's unfamiliarity with the small town of Telgte. But, then, most German readers probably were not aware either of the existence of the historic town of Telgte chosen by Grass for a fictitious meeting of German writers and poets at the end of the Thirty Years' War.

VII. Graphic Arts

The fact that *The Flounder* has not won as wide a reading public and sold as many copies as *The Tin Drum*,[10] the first volume of the popular, so-called "Danzig Trilogy," does not mean that the "Green Days of Grass"[11] in the United States are definitely over. By now another aspect of the author's labors during the last decade or so has emerged more clearly. In fact, Grass spent the years since 1972 only partially with writing a novel that was to be completed by his fiftieth birthday on 16 October 1977. During these years Grass also found a new approach to what had been his original "calling": sculpting and the graphic arts. Since an artist friend showed Grass in 1972 how to work with a needle and copperplate, he has produced some 145 etchings. The resulting prints are receiving more and more international acclaim as the writer-artist is visibly perfecting his technique from year to year. Although there had been exhibits of Grass prints sponsored by Goethe Institutes before 1977, the official introduction of his prints to the American public took place March 1977 at the Weyhe Gallery in New York as part of a "Berlin Now" festival. This included an exhibition of contemporary Berlin art at the New School Art Center and other local galleries, and readings by Uwe Johnson and Günter Grass. At that time the dustcover etching of *The Flounder* already existed; since that time Lee Naiman has been the art dealer for Grass's prints, and Anselm Dreher produced a catalogue of the etchings from 1972 to 1979 that is also available with a short English preface.[12]

In the United States, Grass's etchings have been received not so much as a byproduct of his writing—as was more or less the case in Germany—but as works of fine art in their own right. An awareness that Grass the artist is more than an illustrator of his own prose fiction is discernible in some *Flounder* reviews. Although *Time* and *Newsweek*, for example, chose to reproduce one of the author's numerous etchings of the "Flounder" in their reviews, they were careful not to speculate as to their role in the conception of the book. Actually, the so-called "Middle-Aged Flounder" reproduced by *Time* was not executed until 1978, a year after the novel had been finished. Originally entitled *Mann im Butt*, it shows a distorted self-portrait embedded in the "broadside" of the turbot. The "Flounder" reproduced by *Newsweek* is the second view of the fish in a series of seven, all done in 1977. The series was entitled, "When only the bones were left of the Flounder" *(Als vom Butt nur die Gräte geblieben war)*. In this example the fish is not seen as the perfect specimen pictured on the dustcover of both the German and American editions, but looked at from above, its mouth wide open, as it would appear after having been caught. *Saturday Review* reprinted a 1974 etching entitled, "Inspecting Mushrooms" (*Pilze besehen*) that shows a self-portrait, a pair of eyeglasses, and a pair of mushrooms arranged vertically in this order. *New York Times* combined the dustcover etching with a photoportrait of the author. Some other reviews added drawings of a flounder by their own artists. Does this mean that the subject of the book was demanding some visual representation?

Between August and December of 1980 five exhibitions of selected Grass prints took place in different parts of the country.[13] They engendered some reviews and publications that add a new perspective to the American reception of *The Flounder*. A more comprehensive analysis of Grass's artwork, as seen through the eyes of an art historian, can be found in *The Print Collector's Newsletter*. In surveying Grass's personal history as an artist and in trying to relate his work to European art history Mary Lee Thompson links his technique of printmaking but also his observations of the forms of plants, animals, and humans to Dürer: "He draws the skin of flounder in all its detail of knobby texture as a biological specimen the way Dürer drew the plated hide of the . . . rhinoceros" (59). While Grass's art is related to Dürer in technique, in subject matter it is closer to the demonic images of Bosch and Brueghel, and even to modern Surrealism. With regard to some twentieth-century artists and Expressionists it appears that "the styles of drawing and the specific forms of these artists are less important than the emotional intensity, the Expressionism." This art historian maintains that *The Flounder* "ransacks History of Art surveys as the book's basic structure" and that "Grass chooses artist/writers as key figures in his writing: Dürer, then Möller/Opitz, and Runge/Grimm brothers." In describing the prints Thompson concludes that they do not illustrate or explain the writing or vice versa: "They are images, not narratives. They stand alone, but in series, resisting explanation." As the two major themes she identified sexuality and violence. In comparing *The Flounder* and the etchings produced during the time Grass wrote the novel, the author concludes: "At times the book reads as a tedious document of the discomfort of one lover-of-women with the liberation movement. The prints, on the other hand, are never tedious or tendentious" (59).

In this analysis of Grass's artwork, the Oscar winning film *The Tin Drum*, directed in 1979 by Volker Schlöndorff with the close collaboration of the author, is conceived as a "synthesis of his dual profession of wordsmith and printmaker." Elsewhere the imagery of the film as well as that of Grass's prints has been characterized as "Dream Work" (52) and "Dreamlike Images" (32), respectively. In reviewing the film for *Time* Richard Schickel emphasized its "sharply realized, entirely realistic figures who exist in a palpable, well specified environment." Nevertheless the film is said to have "the dislocating immediacy of a nightmare" (52). A viewer of the print exhibit at Wesleyan University noted, "There is even a portrait on view of the film's Oskar, the boy who refused to grow up" (24). Actually, David Bennent, who played Oskar Matzerath, can be seen in two protraits by Grass, in 1978 with the attribute of an eel, and in 1979, in the softer but scarce lines of a drypoint, the token drummer's sticks attached to his shoulder.[14]

Some four years ago a journalist wrote in *Commonweal*: "A picture, in Grass's case, is not worth a thousand words. His words are too valuable. . . The etchings are interesting and well executed and they make money. They need the novels but the novels don't need them" (44). Today, not a few viewers and reviewers of Grass's writing and artwork would disagree. The immediacy of his graphic images and the bold confrontations of objects and live beings from different realms tend to fascinate many American viewers who have no patience with the author's epic fantasies. In the words of an art reviewer for *New York Post*, "The novels of Grass almost burst with richness from between their covers. This work on the walls was lean, sparse, for all its sexual imagery" (58). This observation is augmented in a recent discussion of "Grass' Sordid Pseudo-Realism [in comparison to] Warhol's Handsome Portraits." Here we read, "The composition itself may be sparse but within the objects included there is detail upon detail and line upon line until the eye reels and the mind rebels" (26). Although this stark, if challenging attempt at comparing and contrasting professes to "being either chauvinistic or hopelessly prejudiced," it demonstrates how Grass's etchings can be viewed rather productively without any interference from the texts that originated in connection with them. The question of the independence of Grass's graphic art is also raised in *Los Angeles Times*: "Grass' etchings are sufficiently expressive to stand alone, but they are greatly enhanced by familiarity with his books" (56). Yet in reporting that

Grass "draws a giant fly on a man's forehead" the reviewer is apparently not aware that the *Portrait mit Schmeissfliege* had a function in the 1980 election campaign in the Federal Republic of Germany. In this as in previous campaigns Grass was supporting the Social Democrats; and when the candidate for the opposition party, F. J. Strauss, made a public statement comparing writers and *literati* collectively to bugs and blowflies, the artist-writer Grass did not hesitate to graphically turn the attribute of a blowfly into a personal and a party symbol in this "Portrait with Blowfly" that found wide distribution on various posters (see KG, 56-58). Although this incident demonstrates how the author, who has always engaged in drawing, even long before he met with the challenging resistance of the copper plate, could conceive a picture worth a thousand words, this process also works in reverse: only the picture that can also stand alone may inspire a thousand words.

The compactness and courage of his views, his willingness to confront any clearcut question head on, and his firm command of the English language have made Günter Grass a favorite of interviewers. On these occasions, when asked about his method of working, he never fails to mention his drawings and poems at the inception of *The Flounder*. As the approach of American reporters tends to be more informal, flexible, and open-ended than that of their European colleagues, such interviews with Grass the writer, Grass the artist, and Grass the socialist have often resulted in elucidating statements on a wide range of subjects. An impressive example of the author's willingness to "Speak Out"[15] when given the chance and the right leads can be found in the *New Republic* of December, 1978 (35). Some less stringent and more pragmatic "Answers by Günter Grass" were reported in the *New York Times* of 17 December 1978 (48). But it was also possible to read English excerpts of Grass's discussion with the editors of *Le Point* in Paris (57).

Some of the interviews with Günter Grass that were recorded during his numerous visits to the United States might well be worth retranslating for his German readers and critics. This is not to say that an author should be considered a competent judge of his work, nor do his views on history, politics, and art deserve more attention than those of the specialists in these fields. But, considering how many questions about *The Flounder* are still awaiting answers from scholars and critics in literature and art, and considering the vast disagreements among the reviewers of the book, an approach that also enlists the author's comments may prove quite productive.

Notes

1. Heinrich Vormweg, "Eine phantastische Totale. Nachtrag zur 'Butt'-Kritik," *TuK*, pp. 94-100.
2. According to the Fawcett Crest paperback edition the book was on the *New York Times* bestseller list for three months. It was on the bestseller list of *Time* from 12 April 1963 to 12 July 1963.
3. Richard Howard, "A Whopper of a Tale," pp. 23-24. In the following, all references to reviews listed in the Bibliography, B/IV/3, will be given by the appropriate numbers in parentheses.
4. "Year's Best," *Time*, 1 Jan. 1979, p. 88.
5. Sigrid Mayer, "*Der Butt*: Lyrische und graphische Quellen," *AoF*, pp. 16-23.
6. See Bibliography, A/II/3.
7. See also Rolf Michaelis, "Mit dem Kopf auch den Gaumen aufklären," p. 19.
8. See Michael Hollington, "Back to the Pisspot," *Günter Grass*, pp. 159-69.
9. Michael Cimino, "Heaven's Gate," *United Artists*. The quote was reported anonymously on NBC Television News in the last week of November 1980.
10. "*The Flounder* has sold some 28,000 copies in the English edition (USA) published by Harcourt Brace Jovanovich in 1978. It was also licensed to Quality Paperback Book Club, and appeared as their April (1979) double selection. Exclusive paperback reprint rights were sold to Fawcett World Library." This information by courtesy of *Helen and Kurt Wolff Books, Harcourt Brace Jovanovich, Inc.*, New York, 18 Nov. 1980.
11. Cf. *Life,* June 1965, pp. 51-56.
12. Anselm Dreher, *Günter Grass. Werkverzeichnis der Radierungen.* (Berlin: Galerie Andre-Anselm Dreher, 1979). The American publication retained the title *Werkverzeichnis* (New York: Lee Naiman Fine Arts, 1979); Grass's preface was translated by Kate Lewin.
13. Cherry Stone Gallery, Wellfleet, Mass., August 1980; Suzanne Gross Gallery, Philadelphia, Pa., 2-27 Sept. 1980; Art Expo New York, Gallery 1980, 28th St.; Davison Art Center, Wesleyan University, Conn., 17 Oct.-23 Nov. 1980; Mirage Editions, Santa Monica, Ca., 7 Nov.-7 Dec. 1980.
14. *Werkverzeichnis der Radierungen*, pp. 271, 279.
15. See also Grass's volume of speeches by the same title (Bibliography, A/II/4).

Appendices

Structural Diagram of *The Flounder**

Month	Period	Place	Cook
1(a)	Neolithic: 2211 B.C.	swamps of the Vistula estuary	Awa, priestess
(b)	Iron Age: Great Migration	swamps of the Vistula estuary	Wigga, priestess
(c)	10th century: Pomorshians converted to Christianity	swamps of the Vistula estuary (Wicker Bastion)	Mestwina, priestess
2	14th century: High Gothic period	Danzig	Dorothea of Montau, Saint
3	16th century: Reformation	Danzig	Margarete ("Fat Gret") Rusch, abbess (1489–1585)
4	17th century: Thirty Years' War, Baroque period	Danzig	Agnes Kurbiella (1619–1689)
5	18th century: Frederic II of Prussia, Age of Enlightenment	Royal Prussian State Farm at Zuckau	Amanda Woyke (1734–1806)
6	Napoleonic period: Romanticism	Danzig	Sophie Rotzoll (1784–1849)
7	19th and 20th centuries	Danzig	Lena Stubbe (1849–1942)
8	Father's Day: June 1963	Berlin (West)	Sibylle ("Billy") Miehlau (1929–1963)
9	1970: Workers' uprising at Lenin Shipyard	Gdańsk	Maria Kuczorra (b. 1949)

* Similar diagrams may be found in Volker Neuhaus, *Günter Grass*, p. 144, and Peter Russell, "Floundering in Feminism: The Meaning of Günter Grass's *Der Butt*," p. 56.

NARRATOR	NARRATOR'S FRIEND	WOMEN'S TRIBUNAL
Edek, fisherman and potter	Lud(ek), fisherman	Dr. Ursula Schönherr, presiding judge
Edek, fisherman and potter	Ludger, a Goth	Helga Paasch
Shepherd Bishop Adalbert of Prague (d. 997)	Prelate Ludewik	Ruth Simoneit
Albrecht Slichting, swordmaker	Ludwig Skriever, woodcarver	Dr. Sieglinde ("Siggie") Huntscha, prosecutor
Runaway Franciscan monk Blacksmith Rusch Lutheran preacher Hegge Mayor Ferber Abbot Jeschke Vasco da Gama	Lud, coppersmith Ladewig, executioner	Ulla Witzlaff
Martin Opitz, poet Anton Möller, painter	Axel Ludström, a Swede	Bettina von Carnow, defense counsel
August Romeike, farm inspector	Ludrichkait	Therese Osslieb
Friedrich Bartholdy Pastor Blech General Rapp, governor	Captain Fahrenholz	Griselde Dubertin
Stobbe (d. 1871), Stubbe (d. 1914), anchor makers	Ludwig Skröver	Erika Nöttke
Writer, formerly engaged to "Billy"	Frankie Ludkowiak	Beate Hagedorn
Writer ("I"), married to Ilsebill	Jan Ludkowski Ludwig Gabriel Schrieber, sculptor	Elisabeth Güllen

German–English Concordance: *The Flounder*

The reader may approximate passages quoted in each of the four editions currently available by referring to the pagination in the columns below (columns I and III denote the pagination of the hardcover editions used throughout the volume).

Col. I: *Der Butt* (Neuwied: Luchterhand, 1977).
Col. II: *Der Butt* (Frankfurt am Main: Fischer Bücherei, 1979).
Col. III: *The Flounder* (New York: Harcourt Brace Jovanovich, 1978).
Col. IV: *The Flounder* (New York: Fawcett Crest, 1979).

GERMAN	I	II	ENGLISH	III	IV
IM ERSTEN MONAT			*THE FIRST MONTH*		
Die dritte Brust	9	7	The third breast	3	13
Worüber ich schreibe	14	11	What I write about	8	17
Neun und mehr Köchinnen	16	13	Nine and more cooks	9	19
Aua	28	22	Awa	19	28
Wie der Butt gefangen wurde	28	23	How the Flounder was caught	20	29
Arbeit geteilt	45	37	Division of labor	34	42
Wie der Butt zum zweiten Mal gefangen wurde	46	38	How the Flounder was caught a second time	34	43
Vorgeträumt	54	45	Dreaming ahead	41	50
Wie der Butt von den Ilsebills angeklagt wurde	56	46	How the Flounder was prosecuted by the Ilsebills	42	51
Fleisch	66	54	Meat	51	59
Wo das gestohlene Feuer kurze Zeitlang versteckt wurde	67	55	Where the stolen fire was briefly hidden	52	60

GERMAN	I	II	ENGLISH	III	IV
Was uns fehlt	70	57	What we lack	54	62
Gastlich von Horde zu Horde	71	59	Hospitality from horde to horde	66	74
Doktor Zärtlich	85	70	Dr. Affectionate	66	74
Gestillt	86	70	Fed	67	74
Die Runkelmuhme	87	71	The wurzel mother	68	75
Demeter	103	85	Demeter	81	88
Wozu ein gusseiserner Löffel gut ist	104	85	What a cast–iron spoon is good for	81	88
Wie ich mich sehe	116	95	How I see myself	91	98
Ach Ilsebill	117	96	Oh, Ilsebill	92	99
Am Ende	120	99	At the end	95	101
Woran ich mich nicht erinnern will	121	99	What I don't want to remember	96	102
IM ZWEITEN MONAT			*THE SECOND MONTH*		
Wie wir städtisch wurden	137	111	How we became city dwellers	107	113
Streit	161	131	Quarrel	127	132
Ein Abwasch	161	131	Dishwashing	128	133
Helene Migräne	175	143	Elaine Migraine	139	143
Manzi Manzi	176	143	Libber, Libber	140	144
Ähnlich meiner Dorothea	178	145	Like my Dorothea	141	146
Wie im Kino	189	154	Like at the movies	151	155

German	I	II	English	III	IV
Die Köchin küsst	295	239	The cook kisses	233	235
IM VIERTEN MONAT			*THE FOURTH MONTH*		
Den Kot beschauen	299	241	Inspection of feces	235	237
Leer und alleine	304	245	Empty and alone	239	241
Von der Last böser Zeit	305	246	The burden of an evil day	240	242
Runkeln und Gänseklein	315	254	Turnips and Gänseklein	249	250
Warum der Butt zwei kalte Öfen wieder befeuern wollte	316	255	Why the Flounder tried to rekindle two cold stoves	249	251
Spät	327	264	Late	258	259
Fischig über die Liebe und Poesie	328	265	Fishily on love and poetry	259	260
Bei Kochfisch Agnes erinnert	341	275	Agnes remembered over boiled fish	270	270
Der soll Axel geheissen haben	342	276	It seems his name was Axel	270	271
Kot gereimt	354	286	Excrement rhymed	280	280
Nur eine hat als Hexe gebrannt	355	287	Only one was burned as a witch	281	281
Unsterblich	361	299	Immortal	286	286
IM FÜNFTEN MONAT			*THE FIFTH MONTH*		
Woggegen Kartoffelmehl hilft	365	293	What potato flour is good for (and against)	287	287
Beim Eichelstossen Gänserupfen Kartoffelschälen erzählt	368	295	Told while pounding acorns, plucking geese, peeling potatoes	290	290

GERMAN	I	II	ENGLISH	III	IV
Wir sassen zu dritt	481	387	Three at table	380	377
Nur Töchter	500	402	Nothing but daughters	395	392
Fortgezeugt	507	408	Continuous generation	401	397
IM SIEBTEN MONAT			*THE SEVENTH MONTH*		
Auch mit Ilsebill	511	409	With Ilsebill, too	402	399
Lena teilt Suppe aus	514	411	Lena dishes out soup	405	401
Eine einfache Frau	515	412	A simple woman	406	402
Alle	526	421	All	415	411
Nagel und Strick	527	422	Nail and rope	416	412
Bratkartoffeln	539	432	Home-fried potatoes	425	421
Bebel zu Gast	540	433	Bebel's visit	426	422
Die Reise nach Zürich	555	445	The trip to Zurich	439	434
Wo ihre Brillen liegenblieben	564	453	Where she left her specs	447	441
Lena nachgerufen	567	455	An obituary for Lena	449	443
IM ACHTEN MONAT			*THE EIGHTH MONTH*		
Vatertag	575	461	Father's Day	454	449
IM NEUNTEN MONAT			*THE NINTH MONTH*		
Lud	629	503	Lud	494	483

GERMAN	I	II	ENGLISH	III	IV
Verspätet	634	507	Late	499	493
Bis zum Erbrechen	635	508	Why she vomited	499	494
Einige Kleidersorgen, weibliche Ausmasse und letzte Visionen	648	519	Vestimentary preoccupations, feminine proportions, last visions	510	504
Das Feminal	655	524	The Womenal	515	509
Auf Møn	670	537	On Møn	527	521
Wortwechsel	677	542	Conversation	533	526
Was wir uns wünschen	678	543	What we wish for	534	527
Mannomann	682	547	Man oh man	538	530
Dreimal Schweinekohl	683	548	Three meals of pork and cabbage	539	531

German–English Concordance: *The Meeting at Telgte*

	Das Treffen in Telgte	*The Meeting at Telgte*
1	p. 7	p. 3
2	15	9
3	22	14
4	28	18
5	33	22
6	42	30
7	49	35
8	55	40
9	61	45
10	68	49
11	74	53
12	87	63
13	95	69
14	108	79
15	114	83
16	127	93
17	133	97
18	142	103
19	149	109
20	156	113
21	168	122
22	175	127
23	179	130

Bibliography

A. Works by Grass (in chronological order according to genre)

I. IN GERMAN

1. Prose Fiction

Die Blechtrommel. Roman. Neuwied: Luchterhand, 1959.
Katz und Maus. Eine Novelle. Neuwied: Luchterhand, 1961.
Hundejahre. Roman. Neuwied: Luchterhand, 1963.
Örtlich betäubt. Roman. Neuwied: Luchterhand, 1969.
Aus dem Tagebuch einer Schnecke. Neuwied: Luchterhand, 1972.
Der Butt. Roman. Neuwied: Luchterhand, 1977.
Das Treffen in Telgte. Eine Erzählung. Neuwied: Luchterhand, 1979.
Danziger Trilogie. Neuwied: Luchterhand, 1980.
Kopfgeburten oder Die Deutschen sterben aus. Neuwied: Luchterhand, 1980.

2. Dramas and Film

Die Plebejer proben den Aufstand. Neuwied: Luchterhand, 1966.
Theaterspiele. Neuwied: Luchterhand, 1970. [*Onkel, Onkel; Noch zehn Minuten bis Buffalo; Die bösen Köche; Die Plebejer proben den Aufstand; Davor*].
(with Volker Schlöndorff). *Die Blechtrommel als Film.* Frankfurt am Main: Zweitausendundeins, 1979.

3. Poetry

Die Vorzüge der Windhühner. Neuwied: Luchterhand, 1956.
Gleisdreieck. Neuwied: Luchterhand, 1960.
Ausgefragt. Neuwied: Luchterhand, 1967.
Gesammelte Gedichte. Neuwied: Luchterhand, 1971.
Mariazuehren. Hommageàmarie. Inmarypraise. Photos Maria Rama. Munich: Bruckmann, 1973.
Liebe geprüft. Bremen: Schünemann, 1973.

4. Political and Theoretical Writings

Über das Selbstverständliche. Reden, Aufsätze, Offene Briefe, Kommentare. Neuwied: Luchterhand, 1968.
Über meinen Lehrer Döblin und andere Vorträge. Berlin: Literarisches Colloquium, 1968.
"Unser Grundübel ist der Idealismus." *Der Spiegel*, 11 Aug. 1969, p. 94.
Der Bürger und seine Stimme. Reden, Aufsätze, Kommentare. Neuwied: Luchterhand, 1974.

209

Denkzettel. Politische Reden und Aufsätze 1965–1976. Neuwied: Luchterhand, 1978.
Aufsätze zur Literatur. Neuwied: Luchterhand, 1980.

5. Interviews

Raddatz, Fritz J. "Heute lüge ich lieber gedruckt. *Zeit*-Gespräch über den *Butt* mit Günter Grass." *Die Zeit* (overseas ed.), 19 Aug. 1977, pp. 8-9. Rpt. in Fritz J. Raddatz. *ZEIT-Gespräche.* Frankfurt am Main: Suhrkamp, 1978.
Arnold, Heinz Ludwig. "Gespräche mit Günter Grass." *Tuk*, pp. 1-39.
Casanova, Nicole. *Günter Grass, atélier des métamorphoses. Entretiens avec Nicole Casanova, traduits de l'allemand et annotés.* Paris: Belfond, 1979.
'Am liebsten lüge ich gedruckt.' Interviews mit Günter Grass." *Der Spiegel*, 2 April 1979, pp. 219-25. [Excerpts from the interview with Nicole Casanova].

II. IN ENGLISH

1. Prose Fiction

The Tin Drum. Trans. Ralph Manheim. New York: Pantheon Books, 1963.
Cat and Mouse. Trans. Ralph Manheim. New York: Harcourt, Brace & World, 1963.
Dog Years. Trans. Ralph Manheim. New York: Harcourt, Brace & World, 1965.
Local Anaesthetic. Trans. Ralph Manheim. New York: Harcourt, Brace & World, 1969.
From the Diary of a Snail. Trans. Ralph Manheim. New York: Harcourt Brace Jovanovich, 1973.
The Flounder. Trans. Ralph Manheim. New York: Harcourt Brace Jovanovich, 1978.
The Meeting at Telgte. Trans. Ralph Manheim, afterword Leonard Forster. New York: Harcourt Brace Jovanovich, 1981.
Headbirths or The Germans Are Dying Out. Trans. Ralph Manheim. New York: Harcourt Brace Jovanovich, 1982.

2. Drama

The Plebeians Rehearse the Uprising. Trans. Ralph Manheim. New York: Harcourt, Brace & World, 1966.
Four Plays: Flood. Mister, Mister. Only Ten Minutes to Buffalo. The Wicked Cooks. Trans. Ralph Manheim and A. Leslie Willson, introd. Martin Esslin. New York: Harcourt, Brace & World, 1967.
Max: A Play. Trans. A. Leslie Willson and R. Manheim. New York: Harcourt Brace Jovanovich, 1972.

3. Poetry

Selected Poems. Trans. Michael Hamburger and Christopher Middleton. New York: Harcourt, Brace & World, 1966.
New Poems (Ausgefragt). Trans. Michael Hamburger. Bilingual ed. New York: Harcourt, Brace & World, 1968.
Inmarypraise. Trans. Christopher Middleton. Photos by Maria Rama. New York: Harcourt Brace Jovanovich, 1974.
In the Egg and Other Poems. Trans. Michael Hamburger and Christopher Middleton. New York: Harcourt Brace Jovanovich, 1977.

4. Political Writings

Speak Out: Speeches, Open Letters, Commentaries. Trans. Ralph Manheim, introd. Michael Harrington. New York: Harcourt, Brace & World, 1969.

5. Interviews

Plant, Richard. "Answers by Günter Grass." *The New York Times Book Review*, 17 Dec. 1978, pp. 14, 31.

B. Secondary Literature (in alphabetical order)

I. BIBLIOGRAPHIES

Everett, George A. *A Select Bibliography of Günter Grass (From 1956 to 1973)*. New York: Franklin, 1974.

Görtz, Franz Josef. "Kommentierte Auswahl-Bibliographie." *TuK*, pp. 175-99.

Neuhaus, Volker. "Literaturverzeichnis." *Günter Grass*, pp. 167-77.

O'Neill, Patrick. *Günter Grass. A Bibliography, 1955-1975*. Toronto: Toronto University Press, 1976.

Woods, Jean M. "Günter Grass: A Selected Bibliography. Parts I, II." *West Coast Review*, 5, No. 3 (Jan. 1971), 52-56; 6, No. 1 (June 1971), 31-40.

II. COLLECTIONS OF ESSAYS

Adventures of a Flounder: Critical Essays to Günter Grass' Der Butt. Ed. Gertrud B. Pickar. Houston German Studies, vol. III. Münich: W. Fink, 1982. [Abbreviated *AoF*; the individual contributions have been listed separately].

Von Buch zu Buch – Günter Grass in der Kritik. Eine Dokumentation. Ed. Gert Loschütz. Neuwied: Luchterhand, 1968.

Grass. Kritik – Thesen – Analysen. Ed. Manfred Jurgensen. Berne: Francke, 1973.

Günter Grass – Dokumente zur politischen Wirkung. Ed. Heinz Ludwig Arnold and Franz Josef Görtz. Munich: Edition Text + Kritik, 1971.

Günter Grass. Ein Materialienbuch. Ed. Rolf Geissler. Neuwied: Luchterhand, 1976.

A Günter Grass Symposium. Ed. A. Leslie Willson. Austin: The University of Texas Press, 1971.

Günter Grass. Text + Kritik. Ed. Heinz Ludwig Arnold. No. 1/1a, 5th ed. (June 1978). [Abbreviated *TuK*; the individual contributions have been listed separately].

III. CRITICAL WORKS IN GERMAN

1. General

Arnold, Heinz Ludwig. "Zeitroman mit Auslegern. Günter Grass' *Örtlich betäubt.*" *Grass*, ed. Jurgensen, pp. 97-102.

Brode, Hanspeter. *Günter Grass*. Munich: Beck, 1979.

Brode, Hanspeter. "Von Danzig zur Bundesrepublik. Grass' Bücher *örtlich betäubt* und *Aus dem Tagebuch einer Schnecke*," *TuK*, pp. 74-87.

Cepl-Kaufmann, Gertrude. *Günter Grass. Eine Analyse des Gesamtwerkes unter dem Aspekt von Literatur und Politik*. Kronberg/Taunus: Scriptor, 1975.

Enzensberger, Hans Magnus. "Wilhelm Meister, auf Blech getrommelt." *Von Buch zu Buch. Günter Grass in der Kritik*, ed. Loschütz, pp. 8-12.

Görtz, Franz Josef. *Günter Grass – Zur Parthogenese eines Markenbilds*. Meisenheim am Glan: Hain, 1978.

Görtz, Franz Josef. "Der Provokateur als Wahlhelfer. Kritisches zur Grass-Kritik." *TuK*, pp. 162-74.

Hamburger, Michael. "Moralist mit Narrenkappe. Die Lyrik des Günter Grass." *TuK*, pp. 107-117.

Jäger, Manfred. "Politischer Kleinkram? Günter Grass, ein Publizist mit Praxis." *TuK*, pp. 133-50.

Kaiser, Gerhard. *Günter Grass: Katz und Maus.* Munich: Fink, 1971.

Kaiser, Joachim. "Die Theaterstücke des Günter Grass." *TuK*, pp. 118-32.

Koopmann, Helmut. "Günter Grass. Der Faschismus als Kleinbürgertum und was daraus wurde." *Gegenwartsliteratur und Drittes Reich.* Ed. Hans Wagener. Stuttgart: Reclam, 1977, pp. 163-82.

Mayer, Gerhart. "Zum deutschen Antibildungsroman." *Jahrbuch der Raabe-Gesellschaft* (1974), pp. 55-64.

Mayer, Sigrid. "Grüne Jahre für Grass: Die Rezeption in den Vereinigten Staaten." *TuK*, pp. 151-61.

Neuhaus, Volker. *Günter Grass.* Stuttgart: Metzler, 1979.

Neuhaus, Volker. "Günter Grass." *Kritisches Lexikon zur deutschsprachigen Gegenwartsliteratur.* Ed. Heinz Ludwig Arnold. 7th supp. Munich: Edition Text + Kritik, Jan. 1981, pp. 1-16, A-L. [With bibliography].

Reddick, John. "Eine epische Trilogie des Leidens? *Die Blechtrommel, Katz und Maus, Hundejahre.*" *TuK*, pp. 60-73.

Plard, Henri. "Über die Blechtrommel." *TuK*, pp. 40-50.

Rohlfs, Jochen. "Erzählen aus unzuverlässiger Sicht: Zur Erzählstruktur bei Günter Grass." *TuK*, pp. 51-59.

Rothenberg, Jürgen. "Grosses 'Nein' und kleines 'Ja': *Aus dem Tagebuch einer Schnecke.*" Günter Grass, ed. Geissler, pp. 136-53.

Rothenberg, Jürgen. *Günter Grass. Das Chaos in verbesserter Ausführung: Zeitgeschichte als Thema und Aufgabe des Prosawerks.* Heidelberg: Winter, 1976.

Tank, Kurt Lothar. *Günter Grass.* Berlin: Colloquim, 1965. 5th, rev. ed., 1974.

Schwarz, Johannes Wilhelm. *Der Erzähler Günter Grass.* Berne: Francke, 1969. 2nd. ed., 1971.

2. On *The Flounder* and *The Meeting at Telgte*

Arnold, Heinz Ludwig, "Grafiker Grass." *TuK*, pp. 101-106.

Bleyl, Hansjoachim. "Danziger Alchemie." *Neue Rundschau*, 88 (1977), 629-35.

Brode, Hanspeter. "Kommunikationsstruktur und Erzählerposition in den Romanen von Günter Grass. *Die Blechtrommel, Aus dem Tagebuch einer Schnecke, Der Butt.*" *Germanisch-Romanische Monatsschrift*, 30 (1980), 438-50.

Burkhardt, Anke, et al. "Geschichten zur Geschichte. Zum neuen Roman von Günter Grass *Der Butt.*" *AoF*, pp. 81-90.

Durzak, Manfred. "Ein märchenhafter Roman. Zum *Butt* von Günter Grass." *Basis*, 9 (1979), 71-90, 261. Rpt. in Manfred Durzak. *Der deutsche Roman der Gegenwart. Entwicklungsvoraussetzungen und Tendenzen.* 3rd, rev. ed. Stuttgart: Kohlhammer, 1978.

Durzak, Manfred. "Die Zirkelschlüsse der Literaturkritik." *AoF*, pp. 63-80.

Haberkamm, Klaus. "'Mit allen Weisheiten Saturns geschlagen': Glosse zu einem Aspect [sic] der Gelnhausen-Figur in Günter Grass' *Treffen in Telgte.*" *Simpliciana. Schriften der Grimmelshausen-Gesellschaft*, 1 (1979), 67-78.

Hildesheimer, Wolfgang. "Butt und die Welt. Geburtstagsbrief an Günter Grass." *Merkur*, 31 (1977), 966-72.

Hoesterey, Ingeborg. "Aspekte einer Romanfigur: Der Butt im *Butt.*" *German Quarterly*, 54 (1981), 461-72.

Hoffmeister, Werner. "Dach, Distel und die Dichter: Günter Grass' *Das Treffen in Telgte.*" *Zeitschrift für deutsche Philologie*, 100 (1981), 274-81.

Jurgensen, Manfred. "Das allzeitig fiktionale Ich. Günter Grass: *Der Butt.*" *Erzählformen des fiktionalen Ich. Beiträge zum deutschen Gegenwartsroman.* Berne: Francke, 1980. pp. 121-44.

Karasek, Hellmuth. "Nora–Ein Suppenheim." *Der Spiegel*, 8 Aug. 1977, pp. 103-105.

Krättli, Anton. "Danziger Butt mit Zutaten: Zum neuen Roman von Günter Grass." *Schweizer Monatschefte*, 57 (1977), 485-93.

Mayer, Sigrid. "*Der Butt*: Lyrische und graphische Quellen." *AoF*, pp. 16-23.

Mews, Siegfried. "Der Butt als Germanist: Zur Rolle der Literatur in Günter Grass' Roman." *AoF*, pp. 24-31.

Michaelis, Rolf. "Mit dem Kopf auch den Gaumen aufklären." *Die Zeit* (overseas ed.), 19 Aug. 1977, pp. 8-9.

Perels, Christoph. "Über den Butt." *TuK*, pp. 88-90.

Raddatz, Fritz J. "' Wirklicher bin ich in meinen Geschichten.' Der *Butt* des Günter Grass. Eine erste Annäherung." *Merkur*, 31 (1977), 892-901.

Michaelis, Rolf. "Kein Treffen in Telgte." *Die Zeit* (overseas ed.), 6 April 1979, p. 13.

Reich-Ranicki, Marcel. "Von dem Grass un synen Fruen." *Frankfurter Allgemeine Zeitung*, 13 Aug. 1977. Rpt. in Marcel Reich-Ranicki, *Entgegnung. Zur deutschen Literatur der siebziger Jahre.* Stuttgart: Deutsche Verlagsanstalt, 1979, pp. 182-92.

Rölleke, Heinz. *Der wahre Butt. Die wundersamen Wandlungen des Märchens vom Fischer und seiner Frau.* Köln: Diederichs, 1978.

Schmid Noerr, Gunzelin. "Über den Butt." *TuK*, pp. 90-93.

Schneider, Rolf. "Eine barocke Gruppe 47." *Der Spiegel*, 2 April 1979, pp. 217-19.

Triller, Anneliese. "Grobe Verzeichnung. Die Darstellung der Dorothea von Montau durch Günter Grass." *Rheinischer Merkur*, 19 Aug. 1977, p. 20.

Verweyen, Theodor and Gunther Witting. "Polyhistors neues Glück. Zu Günter Grass' Erzählung *Das Treffen in Telgte* und ihrer Kritik." *Germanisch-Romanische Monatsschrift*, 30 (1980), 451-65.

Vormweg, Heinrich. "Eine phantastische Totale. Nachtrag zur *Butt*-Kritik." *TuK*, pp. 94-100.

Wallmann, Jürgen P. "Günter Grass: *Der Butt.*" *Neue Deutsche Hefte*, 24 (1977), 585-89.

Williams, Gerhild S. "Es war einmal, ist und wird wieder sein: Geschichte und Geschichten in Günter Grass' *Der Butt.*" *Deutsche Literatur in der Bundesrepublik seit 1965.* Ed. Paul Michael Lützeler and Egon Schwarz. Königstein/Taunus: Athenäum, 1980, pp. 182-94.

Zimmer, Dieter E. "Was heisst Glumse auf japanisch?" *Die Zeit* (overseas ed.), 17 Feb. 1978, p. 19.

IV. CRITICAL WORKS IN ENGLISH

1. General

Cunliffe, W. Gordon. *Günter Grass.* New York: Twayne, 1969.

Diller, Edward. *A Mythic Journey. Günter Grass's Tin Drum.* Lexington: The University Press of Kentucky, 1974.

Enright, D.J. "Casting Out Demons." *New York Review of Books*, 3 June 1965, pp. 8-10.

Forster, Leonard. "Günter Grass since the Danzig Trilogy." *University of Toronto Quarterly*, 47, No. 1 (1977), 56-73.

Hollington, Michael. *Günter Grass. The Writer in a Pluralist Society.* London: Boyars, 1980.

Leonard, Irène. *Günter Grass.* New York: Harper & Row, 1974.

Mason, Ann L. *The Skeptical Muse: A Study of Günter Grass' Conception of the Artist.* Berne: Lang, 1974.

Miles, Keith, *Günter Grass.* New York: Barnes & Noble, 1975.

Reddick, John. *The "Danzig Trilogy" of Günter Grass.* New York: Harcourt Brace Jovanovich, 1975.

Tank, Kurt Lothar. *Günter Grass.* Trans. John Conway. New York: Ungar, 1969.

Yates, Norris W. *Günter Grass. A Critical Essay.* Grand Rapids, Michigan: Eerdmans, 1967.

2. On *The Flounder* and *The Meeting at Telgte*

Angress, Ruth. "*Der Butt* – A Feminist Perspective." *AoF*, pp. 43-50.

Butler, G[eoffrey] P. "Grass Skirts the Issue: A Reaction to *Der Butt.*" *Quinquereme. New Studies in Modern Languages*, 2, No. 1 (1977), 23-33.

Durrani, Osman. "'Here Comes Everybody': An Appraisal of Narrative Technique in Günter Grass's *Der Butt.*" *Modern Language Review*, 75 (1980), 810-22.

Forster, Leonard. "An Unsystematic Approach to *Der Butt.*" *Festschrift for E. W. Herd.* Ed. August Obermayer. Dunedin, New Zealand: Department of German, University of Otago, 1980, pp. 55-77.

Hollington, Michael. "Back to the Pisspot." *Günter Grass. The Writer in a Pluralist Society*, pp. 158-69.

O'Neill, Patrick. "The Scheherazade Syndrome: Günter Grass' Meganovel *Der Butt.*" *AoF*, pp. 1-21.

Russell, Peter. "Floundering in Feminism: The Meaning of Günter Grass's *Der Butt.*" *German Life and Letters*, 33 (1979-80), 245-56.

Schade, Richard. "Poet and Artist: Iconography in Grass' *Treffen in Telgte.*" *German Quarterly*, 55 (1982), 200-211.

Stern, Guy. "*Der Butt* as an Experiment in the Structure of the Novel." *AoF*, pp. 51-55.

Thomas, Noel L. "Günter Grass's *Der Butt*: History and the Significance of the Eighth Chapter ('Vatertag')." *German Life and Letters*, 33 (1979-80), 75-86.

Ulfers, Friedrich. "Myth and History in Günter Grass' *Der Butt.*" *AoF*, pp. 32-42.

Willson, A. Leslie "The Numbers Game." *AoF*, pp. 56-62.

3. Reviews (compiled by Sigrid Mayer)

a) *The Flounder*

1 Adams, Phoebe-Lou. "*The Flounder* by Günter Grass." *Atlantic Monthly*, Dec. 1978, p. 98.

2 Anonymous. "Fish Tale." *Horizon*, Oct. 1978, p. 14.

3 Anonymous. "The Flounder." *Publishers Weekly*, 18 Sept. 1978, p. 162.

4 Anonymous. "The Flounder (Fawcett Crest)." *Publishers Weekly*, 3 Sept. 1979, p. 95.

5 Anonymous. "Grass, Günter. The Flounder." *Kirkus Reviews*, 1 Sept. 1978, p. 962.

6 Anonymous. "Günter Grass. Der Butt." *Booklist*, 1 May 1978, p. 1417.

7 Anonymous. "Günter Grass. Complex, but Worth it." *Economist*, 28 Oct. 1978, p. 126.

8 Anonymous. "Günter Grass. The Flounder." *Booklist*, 15 Sept. 1978, p. 155.

9 Anonymous. "More November Titles." *National Review*, 10 Nov. 1978, p. 1424.
10 Anonymous. "New in Paperback: Fiction." *Washington Post Book World*, 6 Jan. 1980, p. 15.
11 Anonymous. "Notes in Brief." *German Quarterly*, 51 (1978), 23.
12 Ascherson, Neal. "A Fish Out of Water." *Observer* (London), 8 Oct. 1978, p. 30.
13 Benjamin, Jessica. "The Fish That Got Away." *Ms.*, Dec. 1978, pp. 41, 44, 78.
14 Burgess, Anthony. "A Fish Among Feminists." *Times Literary Supplement*, 13 Oct. 1978, p. 1141.
15 Clark Jr., Lindley H. "A Christmas Potpourri of Books." *Wall Street Journal*, 8 Dec. 1978, pp. 17-18.
16 Clemons, Walter. "Fish Story." *Newsweek*, 6 Nov. 1978, p. 99.
17 Cloonan, William. "The Flounder by Günter Grass." *New Boston Review*, 5, No. 1 (Sept./Oct. 1979), 3-4.
18 Dennis, Nigel. "The One That Got Away." *New York Review of Books*, 23 Nov. 1978, pp. 22-23.
19 Dickstein, Morris. "An Epic, Ribald Miscellany." *New York Times Book Review*, 12 Nov. 1978, pp. 12, 66.
20 Enright, D. J. "The Sex of Power." *The Listener*, 26 Oct. 1978, p. 537.
21 Fenton, James. "Ins Archiv." *New Statesman*, 13 Oct. 1978, pp. 478-79.
22 Fine, Warren. "Review." *Prairie Schooner*, 53 (Summer 1979), 190-91.
23 Fremont-Smith, Eliot. "The Flounder." *Village Voice*, 20 Nov. 1978, p. 103.
24 Gonzales, Shirley. "Fantastic Inner Visions of Novelist–artist Grass." *New Haven Register*, 2 Nov. 1980. (Review of an exhibit at Wesleyan University's Davison Art Center).
25 Grass, Günter. "The Flounder. First Look at a New Novel." *Playboy*, Dec. 1978, pp. 136-38, 140, 360, 362.
26 Hanson, Bernard. "Grass' Sordid Pseudo-realism; Warhol's Handsome Portraits." *Hartford Courant*, 23 Nov. 1980, Sec. G, pp. 2-3.
27 Hatfield, Henry. "Günter Grass. *Der Butt.*" *World Literature Today*, 52 (Spring 1978), 273-74.
28 Hayman, Ronald. "The Undercooked Flounder." *Books and Bookmen*, Dec. 1978, pp. 30-31.
29 Howard, Maureen. "New Books in Review." *Yale Review*, 68 (Spring 1979), 438-39.
30 Howard, Richard. "A Whopper of a Tale." *New Leader*, 4 Dec. 1978, pp. 23-24.
31 Jaesrich, Hellmut. "Günter Grass' Tall Tale: A Fishy Story." *Encounter*, Feb. 1978, pp. 46-48.
32 Johnson, Lincoln F. "Dreamlike Images Fill Grass Prints." *Baltimore Sun*, 8 April 1978. (A review of an exhibit at the Baltimore Museum of Art).
33 Judd, Inge. "Grass, Günter. *The Flounder.*" *Library Journal*, 1 Sept. 1978, p. 1660.
34 Keller, Karl. "Man's Will vs. Woman's Will." *Los Angeles Times*, 1 Oct. 1978.
35 Kinkead, Gwen. "The Novelists. Günter Grass." *New Republic*, 23 & 30 Dec. 1978, pp. 25-28. [Interview].
36 Kramer, Hilton. "Art: Gunter Grass, Portraitist." *New York Times*, 15 April 1977, Sec. C, p. 18.
37 Kurcfeld, Michael. "Günter Grass." *New West*, 17 Nov. 1980. (A review of an exhibit at Mirage Editions Gallery, 1662 12th St., Santa Monica, California).
38 Learmont, Lavinia. "London. Gunter Grass – Patrick Seale Gallery." *Art and Artists*, Dec. 1978, pp. 42-45.

38a Leonard, John. "Books of the Times." *New York Times*, 9 Nov. 1978, Sec. C, p. 24.

39 Maloff, Saul. "The Hand That Holds the Ladle. . . ." *Nation*, 23 Dec. 1978, pp., 707-708, 710.

40 Mays, John Bentley. "Petronius Would Have Been Proud." *MacLeans Magazine*, 4 Dec. 1978, pp. 62-63.

41 McPherson, William. "A Fish Story." *Washington Post Book World*, 5 Nov. 1978, Sec. G, pp. 1, 4.

42 Milton, Edith. "The Flounder." *New Republic*, 23 & 30 Dec. 1978, pp. 32-33.

43 Mitgang, Herbert. "Grass: 'The Flounder' Misread as Attack on Feminist Thought." *Chapel Hill Newspaper*, 7 Jan. 1979.

44 Moorcroft, Marilyn. "Floundering with Grass." *Commonweal*, 8 July 1977, pp. 435-38.

45 Nordell, Roderick. "Grass's Indulgent Feast." *Christian Science Monitor* (Eastern Edn.), 3 Jan. 1979, p. 19.

46 Paulin, Tom. "Recent Fiction." *Encounter*, Jan. 1979, pp. 54-55.

47 Perez, Gilberto. "Fiction Chronicle." *Hudson Review,* 32 (Fall 1979), 478-80.

48 Plant, Richard. "Answers by Günter Grass." *New York Times Book Review*, 17 Dec. 1978, 14, 31.

49 Read, Piers Paul. "Twilight of the Men." *Spectator*, 14 Oct. 1978, pp. 18-19.

50 Revzin, Philip. "Trials of a Male Chauvinist Fish." *Wall Street Journal*, 1 Nov. 1978, p. 22.

51 Sale, Roger. "Big Fish, Mythical Fish." *Chicago Tribune Book World*, 29 Oct. 1978, pp. 1, 6.

52 Schickel, Richard. "Dream Work." *Time*, 28 April 1980, p. 76.

53 Sheppard, R. Z. "A Turbot de Force." *Time*, 23 Oct. 1978, pp. 104, 106.

54 Simon, John. "What's Cooking?" *Saturday Review*, 11 Nov. 1978, pp. 57-59.

55 Simonsen, Sofus E. "Books of 1978: The Flounder." *Magill's Literary Annual*. Englewood Cliffs: Salem Press, 1979, pp. 226-30.

56 S.M. "The Galleries." *Los Angeles Times*, 14 Nov. 1980, Sec. 6, pp. 7, 9.

57 Suffert, Georges and Ursula Zentsch. "A Passion for Counter-Reality." *Atlas World Press Review*, June 1979, pp. 30, 31, 34.

58 Tallmer, Jerry. "Ink for Writing, Ink for Etching." *New York Post*, 23 April 1977, p. 24.

59 Thompson, Mary Lee. "Günter Grass Prints." *The Print Collector's Newsletter*, 11, No. 4 (Sept./Oct. 1980), 117-20.

60 Tomalin, Claire. "Coup de Grass." *Punch*, 25 Oct. 1978, pp. 702-703.

61 Updike, John. "Fish Story." *New Yorker*, 27 Nov. 1978, pp. 203-206.

62 Vinocur, John. "In Any Language, Grass Chooses His Words With Care." *New York Times*, 26 Jan. 1980, p. 2.

63 Williams, David. "Home of Lost Classics. Paperbacks." *Punch*, 26 March 1980, p. 533.

64 Zimmer, Dieter E. "Was heisst Glumse auf japanisch?" *Die Zeit,* 17 Feb. 1978, p. 19. English translation in *The German Tribune*, 26 February 1978, p. 10.

65 Zweig, Paul, "Too Many Cooks." *Harper's,* Dec. 1978, pp. 80-81.

b) *The Meeting at Telgte*

66 Davenport, Guy. "Günter Grass: Rebuilding a Ravaged Language." *The Washington Post Book World*, 9 Aug. 1981, p. 5.

67 Gray, Paul. "Poets in Search of Peace." *Time*, 18 May 1981, p. 87.
68 Leonard, John. *"The Meeting at Telgte."* *Books of the Times*, July 1981, pp. 314-16.
69 Newlove, Donald. *"The Meeting at Telgte."* *Saturday Review*, May 1981, p. 71.
70 Spender, Stephen. "Elbe Swans and Other Poets." *New York Review of Books*, 11 June 1981, pp. 35-36.
71 Ziolkowski, Theodore. "Historical Analogy." *New York Times Book Review*, 17 May 1981, pp. 7, 22.

Index

This index of names and titles of works includes persons of at least some degree of historical and/or literary-artistic significance—regardless of whether they appear in a fictional context. Purely fictional figures (except those in well-established myths) have, as a rule, not been listed.